MORE KETCHUP THAN SALSA

D0746672

JOE CAWLEY

WWW.JOECAWLEY.CO.UK

MORE KETCHUP THAN SALSA

www.joecawley.co.uk

Table of Contents

CHAPTER 1

It was whilst holding aloft a not altogether pleasant-smelling mackerel that the decision was made. Blood dripping from a rabbit dangling overhead tinted the cold water from the fish and rolled down a white sleeve. The March rain hammered on the rotting tin roof high above the stall and where there was more rot than metal columns of water plunged onto the shuffling shoppers below. Their faces were drawn and bleak like a funeral cortege following the last remains of hope. From life they expected nothing – save a nice piece of cod at a knockdown price. Northern England in March. Northern England for most of the year, in fact. I was 28. There had to be more. I lowered the fish to eye level, 'Is this my life?'

The fish said nothing but I already knew the answer.

I had worked on Bolton market for six months forcing myself out of bed at 3.30 every morning to spend 11 hours knee-deep in guts and giblets, selling trays of dubious fish and chicken at three for a fiver. The freezing cold and the smell I had grown used to but the pinched expressions of fellow passengers on the bus journey home still brought about a great deal of embarrassment. It couldn't be denied, in the inverted language of market traders I was lemsy (smelly) from deelo (old) fish.

Word inversion was useful when you didn't want customers to understand. 'Tar attack!' would have all the workers scuttling for higher ground onto splintered pallets or battered boxes of chicken thighs stacked at the back of the stall as a rat the size of a bulldog decided it was time for mayhem.

Originally dubbed the poor man's market in what was a working man's town built on the prosperity of the local cotton mills, Bolton market was subsidised by the council to provide cheap food and clothing for low-income workers. (In a flourish of affluent delusion it has since been completely refurbished and modernised. The rats get to scamper around on fitted nylon carpets amid designer lighting franchises. An elegant coffee shop offering vanilla slices on dainty china now occupies the spot where once the best meat and potato pie butties in Lancashire were messily consumed by fishy-fingered stall workers like me.)

It was an undemanding job both physically and mentally, which suited me fine. Stress was for the rich and hardworking, characteristics that were never going to be heading my way. That's not to say that I was content. A string of menial jobs had taught me that contentment is not always found on the path of least resistance but I had found myself meandering towards that monotone British lifestyle of school-job-pension-coffin, and something needed to be done, fast.

I had grown bored with the same old stallholder banter – 'We're losing a lot of money, but we're making a lot of friends,' or 'Oh yes love, it *is* fresh, it *will* freeze.'

I was becoming weary of the merciless teasing of old ladies as they stood at the stall with purses wide open, names inadvertently displayed on their bus passes.

'Hello, Mrs Jones. Fancy seeing you here.'

From beneath a crocheted hat the gaunt figure would try to force a vague recollection. 'I... err...'

'You remember me, don't you, Mrs Jones? I used to come round your house for tea every Friday.'

'I... I think I do. Yes, yes. Now I remember,' she would say with a weak smile.

Even the daily competition to land a rabbit's head in Duncan's hood had lost its appeal. Duncan was a mentally retarded hulk who, although teased mercilessly by the market crew, was also well looked after by them. They gave him pocket money that he spent on *Beano* comics and Uncle Joe's Mintballs, and made sure that no harm came to him from occasional gangs of skinheads that, for want of anything more constructive to do, would try to beat him senseless.

At six-foot-four, eighteen-stone, with no neck and an unappealing habit of walking around with his cheeks puffed out and his bottom lip investigating the underside of his nose, he was not what most able-sighted people would term 'attractive'. If one of the workers did manage to score a rabbit he would charge at the victor, bellow obscenities and curse them with death threats until his attention was distracted by one of the girls. At this point all aggression would dissipate as he embellished the gurning with a damp pout. 'Give us a kiss,' he would demand in such a commanding voice that were it not for his spectacular ugliness would have been hard to refuse.

'Hey, boss,' I shouted, jerking my head back from the open box of chicken thighs, 'you can't sell this. It stinks.' Pat continued pulling at the innards of a rabbit.

'Dip it in tandoori and put it out as five for a fiver.' I looked down at the poultry pieces glowing green.

'No. I mean it really stinks. You'll kill somebody with this.' Pat lifted a red-stained sleeve above his shaved head and breathed in the blend of blood and body odour. His shoulders rose as his round torso filled with the sweet smell.

'You've been here six months. Don't start getting a jeffin' conscience on me now,' he grunted. He pointed the sharp end of a filleting knife towards me. 'Get it sold. Anyway, the dead can't complain.'

I dipped each piece in the bucket of rust-coloured spice then chucked them all in the waste bin when Pat turned his back to have a word with one of the girls who had lost a false nail inside the rainbow trout she was gutting.

I decided that I should dispose of his lethal produce more permanently and wheeled the bin outside to the main rubbish collection point. The sky had given up on any attempts of clarity and had slipped into dull grey pyjamas, sucking the last remnants of colour from Ashburner Street. When had life turned grey? I asked myself. Where was the excitement, the glamour, the anticipation of things to come?

A voice answered: 'Come on, Tinkerbell. There's fourteen rabbits waiting for decapitation in here.' Pat was poking his ruddy cheeks around the huge sliding doors, an ill-timed intrusion on the meaning of life.

A nine-to-five had never been a burning ambition. Neither for that matter was a five-to-four. I had long aspired to be a musician – well, a drummer at least. I'd answered the ad in my head and spent 14 years in an interminable interview.

Rock Star Wanted

Requirements: The ability to sit on your arse, make a lot of noise and become famous.

Remuneration: Unbelievable.

Perks: Aplenty.

But try as I might, I was always several beats behind stardom. A sporadic booking at Tintwistle Working Men's Club was the closest I'd got to Wembley Stadium, which was more than 200 miles further up the pop ladder of success.

My battered old Pearl drum kit now gathered dust at the back of a garage in Compstall while my life did the same at the back of a fish stall in Bolton. I desperately needed an out.

'*Hola!*' Two hands covered my eyes from behind.

'I thought you weren't back 'til tonight,' I said and planted a kiss on Joy's cheek. She'd just returned from a girls' week in Tenerife.

'I got the flight time mixed up so I thought I'd surprise you. You smell nice.' She peeled a phlegm of chicken skin off my neck.

'Pat's trying to offload some killer chicken. I've chucked it in the bin. You look well. Had a good time?'

'Yeah great. But listen, I've got some news. Big news. Meet me in the Ram's after work.' She winked and ran to the bus stop where the number 19 had just sprayed a line of rain-stained shoppers.

The rest of the afternoon passed just like any other. Terry came round to see if any of us had orders for him. 'There's a lovely brass table lamp I saw in Whitakers,' said Julie, Pat's wife. 'Green glass shade, second floor, next to the clocks.'

'Can you get me a clock, Terry? Nothing too fancy. Wooden perhaps. Something that'll look nice above me kitchen door,' asked Ruth, interrupting the customer she was serving.

Debbie, Pat and Julie's daughter, flapped her arms excitedly. 'Terry, Terry, me Walkman's bust. Get me a good one, will you? And don't forget the batteries this time.'

Terry scribbled the orders on a scrap of paper. 'Joe? Any more CDs?'

'If you can get *Thrills 'N' Pills anB ellyaches* I'll have that.'

'Hey, if it's pills you want, you only need to ask.'

'No, it's the new Happy Mondays CD.'

'Oh, OK,' he said, disappointed, 'I'll see what I can do. But if you *d* want pills,' he tapped his nose conspiratorially, 'I know a man.'

Terry returned at the end of the day, red-faced and panting. He dragged a large, leather holdall behind the stall.

'Littlewoods are here,' shouted Julie. We grouped around Terry who opened the bag and passed around the various items like Father Christmas on day release. Price tags were strung around the clock and table lamp and my CD still had the security tag attached.

'I'll be back on Saturday to settle up,' he said and scuttled off into the crowd with the empty bag.

I continued to push out 'tish' at three for a fiver and mechanically joined in the banter. We wolf-whistled at passing girls and then shouted after them as they turned and blushed, 'Not you love. Don't flatter yourself.' Monotony could be so cruel.

The Ram's Head was not the obvious choice for a celebratory reunion but it was run by Leonard, the only landlord who would put up with the aroma of stale trout. A previous and unsuccessful career in boxing had left him nasally advantaged when it came to our patronage.

There were half a dozen drinkers scattered about the perimeter of the high-vaulted room. Most sat alone. Their eyes tracked what little movement occurred beyond Leonard methodically drying glasses with an aged tea towel. A Jack Russell lay across the feet of one man. It yawned at the lack of antagonists whilst its master carefully rolled a cigarette as if in slow motion.

Brass wall lights topped with cocked green shades cast the room in a sickly pallor throwing sallow circles of light onto the once-white wallpaper now jaundiced through decades of low-grade tobacco.

The only sounds were phlegmatic coughs and the deranged melody of a fruit machine happy to have found a friend. Joy was feeding it 50-pence pieces with one hand, jabbing at the nudge buttons with the other. Her tan had attracted the attention of two investment advisers dressed in no-brand tracksuits who were teaching her about consecutive bells and lemons. Lessons in slot machine skills she certainly did not need.

'Pint and a half please.'

'Joy's at it again.' Leonard smiled a toothless smile and nodded at the machine.

'No stopping her, I'm afraid. She insists it'll pay off one day.'

I carried the glasses carefully across the threadbare carpet and blew on the back of her neck. 'You winning?'

'Nearly. Have you got any fifties? I think it'll hold on two bars.' The two lads peered inside the machine trying to see if was worth risking their beer money.

'Come on.' I motioned to a table under a window. A karaoke poster written in yellow marker pen obscured most of the outside view which would have been the damp remnants of Bolton's first ever bicycle shop.

'So what's this great idea then? You give all your money to me and I stop it disappearing inside those stupid machines?'

She took a sip and raised one eyebrow. 'You're gonna like it.' She paused to take another sip then smiled again. I smiled back. 'So come on then.'

I'd known Joy ever since she'd pushed me backwards off the top of the slide at nursery school. She was an experimental child but compassionate with it. As soon as my head had hit the floor she slid down and ran around to peer in my face. 'You dead?' she asked. I managed to smile crookedly as Miss Cornchurch dragged her off by the arm before I passed out.

But I took solace in the fact that I was not the only one bullied by Joy. In fact, she was so impressed by my not dying that she took on the role of protector and regularly pushed other kids from the slide if I wanted to have a go. She also insisted that I push *her* off, as she was curious to see what it felt like to fall so far. I declined the offer.

We sailed through primary school as a tag-team of cutesy cheek and imaginative excuses. I would help her with her homework and she would steal me penny chews as a reward.

As pre-teens we had only once stepped over the line of platonic friendship. It was Saturday night and her parents had left us playing Buckaroo whilst a romantic western flickered in the background. Joy's attention was diverted from the kicking mule by a passionate scene involving a feisty cowgirl and cowboy.

'Kiss me like that,' she commanded and pulled my face against hers. I remember the taste of liquorice toffees and wondered if this is what she tasted like to herself all the time. We remained eye-to-eye for about a minute until, unimpressed, Joy pulled away and silently placed another bucket on the donkey's backside. Romance didn't surface again for a long time although we both maintained a mutual disrespect for each other's juvenile *amour*s.

Although in different levels of classes at comprehensive school, we would still hang around with each other during most lunch breaks and after school, plotting horrific revenge on the teachers that had dared to reprimand us. I was usually no more than an accessory but due to my pubescent lanky stature I had taken over the mantle of protector. And boy, did she need it. A cheeky smile and sparkling eyes could redeem her of most crimes but there were times when physical intervention was unavoidable.

We finally became an item after an unplanned holiday together. Joy's boyfriend had dumped her just days before departure, accusing her of spending more time with me than with him. It all came to a head outside the Dog and Partridge in Hazel Grove when I was invited on what her boyfriend thought was going to be a cosy tête-à-tête but turned out to be a tête-à-tête-à-tête.

On a campsite in southern France, fuelled by too much alcohol and exposure to naked flesh, intimacy was inevitable. The holiday romance continued after we returned home and still did three years later inside a dingy pub in Bolton.

'How do you fancy moving to Tenerife?' Joy peered over the rim of her glass. Her eyes searched mine.

'Uh... why?'

'We've been offered the chance to run a bar, only it needs two couples to run it, so I said I was married.'

'To who?' I shrieked.

'To you, you numpt! Who else? I said we could run it with me as bar manager and you as the chef and...' Her speech accelerated as it always did when she was trying to steamroll me.

'Hang on, hang on.' I raised a hand to slow down the onslaught. 'Who would offer to let two people who have hardly any experience of pouring a pint let alone running a bar in a foreign country, take over a bar?' I knew as soon as I had said it that our previous careers may have deviated slightly from fish filleters to nightclub management. Joy confirmed that she had exaggerated our talents slightly *and* distorted the actual financial arrangements.

It transpired that we weren't expected to just run it; we were expected to buy it.

'What exactly are we supposed to buy it with? Fish heads?' I spluttered when the actual truth came out.

'No. We can borrow it,' replied Joy. Her straight face implied that there was something else she wasn't telling me.

'How much?'

'A hundred-and-sixty-five grand... more or less.'

I blinked twice. Hard. My pint remained suspended halfway between my open mouth and the beer mat. This was surely some seafood-induced dream. Believing that this was just another of Joy's get-rich-quick schemes that would fizzle out as fast as previous plans, I decided to humour her.

'You said two couples?'

Joy continued. 'I didn't tell you but I got a phone call from your stepdad before I went to Tenerife. He said that the bar on El Beril, where his apartment is, had come up for sale and he was thinking of buying it as an investment. He asked me to collect the books for him to take a look at. When I called in, the owner said why don't I take it over. Anyway, when I got back this morning Jack came to pick up the books and I joked about us two running the bar for him. Before I saw you he'd just called to say he'd been talking to your mum and they both thought it was a good idea. We go into partnership with your brother and they'd help us raise the money.'

'Whoa, whoa, whoa,' I interrupted. This was in danger of becoming serious. 'From having a bar job in Tenerife, we've gone into partnership with my brother and into debt with Jack to the tune of a hundred-and-sixty-five grand. All on an island two thousand miles away with a population that doesn't speak English. And all behind my back. Where exactly does my opinion come into all this?'

Joy became defensive as she always did when she was on the offensive. 'Calm down. It's just an idea. Just forget I ever said it and tomorrow we can go back behind that crappy stall and stink of fish for the rest of our lives.'

Several pints later – I suspect that they had been laced a little – the whys and wherefores had progressed to whens and hows.

CHAPTER 2

I hadn't seen my brother for several months. Like me he was drifting through life waiting for an opportunity to be handed to him on a plate. Over the three days since the seed of the idea had been planted, I assumed that like me he'd begun to think that this could possibly be it.

Joy, myself, David and his girlfriend Faith had arranged to discuss the idea in The Stage Door pub in Manchester. It was next to the Palace Theatre where a degree in sociology and history had enabled my elder brother to secure the lofty position of box office assistant.

Although we were virtually neighbours in age – there were only 11 months between us – we were poles apart in character. I was the practical brother, he was the creative one. I had logic, he had intellect. Ask about the social order of the Napoleonic age or the consequence of community breakdown in the 1980s and my eyes would glaze over, saliva would forge a path down my chin and my brain would start blowing raspberries. David, however, would casually launch into a scholarly diatribe over the shame of the proletariat and the fortitude of Karl Marx and then try and flog you two tickets to see Widow Twankey starring Keith Chegwin.

University had taught him many things: how to dress like an East European chimney-sweep; how to smoke out of the side of his mouth like an aristocrat; how to behave like a socialist; and how to make £1.50 last a fortnight. Only on weekdays though. On the odd weekend when he would return to Mum and Jack's house he muttered about the capitalist extravagances of home life before indulging himself in a bathroom full of designer toiletries, a kitchen full of food and a car full of petrol. I suspected that David, like me, was also ready for an out.

'Well!' I exclaimed, starting the discussion. 'What do you think?'

'We're all for it,' David replied. 'We think it's a great opportunity...'

'*You* do,' interrupted Faith looking up at my brother. Physically they were complete opposites. David had the physique of a retired rugby player but the heart of a teddy bear. At six-foot-two he was a good 12 inches taller than Faith who, with her tiny, doll-like features, seemed too delicate for a man with hands the size of bin lids. Her skin was porcelain white, a nose stud and four gold earrings provided a gilt-edge. She looked like a fragile piece of china but her apparent frailty was used to good effect. David would fuss round her like she was a vulnerable child.

Where David merely had to breathe his words to be heard, Faith had to project her voice with all the force of a shout but without the volume just to reach ears that were rarely close by. 'It's a huge risk for me. I'd be giving up my career to gamble on this,' she strained. Faith's career had so far reached the dizzy heights of assistant manager at a Virgin Records store in Altrincham. We were not playing with high stakes here. 'I mean, none of us have any experience of working behind a bar, in a kitchen or running a business,' she continued.

'I've worked in my mum's café and Joe and David have both had bar jobs. It's just the next step, that's all,' said Joy.

'Selling pies and serving tea is hardly the same as owning a restaurant,' argued Faith.

'We'll learn,' countered Joy.

'That's a bit flippant considering we'll be in debt for a hundred-and-sixty-five-thousand pounds. It'll be an expensive lesson if we get it wrong.'

'We'll just have to make sure we don't then, won't we?'

'What about my cat? I can't leave him.'

'Surely a cat isn't going to make the difference between going and staying?'

'I've had him a long time.'

'He's not even your cat. He's David's.'

'He still loves me though. I can't leave him.'

'Well, buy him some sunglasses and bring him along. He looks like he could do with a holiday.'

'I'm being serious.'

'So am I.'

This was not a good start to a business partnership. David and I let the girls slug it out for a while as we bought another round of drinks.

'You know that Mum and Jack said that they'd only lend us the money if we all went?' I reminded David.

'I know, but I'm not sure if Faith's got it in her. You know what she's like.'

I wasn't sure if any of us had it in us to leave the comfort zone of un-demanding jobs in familiar surroundings and put ourselves in debt through owning a business that we knew nothing about – on an island of which we knew even less. Although spurred on by Joy's reckless enthusiasm to give it a go, Faith's contrary attitude had raised uncertainty about the wisdom of Mum and Jack's plan. I began to wonder if we were really ready for it. This was a commitment, the very thing that I had done my best to avoid all these years. A small part of me hoped that Faith would say no and we could sink back into the cosiness of a life without change, responsibility or effort.

Although Jack's offer to lend us some of the money and help arrange a mortgage for the bulk was a generous, and perhaps foolish, one, the rate of interest that we'd be paying back was a lot more than the rate he would have gained by holding the same money in a bank. At the end of the day it was a business proposition that was intended to benefit him as well as us. Financial gain was always behind any reasoning of Jack's.

The appeal of investing in a bar on the same complex as his apartment would satisfy many whims. He could waltz in and out, help himself to large brandies and puff on fat cigars. He would have achieved most men's dream to own their own pub but without having to deal with the petty whims of a drunken Joe Public.

An added bonus of course was that his two stepsons would finally have 'proper jobs' rather than messing about with mackerel, Karl Marx and Wid-ow Twankey.

If there was a certain amount of self-interest in the proposition, there was also a smattering of sense in Jack being the one to suggest it. After decades of flogging houses on the home front, he had retired from his UK partner-ship the year before and had set up a similar venture for property investors overseas. Tenerife was the first port of call as residential tourism was just starting to follow in the footsteps of its package holiday popularity. For UK investors seeking a red-hot winter bolthole whilst the rest of Europe turned blue, the Canary Islands had recently emerged as a leading contender, with one advantage over the Spanish Costas – winter sun.

Located less than 100 miles from the coast of North Africa, the seven islands making up the Canarian archipelago had all the assets that a North European citizen looking to escape grey winters could ask for. A growing expat community embraced the perma-sunshine, an eternal spring climate and safe bathing.

Historically this septuplet of islands had drawn the attention of many British visitors, most of them unwanted. In 1585 the Canarians beat off Sir Francis Drake as he tried to conquer La Palma. In 1797 Nelson and his arm parted ways during an ill-timed attack on Santa Cruz de Tenerife. And whilst docked off the same island in 1832, Charles Darwin was thwarted in his lifelong ambition to explore the archipelago because of the risk of a cholera epidemic.

Perhaps with all the chronicled exploits of the early visitors it was surprising that it wasn't until the late 1980s that the masses cottoned on to the appeal. For Joy and me though, it wasn't the beaches, pine forests or volcanic badlands that had provided the lure. If Jack had diverted his attentions towards pig farming in Lithuania and dangled a means of becoming swine entrepreneurs I think we would have been equally enthused. It was merely the dream of an adventurous escape from our usual drudgery, but with the added incentive of daily sunshine and a potential pot of gold if we managed to avoid spectacular failure.

The problem now was that this dream had grown dangerously close to becoming reality and for me that would mean having to swap the excitement of making plans with the horror of having to follow them through. But the decision was now down to Faith.

Despite several more remonstrations about what a crazy, illogical plan it was for herself and the cat, Faith finally, though reluctantly, agreed to come. Having overcome our own personal doubts, Faith's decision took us to Phase II. We had to start preparing to move.

For Joy and me the most pleasant part of Phase II was leaving the market.

But that would only come after the most unpleasant part – telling Pat.

He was in a particularly vicious mood that day. 'You're not going to sell that fish by whispering, Joe, for jeffin's sake, shout.'

'Three fish for a fiver! Fresh in today!'

'That's not shouting. That's talking. Scream it out, you nancy.'

'THREE FISH FOR A FIVER! DON'T BE SHY, COME AND BUY!'

'Joy, shift those chicken legs. They've been out of that jeffin' freezer three times now. If they have to go back in one more time you're going in with them. Sandra! What the bollocks...?'

Sandra worked alone on the shellfish 'department' slotted at right angles to the fish and chicken stall. She was allowed to run it how she pleased and was a particular favourite of Pat's. This was just as well as the slightest hint of a reprimand would make her reach for the Kleenex. Today however, wasn't even a good day for Sandra.

Occasionally, apart from the run-of-the-mill fish like cod, halibut and hake, Pat would take delivery of some unusual marine life. This was partly to show off to the other fishmongers in the market and partly to keep the attention of his regular customers.

Emerging from the cold, dark, hush of Ashburner Street into the brightly-lit riot of early morning stall preparation was a slap in the face. Finding yourself eye-to-eye with a creature that you wouldn't normally expect to come across in Bolton town centre was heart-stopping.

I was deep in thought about warm quilts and soft pillows, hands burrowed in my donkey jacket, collar turned up in defence against the biting chill, when suddenly what appeared to be a large shark was grinning at me from atop a trestle table in the middle of the market hall. The apparition was indeed a three-metre shark, Pat's latest 'attention-grabber'. It had certainly got mine. Pat's beam matched the shark's as he noticed my shock. 'Think you can sell that?' he asked.

'It's a shark,' I said.

'Top marks, Einstein. I can see education's not been wasted on you.'

But this morning it was fauna of a different kind that was destined to draw the gapes of Bolton's plastic bag brigade. A fresh delivery of live crabs had arrived and Sandra had carefully arranged a dozen of them on their backs, little legs cycling in unison between the cockles and mussels.

Unfortunately, a sympathetic pensioner had noticed they were upside down and had turned them back the right way whilst Sandra was off chasing a young boy who had helped himself to a fistful of crabsticks.

Sandra returned to find a man in a cloth cap and a woman with no teeth hopping youthfully in front of the stall. The upright crabs, having sensed a window of opportunity, had hurled themselves off the edge of the stall and were scuttling for their crusty lives between wellies and moon boots in a bid for freedom. The good people of Bolton, unaccustomed to such crustaceous attacks, had also fled, missing another window of opportunity around the other side of the stall as Pat had sanctioned an emergency plan of four trays for a fiver plus a free bag of tandoori chicken in a bid to woo the fleeing shoppers.

The crabs were eventually herded together but not before word had got out that Pat's stall should be given a wide berth. Trade that day remained slack. Worse than that, the other stallholders had gained enough ammunition to goad him in the Ram's Head for a very long time.

At the end of an unprofitable day, Pat's ruddy cheeks were scarlet, his mood black.

'Pat, can we have a word?' said Joy. Pat grunted and kicked a box of chicken legs towards the freezer for their fourth frosty sleepover.

'We've bought a bar in Tenerife,' I said. Pat stopped kicking and looked up. His eyes narrowed and his cheeks glowed furiously. He was in no mood for jokes, especially if they were on him.

'What d'you mean you've bought a bar? A toffee bar maybe. How can you two buy a jeffin' bar on three quid fifty an hour?' He turned his back and shooed us off with a flick of his hand. 'Piss off. I can't be doing.'

'So we're going to have to hand in our notice,' continued Joy.

'You're serious?' We waited for an explosion after the pause. 'Do you want a barman?' Pat had turned round again. He was looking from me to Joy and back again. We both let out a nervous laugh.

'No, I'm pleased for you. You've both worked hard. We all had a bet on how long you'd stick it out when you first came working here. We gave Joe one day and you two weeks. Didn't think you'd both hack it. You proved us all wrong. Just let me know a week before you're leaving so I can get someone else in.' He turned round and shoved the chicken with his foot as we strode off. 'And don't forget,' he shouted, 'if you *d* ever need a barman…'

When the rest of our stall colleagues heard the news, they were sceptical. They expected to see us reappear at one of the other stalls further down the market selling mixed bags of sweets or bundles of low-grade toilet rolls.

The send-off on the last day was full of warm-hearted well wishes. Old fish innards and chicken bits were cheerily stuffed down our clothes and we were both forced to wear rabbit carcasses on our heads for a good deal of the day.

A couple stopped in front of the stall with mouths agape. They both had matching lilac shell suits and absurdly orange-tinted tans. 'Why have you got rabbits on your heads?' asked the man, understandably bemused.

'Because it's our last day,' answered Joy.

'Oh,' he replied, as though this was a reasonable explanation.

'Why are you orange?' said Joy.

'It's called a suntan, love,' said the lady.

'I see. Been away?'

'Yes, we've just come back from Tenerif-ey,' smiled the lady.

'More like Shirley's Sunarama on jeffin' Hardwick Street,' muttered Pat as he passed behind carrying a box Terry had just delivered.

'Tenerife!' exclaimed Joy.

'Yes, we own a villa out there. We try to get over as much as possible, you know, to get away from this frightful weather.' Her voice had suddenly jumped up a couple of social classes to underline her ownership status. 'Have you been?'

'Oh aye,' said Joy brightly. 'We've bought a bar restaurant there. We're moving in a few days. Maybe we'll see you there.'

'Yes... you might well,' answered the woman faintly. The exclusivity of her status was in danger of being cheapened by a market trader of all people! She didn't like it whether it was true or not. The woman was no newcomer to the market and had been on the receiving end of teasing before. You couldn't blame her for doubting that a couple of fishmongers wearing rabbits on their heads had bought a business on *her* island.

'I'll miss you,' said Sandra at the end of the day. A solitary tear dropped onto a bag of peeled king prawns. 'Here, take these,' she blubbered. She checked if Pat was looking and handed us the seafood as a farewell gift.

Pat immediately shouted us over. 'You three, over here now!'

'Shit,' said Sandra. 'Might be needing a job meself now.'

'We all clubbed together and bought you something for the bar,' said Pat. The others were standing around watching. He handed us a box. Inside were an elaborately framed dartboard and two sets of darts. 'I bet your bar doesn't have one of those, does it?'

'No, I'm sure it doesn't,' I said. 'Thanks, Pat. Thanks, everybody.' We were touched that Pat had taken the trouble to arrange a going away gift, irrespective of the fact that the price tag signalled Whitakers of Bolton had unwittingly donated it.

Pat had spared us a final end of day clear-up. We were keen to get home to start packing. There were only three days to go before we were due to fly out and suddenly it seemed like we had a mountain to climb. I wasn't ready, neither physically nor mentally.

I had intended visiting the haunting ground of my schooldays in Glossop. Subconsciously I wanted to be in a place where anxiety, responsibility and financial burden had yet to surface. I wanted to recapture those carefree feelings of walking to Su's at lunchtime when the biggest decision was whether to have batter bits with my chips.

I wanted to stand outside the Surrey Arms where my first serious relationship was sealed with a long kiss, when nothing in the world mattered apart from spending every minute of every hour with Lesley Allen. It was a sensation that I desperately wanted to recapture to clear the whirlwind of emotions currently wreaking havoc in my head.

I wanted to go to Old Glossop at the edge of the Pennines, to wander into the hills and gaze over Derbyshire life. It was there that I always had time to think, safe in the knowledge that at home my mum would have cooked my tea, washed my clothes, been to work and still have the patience in the evening to devote all her time and love to my brother and me. She was the one who had absorbed the anguish of teenage angst, soaked up the grief of broken relationships, made all the plans for our better future whilst my dad busied himself in making a career, always miles away from his real responsibilities. I could see now that my dad had passed down his commitment-aversion genes. I too had developed a phobia of being trapped in a situation with no means of escape.

But my nostalgic journey was not to be and I continued with the material aspects of emigrating. Packing for a new life involves a bit more than throwing in a few shirts, a pair of flip-flops and a good book. Everything that I had collected had some meaning and each time I was coerced into taking things out of my suitcase to throw away it felt like another nail in the coffin of my life to date.

Despite the wrench of packing for a new life and packing up my old one, all was going according to plan until we got a phone call from our *g storia*, the person who was sorting out the paperwork for us in Tenerife. 'Slight problem. I can get work permits and residence permits for the two lads as joint owners, but not the girls. I've just found out the only way we can make them legal is if you're married, in which case the wives automatically become residents. You'll all have to get married, quickly.'

As much as our hearts were racing at the thought of swapping the two-tone grey of Bolton for the multi-coloured hues of a life in the sub-tropics, Joy and I were adamant that marriage was not a thing of convenience. The threat of wedding chimes set off alarm bells and we said no. The whole move was in jeopardy once again.

Even Faith was disappointed. They had already agreed to get married if it meant we could still go ahead with the plan. They were not amused at our refusal.

'We're prepared to sacrifice so much and you won't budge at all,' complained Faith at an emergency meeting.

'We are not being told when to get married,' I said. 'We'd rather forget the whole idea.' Secretly, although I loved Joy, I had no intention of getting married at all, ever. My parents had got divorced and I was not convinced that wearing top hat and tails for a day whilst paying for a knees-up for distant relations was the key to an eternal romantic union.

In the meantime, David and Faith frantically set about organising their wedding, convinced that we would change our minds. It was only amidst a flurry of international phone calls between Jack and our *g storia* that she admitted she may have been a little over-emphatic in using the phrase '*have* to get married'. We could still go ahead with the move but the legalisation process would take a lot longer, that's all. The risk was that, in the meantime, should Joy and Faith get caught without either work permits or family connections they would more than likely be deported. Naturally my brother and his wife-to-be were a little miffed at this eleventh-hour revelation but it was too late to back out, so they proceeded with their big day anyway.

Thus, on a blustery Saturday less than three months since the original business idea had surfaced, and in the presence of a select nearest and dearest, my brother and his girlfriend duly whispered 'I do' at a registry office in Salford. The bride, in an inauspicious display of doom and gloom, draped herself from head to toe in flowing black with matching bonnet, boots and mood.

The dashed affair was completed in traditional fashion: the hat competition was won by Aunty Beryl who managed to force an astounding union of millinery and garden mesh; confetti and insults were hurled with equal verve; tearful emotion became more contagious in direct proportion to the amount of alcohol consumed; and opposing relations were loudly hailed as potential new friends whilst quietly cursed as pains in the neck.

All the hellos quickly turned to goodbyes as the last drops from upturned bottles of Beaujolais dripped onto white linen. The following day we were leaving England to start a new life. The honeymoon was already over.

CHAPTER 3

To wake up in the morning and realise that this is the day every aspect of your life will change forever is, to put it mildly, a tad daunting. Try as I might, I couldn't get back to sleep to delay the inevitable. A tinge of excitement at the start of something new was overshadowed by a cocktail of worry: anxiety that it was too late to stop the momentum; fear that we were stepping into the unknown and into a huge debt that would be hung round our necks for a good number of years; and panic that we had lost something – vital paperwork, passports, our minds. Yesterday I had gained a sister-in-law. Today I was to gain a new life, new identity and new prospects. Excitement and anxiety see-sawed continuously. A life with fish seemed years ago and my thoughts were now racing in one direction, towards what lay ahead. Final packing and the drive to the airport were incidental, a fuzzy montage of checking, re-checking and re-re-checking. I felt like an obsessive-compulsive.

Money? I patted my pocket. Phew... or was it? I thrust my hand into my pocket and let out a sigh. Yes, money. Was it all there though? Had I dropped some? I remembered pulling the keys out of my pocket to give to Joy. Were some of my hard-earned fish funds lying invitingly on the wet pavement outside Joy's mother's house? I pulled out the wad and counted it again. All there. Or was it? Had I counted it wrong? I pulled it out again. 10, 20, 30, 40... 'Pack it in. You're going to lose it.' She snatched it from my hands and folded it in her purse.

I was surprised just how calm she was despite having just waved good-bye to her mother. Joy had an inner strength and a practicality that was beyond me. When the going got tough, whilst I'd look for my coat, Joy would take hers off to wade right in. For her, avoiding trouble and strife was not an option. If she set out to do something she would continue unfalteringly in a straight line until the mission was accomplished. I would veer right and left haphazardly trying to find a way round the hard work and confrontation. Some would call it lazy, I preferred creative meandering. However, creative meandering was not an option now.

David and Faith were to catch a later plane via Madrid so they could accompany Mal the cat on his journey. They would meet us at the bar tomorrow.

As the taxi neared Manchester Airport my nerves called a brief truce. The general mêlée and the whiff of aviation fuel transported me to a time when personal responsibilities involved nothing heavier than returning to the house with the same clothes I went out in and not being caught with a finger up my nose.

This airport 'buzz' started the day my brother took possession of our first aircraft registration book. We both had an alarming lack of hobbies during our junior school years, a situation that our mother set about rectifying with no little verve and haste. Horse-riding lessons had gathered pace until we both outgrew the pastime – literally. My brother and I were not lacking in stature during our pre-teens. Our assigned ponies, unfortunately, were. Short horse plus long rider equals public embarrassment. Merrylegs and I had to part.

Judo was an equally short-lived pastime. Although our mother took great enjoyment from getting us out of the house on a Saturday morning so she could hoover in peace, the appeal of handing over money to a man who repeatedly threw us to the floor soon waned.

It was thus, with some poorly disguised horror, that we announced to friends and family that we had joined the ranks of dumbfounded young (and not so young) anoraks on the viewing gallery at Ringway International Airport.

Any airport now instantly invokes memories of sipping tepid Vimto from within the deep safety of an oversized snorkel jacket hood. At regular intervals the sound of rain pattering on polyester would be drowned out by the exciting screams and whistles of a jet taking off or landing no more than a few hundred yards away. Screwing my eyes up I would read the registration number out to my brother with a mouth full of egg mayonnaise sandwich.

'Bvhee, voy, phthee, thow, thow, thuren.'

My brother, adept at translating my gobbled observations, would then meticulously scan through our handbook checking for BYC 227.

'Nope. Already got it,' he would announce more often than not. Occasionally I would sneak a glance at the more accomplished spotters' records. Their pages always seemed to have more entries than ours. Written notes and scrawled observations filled their pages. 'It's not a competition,' my brother would remind me. Even then I remember having feelings of inadequacy; too few numbers, not enough equipment, tiny Thermos flask. We had no short-wave radio to listen to the mysterious dialogue between pilots and the control tower. It was something that we always aspired to, but that was what plane spotting and most other 'collecting' hobbies were about. It wasn't about having, it was about wanting. Even the fully loaded top dog of the viewing gallery would watch enviably as a bulky piece of metal lifted itself from the rain-stained tarmac of monotony to head for unimaginably more colourful skies beyond our horizon. We all wanted to go, but this was the closest a pale 11-year-old, with just enough money for a bus ticket home and a two-pence piece for the rusty observation binoculars was going to get. I should have realised then that I would always be striving for more. Contentment was forever going to be sadly beyond my grasp. It's not unhappiness or dissatisfaction at what you already have, more of an obsession with not wanting to miss out on another opportunity that you know is out there.

'Opportunistic' was one of the terms that my dad had used to describe me after he had divorced us. It was a rare acknowledgement that he had taken enough interest in his sons to warrant making a judgement and even then it was in the form of a written word on his suicide note. I was more taken aback by the fact that I had received a personal letter from him than the fact that he had taken his own life.

After all of his years of searching for something away from his family he had come to the jolting conclusion that his can of contentment was forever going to be perched on a shelf just out of reach. I was intensely aware that I was shopping with a list that was potentially as unattainable.

Joy's father, Arthur, had arranged to meet her at the airport to say goodbye. Urgent business had called on the day of his daughter's emigration. Bolton Wanderers were playing Tranmere Rovers in the Third Division playoffs at Wembley. As soon as the fat lady started singing Arthur had promised to make all haste back north to wave us off. Unfortunately (unless you're a Tranmere fan of course) Bolton lost 1–0 and the post-mortem took a lot longer than expected. This, combined with a particularly popular day for enjoying the M1 meant that the final boarding announcement came well before Arthur.

'We'd better make a move,' I suggested. I had bid my farewells to my mum and stepfather at their house. Similarly with Joy's mum, Faye. Even though Joy was primarily the instigator of the idea I still felt a pang of guilt at having been partly responsible for the decision that took her away from her family. She was the youngest of five offspring, the only girl. I sensed her mother in particular was not overly happy that her daughter had fled the nest for a distant land.

Faye and Arthur were traditional parents who had cemented a close bond amongst their children. Their four sons all lived within two miles of each other and were regular visitors at the house. I felt like I was stealing Joy from this nurtured and protected environment and risking her happiness two thousand miles into the unknown. Although Joy was initially the most excited about the idea, I sensed that she still got her lead as to whether it was a sensible idea from me. If I had said no, she'd have been just as happy.

Joy continued nursing a paper cup of coffee, gazing towards the airport entrance. 'I can't go without saying goodbye to Dad.' Her eyes had started to well up. 'Two more minutes. He's probably broken down.' Just as she finished the sentence, Arthur burst through the doors puffing and panting.

'Bloomin' broke down,' he affirmed.

After prolonged and tearful clasps, Joy's farewells were complete, albeit a touch rushed.

Once on board I idly mulled over the fact that I was about to embark on an exciting life in a foreign land. I watched as the cabin crew ran through their regular repertoire of useful information, pointing out which doors we were to calmly file out of if the plane plummeted to the ground and revealing the technical intricacies of how to buckle and unbuckle the seat belt. Suddenly a moment of panic jolted my mind.

Foreign! I thought, and then again a bit louder. *Foreig!* As in foreign language! It was one of the many elements of emigrating that I had pushed to the back of my mind. How was I going to communicate with the delivery companies? What if I got lost on a shopping mission? I rummaged through my carry-on bag and whipped out a handy phrase book. The panic increased as I tried to ingest every expression that I thought I might possibly need, but it was no good. Spanish words went in one ear and plopped right out of the other. There was too much to learn. Why don't these books just include general phrases that could be applied in a variety of situations like, 'Say nothing unless it's in English'? Instead they include specifically useless expressions such as, 'My hat is on fire and I don't seem to have any water. Do you know where I may be able to purchase some?'

I gave up and consoled myself with a Jack Daniel's. We were actually doing it. I was actually being responsible for my own future. I had always chosen ventures that implied no binding allegiance. It was holistic claustrophobia, keeping my options open. I figured this is what it must be like to be a grown-up and felt strangely elated. I was finally committing myself to something that had no way out, something I had to see through whether I liked it or not. If the going got tough this time, I'd have to rough it out, ride the wave, sink or swim. I slammed the cabin crew call button for an emergency refill.

Being served alcohol in your seat is one of the few redeeming factors about flying. This aside, it seems that the comfort of passengers is well down on the list of priorities for most charter airlines, just below 'making sure there are ample miniatures available for the cabin crew to take home' and 'making sure the captain has credit on his Visa in case the plane runs out of fuel'.

Seating arrangements are absurdly inadequate unless you're prepared to pay extra for the privilege of being responsible for fathoming out the sequence of lever-yanking necessary to operate the exit door after an unscheduled freefall. I was also the victim of an incessant recliner. The only way I could read the in-flight magazine was to rest it on the bald pate of the man in front who had reclined so much that I managed to pass a good few minutes counting the moles on his head.

The joys of having someone inconsiderate in front can only be equalled by having an oblivious individual behind and I had scored in both directions. Every 20 minutes or so the incontinent grabbed my seat to lever himself up, catapulting my head as he battled to clamber over his neighbours on numerous scurries to the toilet.

This made reading impossible and for want of anything better to do,

I paid a visit to the toilet myself. I have to admit to having a fascination with these sites of sensory overload. They're like giant Fisher Price Activity Centres. The combined aroma of cleaning fluids, cheap soap and a dozen lingering perfumes confuse your sense of smell whilst the unfamiliar sounds of droning engines, creaking plastic and 'whoosh' of water being magically whisked away lead to disorientation. A barrage of notices add to the chaos, warning of dire consequences for disposing of paper products in the waste disposal unit or waste products in the paper disposal unit. *Wipe round to clean. Lift up to drain. Push down to flush. Press in to call. Slide across to close. Pull out to open.* In a state of increasing panic I struggled to fulfil all my obligations and with one hand hastily trying to hitch up my trousers, the other unwittingly resting on the call button, the door flew open.

'Can I help you, sir?' enquired the stewardess, holding the door open a bit wider and for just a little longer than I deemed necessary.

'You were a long time,' noted Joy on my return.

'Just trying to pass the time,' I replied, deliberately disturbing the slumber of my bald lap-mate with a well-placed elbow.

I spent the remainder of the flight staring at the clouds or squinting at re-runs of the sitcom *Terry and June* that seems to be compulsory viewing for those restrained in padded seats, locked inside metal cells miles away from populated areas.

After four hours the captain announced our descent. Out of the window the peak of Mount Teide, Tenerife's sleeping volcano, poked through the cloud cover below. The ethereal vision of our new homeland obscured by cloud yet signalled by the impressive point of Spain's highest mountain added to the apprehension of entering another world, another life even.

We touched down, waved our passports at the disinterested customs officials and awaited the arrival of four mismatched suitcases, three borrowed holdalls and a square, plastic flight bag that nowadays is usually only sported by those passengers who still insist on travelling in 1970s safari suits with hair severely parted in a cut-along-here-for-lobotomy fashion.

We had been happily reunited with half of our baggage but then cases from another flight began to mingle with ours. The tannoy garbled in Spanish and then repeated the message in equally unintelligible English. Something about not using hairdryers on horses.

A rotund German lady with exceptional BO had stolen my view and I leaned a little closer to the conveyor belt. As I did, an overhanging Samsonite rushed from behind the lady and struck me square in the groin, lifting me up slightly and carrying me along for a couple of inches. Now I had tears in my eyes and an intense urge to lie down to contend with, as well as the pungent sumo obstructing my vision.

'That's our case on that belt over there,' said Joy, pointing to the adjacent carousel.

After relaying back and forth, rounding up the remainder of our wayward luggage, the air rife with the fragrance of squelching armpits and with a nagging ache lingering in my gonads, we were welcomed to Tenerife.

The arrivals hall was a bright but characterless warehouse stocked with a mixture of tanned locals and tour reps in dizzy florid blouses. Each held a board with their company's name emblazoned across it. Every tour operator that I had ever heard of, and a lot that I hadn't, seemed to be represented here. Some already had flocks of bewildered, washed-out faces huddled around them, fathers relieved that all responsibility had been passed to someone who knew what the hell to do next.

Joy and I pushed the trolleys through the milling crowd and emerged blinking into the glaring sunshine of our new country of residence. Hot blasts of air swept over us as we wheeled down the endless line of people waiting for a taxi. Overhead, a piercing blue stretched from the glittering Atlantic beyond the runway to where the mountaintops gashed the sky several miles inland.

Families herded their belongings together. Their holiday started here and shirts were already off, revealing pasty torsos desperate to be toasted. As with all travel, replacing familiar surroundings with the unknown fires an electric charge that awakens a sense of adventure. Even those whose pool of adrenalin had long been suffering a severe drought were caught in this buzz of excitement.

Ahead in the queue a beer belly flapped up and down like an elongated can-can dancer as its exuberant owner heaped embarrassment on his two young daughters with a middle-age rave.

'Daaaad! Grow up. Everyone's looking. Stop being stupid.'

'Holiday-hey... celebrey-yate. Don't be boring. We're on holiday now. Come on, pet, get in the spirit.'

'Gerroff, you nutter.' His wife rolled her eyes at her scarlet-cheeked daughters.

We were in no position to judge. In fact, there was a tinge of jealousy at the sight. Shamelessly embarrassing yourself was an expression of joyous freedom. This man had broken free for a fortnight away from a life of responsibility. I was just entering one. It had seemed exciting two thousand miles away but now it was all too real. What if we failed? What if we couldn't stand the heat? What if we burnt down the bar and had to return to the fish market to pay off our debts? I began to calculate how many trays at 'three for a fiver' we would need to sell to pay off one-hundred-and-sixty-five-thousand pounds.

'Ninety-nine-thousand trays of fish if we don't get the bus.'

'Sorry?' said a startled Joy, lost in her own private thoughts.

'That's how many trays we'd have to sell to pay off the debt if it all went wrong, but we'd have to walk home.'

Obviously she didn't think it worthy of reply and just shook her head in a despairing manner, quietly pleased that something familiar had surfaced in this alien land even if it was only my anxiety.

The gleaming white Mercedes continued to line up alongside like bullets fed into a gun. When we eventually reached the front of the queue, eager for a friendly gesture I smiled at the driver and tried out the only words of Spanish that had clung to my memory.

'*Buenos días. Que tal?*'

The taxi driver didn't even bother to look up as he snatched the cases from my helping hands. What if I couldn't learn the language? What if everybody hated us as new owners? What if the locals resented us and tried to ruin our business? I thought about all the big lads at the market who we could invite over to defend our holding in the event of an attack. Mac was the first. You wouldn't want to mess with Mac. He wasn't the biggest of men but with his skinhead, sunken eyes and chiselled jaw he was not to be messed with. Yeah, he'd come over. I began to feel a little more relaxed as I constructed an imaginary army of fish-reeking soldiers.

Our heads shot back as we were fired up the winding dual carriageway towards the motorway. Along the dusty roadside advertising hoardings urged us to sample Dorada beer. A sample was not what I needed right now. Bring two barrels and a straw and leave me alone in a dark corner for about a month. Another billboard welcomed us to 'Tenerife, the beautiful isle'. I was failing to revel in any beauty at the moment. Claws of spiky cactus leapt from the lava like witches' hands. Either side, tumbled rocks littered the terrain like the aftermath of a stone-throwing riot. It could have been Arizona; it could have been Kabul.

We slid from side to side as the driver dodged in and out of the slower traffic, slamming his hand hard on the horn as a small rent-a-car crammed with four pairs of eyes obstructed his way. None of the words aimed at the driver were recognisable but I could guess the gist. He continued to complain as we passed the poor tourists who had hurriedly swerved out of the way to let him pass. As we did he flicked a desultory gesture at the ashen driver. I felt partly responsible and, being British, wanted to apologise but instead exchanged fearful glances, unaccustomed souls at the mercy of a foreign foe.

On the two-lane motorway, the 120 speed limit signs rushed past at 150 kilometres an hour. The driver had wound his window down, which provided a pleasant breeze for him but left us in the back to be buffeted by the gale. The skin on our cheeks raced for shelter around the back of our heads and our hair became a rave of hysterical strands. To compensate for the noise, he turned up the radio. Snatches of Spanish wailing warning of an unpleasant death for all foreigners rattled my eardrums.

When we finally careered off the motorway, my relief was immense. We followed a winding road through a walled banana plantation. Explosions of fluorescent pink bougainvillea burst forth at every curve on the quiet route down towards a sparkling sea. Finally the low terracotta roofs of our new community, El Beril, came into view.

We turned into the complex and drove through a paved parking area that was shared by the Altamira Aparthotel to the north and the El Beril complex to the south. These were the only two developments on this stretch of southern coastline. The glitter of Playa de Las Americas was a two-mile hike around a trio of barren headlands.

El Beril comprised around 100 bungalows and two-storey apartments. Half of them occupied a small plateau about 20 metres above sea level, the other half followed a slight incline down to a shingle beach. Most of the housing faced seawards. Even those furthest from the sea looked over the roofs in front and shared a magnificent view of La Gomera, Tenerife's closest neighbour rising from the ocean around 20 miles away.

The complex was still in its infancy, evident from the stretches of unpaved walkways and loose wires that protruded from open electricity boxes. A cluster of unfinished apartments was tagged on to the back of the complex, seemingly an afterthought from the developer. An ocean breeze stirred some loose powder into dwarf whirlwinds that danced between a cement mixer and a wheelbarrow before collapsing like broken marionettes.

Joy, now sporting a just-got-out-of-the-washing-machine look, paid the taxi driver as I heaved our luggage onto the pavement. Happy holidaymakers wandered across the car park from the adjacent hotel in flowery shorts and shiny new sandals. Were these the same happy souls who would be face to face with us in the next few days demanding full refunds and a pound of flesh for poisoning their children and ruining their holiday?

Some 10 feet below where we were standing, through black iron railings, stood the Smugglers Tavern. It occupied the two penultimate *locales* on the left. The turret-like end unit was empty, as were the two to the immediate right. Next to these appeared to be an office of some sort. A British supermarket had taken over the second unit from the right at the other end, furnishing the patio outside with an assortment of inflatable swimming aids and my first reassurance that we were still on the same planet – the red mastheads of British tabloids.

One more unit remained empty in the corner, its patio in permanent shade from a footbridge that crossed from the car park to the upper level of commercial units. Here, wafts of paella drifted from Bar Arancha, a small Spanish tapas bar, into several neighbouring timeshare offices.

The Smugglers Tavern appeared full, inside and out. There must have been 20 white plastic tables outside without a spare seat at any. I presumed it was just as busy inside as people scurried in from the mid-afternoon sun. Everybody looked content, a postcard snapshot of happy holiday diners. We'll soon put a stop to that, I thought.

Our temporary home was a small bungalow facing Las Americas at the southern edge of the complex. Temporary because the owner was selling it and we would need to vacate as soon as it was sold. It had been decided that David and Faith should get the only long-term rental apartment that was available due to their feline impediment – Mal the cat.

Our apartment belonged to the president of the community who knew my stepfather from his business dealings here. All the properties were more or less identical apart from the number of bedrooms. Ours had just one, to the left of the front door as you walked in. It was barely big enough to house a double bed and still leave enough room to manoeuvre around. A small bathroom faced the front door and down a short hallway to the right was the living area and open kitchen. The walls were a cooling white, interspersed with shelves and a worktop of honey-toned pine. Beige marble tiles covered the floor, which gave the apartment a beguiling touch of quality. Sliding doors at the far end of the lounge – though I use 'far' in the loosest sense of the word as they were only four paces from the kitchen – led onto a small square patio, from which we could gaze across the curving Bahia del Duque (Bay of the Duke) to the vertical excesses of Playa de las Americas.

We spent the rest of the day unpacking and then had a wander round. The sunlight illuminated the newly painted white walls to the extent that it hurt my eyes. Our apartment was about a hundred yards from the black volcanic sand and shingle beach that stretched north to the nearest village of La Caleta, about a mile away. Here a huddle of one- and two-storey houses clung to the base of a rocky hillside, overlooking a tiny harbour dotted with bright blue and red fishing boats.

Behind El Beril white farm buildings sat on the shelves of the terraced slopes, above which were patches of green pine forests that decorated the hem of the omnipresent volcano. There hadn't been an eruption on the is-land since 1909 so I figured in my usual frame of cheery resignation that one was about due.

That night we both lay on top of the sheets unable to sleep, listening to the high-pitched excitement of a mosquito as it chose its next supper venue. For such a tiny creature I have to say it has a helluva loud squeal and the more I flailed the louder it became. There aren't many more irritating noises than what sounds like a dentist's drill kamikaze-ing at your head so in the end, armed with a size 10 flip-flop in each hand I stood on the bed, head slightly cocked waiting for the manic giggling to return.

Thwack-thwack.

I let off both barrels of the flip-flop cannon causing a snowfall of plaster flakes to drift slowly onto Joy's head.

'Eeeeeeeee.'

It danced away towards the window. Keeping my eyes firmly fixed, I followed its path, treading on Joy's leg along the way. Her exasperated in-takes of breath were getting louder but I was sure she would thank me in the morning when she awoke without her ankles displaying the remnants of last night's dinner party.

The curtains were open and I caught sight of a cavorting couple. They temporarily disentangled when they noticed an underpant-clad warrior beating his bedroom wall with over-sized footwear. I smiled and waved a flip-flop at them to demonstrate that I wasn't really crazy.

In the meantime, the mosquito had settled down at a cosy table for one on Joy's left ankle. It seemed distracted as it read the menu so holding my breath I slowly raised a hand.

'DON'T EVEN THINK ABOUT IT! Get back in bed and stop being an idiot.'

Meekly I obliged but I kept hold of one of my weapons just in case. As it was, my ungainly battle tactics weren't needed again. My eyes jerked open as from behind the curtain a huge lizard sprinted over to where the gloating insect was now resting and disposed of it with one quick flick of its tongue. Great, we now had a carnivorous reptile to fend off instead. If we could just find a large cat to dispose of the lizard, then a mean dog to clear up the cat, a vicious bear to get rid of the dog... and so on.

It must have been an hour later before I finally dozed off with my head full of spiralling images of creatures at ascending levels in the food chain.

Then without warning Joy let out a scream. As we both sat bolt upright she screamed again and head-butted me on her rapid evacuation from the room. With a throbbing temple, swirling confusion and not a little fear, I raced after her.

'Something just fell on me. Something heavy. Go and see what it is,' she blubbered.

With one hand rubbing my forehead and the other holding a not very menacing toilet brush, I edged back into the bedroom with Joy peering over my shoulder. Expecting a puma to leap out or a rabid bat to fly at me from any angle, I menacingly flicked the loo brush back and forth epée-style. It became quickly apparent in the sparsely furnished bedroom that whatever beast had ventured in had also ventured out again. It was only on closer inspection of the bed that we realised what had actually attacked Joy was the fitted sheet as it pinged free from the mattress. I added the toilet brush to my arsenal at the side of the bed and we recommenced what was left of a fitful night's sleep. Tomorrow we had to learn how to pay back £165,000, and we had four days of tutoring in how to do it. We'd both slept better.

CHAPTER 4

The sun filled the bedroom with an unearthly resonance that demanded we wake. I had one of those split second 'where am I?' moments before the rabid butterflies began to gnaw on the inside of my stomach. A new life began today. Not a trifling matter to ponder before even a bowl of Cocoa Puffs had passed my lips.

At 7.45 a.m., the sun was already baking the pine furniture in the lounge, releasing an unusual warm-wood odour, a substitute for the damp plaster smell that I was accustomed to in Bolton. I filled the kettle with warm water from the cold tap and removed the jar of Carioca coffee from a plastic bag containing a basic welcome pack from *el presid nte*. There were two cans of San Miguel beer, a bottle of water, a carton of semi-skimmed milk and a jar of apricot jam. No bread, just the jam. Eating was out of the question anyway and after showering and putting on shorts and T-shirts we set out for the bar in anxious silence.

We decided to take the scenic route, walking around the perimeter of the complex down past the sea and back up what I breathlessly dubbed Cardiac Hill. Two or three florid bathing caps bobbed in the gentle wake a hundred yards from the rocky beach where neatly folded towels lay waiting like faithful pets.

For the last few working days at the market, a vision of early morning dips in the warm ocean provided a constant distraction from my ice-cold fingertips and interminably damp feet. It was one of many anticipated pleasures, but for now it would remain just that.

The supermarket was already busy with holidaymakers clutching cartons of milk, sticks of bread and yesterday's editions of the *Daily Mirror* and *The Sun*. One man, dressed in knee-length, green Hawaiian shorts and with a white T-shirt tucked in at one side only, shuffled across the car park reading the day-before-yesterday's sports news. An open-top Porsche narrowly missed him as it screamed past in first gear. The young blonde driver acknowledged the close call with the barest of sideways glances whilst the oblivious sports fan carried on reading.

It was nine in the morning and Mario, one quarter of the previous partnership – in ownership, not in bulk (he made up four-fifths in that department) – was already slicked in sweat as he carried two crates of empty Dorada beer bottles to the outside store cupboard.

Mario was the kind of man that casting directors would have hunted high and low to play the part of an archetypal ice cream vendor. His chubby face was decorated with a handlebar moustache and two other tufts of hair protruded above his ears like upturned question marks. His hairy belly poked out from between a grubby white T-shirt and an inadequately-sized pair of blue shorts. 'It's flickin' hot,' he smiled, 'You gonna love it.' I sensed more than a hint of sarcasm in his voice. The worry fairies set to work.

'I show you how for four days, then you on your own. Piece a cake. I tell you who's trouble and who's OK. OK? OK, let's go.'

In a kitchen obviously never designed for such a large gathering, the three of us pressed together as Mario demonstrated the correct place to hit the fridge door so that it would open; the culinary implement most suitable for turning off the gas in an emergency (a pair of tongs), which knife he used for chopping salads, which he used for paring fruit and which he used for slicing meat (the same knife as it happens). He also exhibited which cloth to use for drying dishes, holding hot pans and wiping sweat off his face and fat belly – as feared, the same cloth for all tasks.

You may have gathered, as we had by this early stage, that the health and hygiene efforts of the Smugglers Tavern were a little deficient. Joy and I gave each other panic-filled glances and at every new revelation her nostrils flared in horror. We made mental notes for sweeping changes.

After an hour the heat was unimaginable. We may as well have been swimming. Perspiration turned our clothes several tones darker. Mario was still moving around with an uncanny speed considering his bulk and I guessed the temperature was something that we would also eventually get used to.

He showed us how to prepare the local spud accompaniment, *papas arrugd as*, or Canarian potatoes, using a pan that could house a family of four, and a kilo of sea salt. Then, after an interactive tour of the general workings, we trailed our mentor to the cash and carry where a juggernaut-like trolley was piled with such goodies as 24-packs of tuna, beans and corn.

When we returned, David and Faith were inside the bar with Jan, Mario's wife. Jan was humming to herself, flicking a feather duster at the mirrors and bottle shelves that occupied the back of the bar area. David and Faith sat on tall bar stools 'testing' the beer.

'How's Mal?' I asked, sensing from Faith's face that all had not gone to plan.

'He's been detained,' she replied frowning, 'in Madrid.'

Apparently the reams of paperwork in his personal flight bag were not sufficient to warrant a smooth and direct transition from Salford to the sub-tropics and he had been bound over by a zealous customs official in Madrid until the missing form could be located and faxed through.

A succession of phone calls had indeed located the necessary piece of paper and all being well Mal would be enjoying some in-flight Whiskas on the last leg of his journey tomorrow.

'Well, it's all ours now,' I said looking round as Jan took her humming and flicking outside. The bar hinted at mock Tudor. Between the black-painted beams, the white ceiling was turning a grubby yellow. Horse brasses behind the bar and on the walls looked absurdly out of place in this sunny clime.

'They'll have to go,' said David. 'And those.' He nodded towards two fluorescent yellow posters that had started to curl off the two floor-to-ceiling windows either side of the main door: 'Tonites specal – leg of labm – 750ptas' and 'Open 6 too midnite'. They looked like they were written by a two-year-old during an earthquake.

Bench seats around the walls were complemented by a mixed array of black, wooden chairs that surrounded eight rectangular tables. They were protected by faded pink tablecloths which were in turn enveloped in thick sheets of clear plastic. This top layer had acquired a patchy adhesiveness due to two years of alcoholic spillages. Sweat was rolling off our arms leaving small pools of water on the surface.

This stickiness was nothing compared to what carpeted the terracotta floor tiles behind the bar. For some reason this region seemed to have been a mop-free zone with the previous owners. The bar area was overrun with gas bottles, soft drink canisters, beer barrels, fridges and drink coolers. Thin yellow tubes ran in all directions, looping around each other like a treacherous roller coaster before disappearing into the many black recesses. All this in an area not much bigger than a double bed. What clear floor space remained was tar-black. Every step involved a 'schlup, schlup' to free footwear from the glue-like texture.

We drew up a long list of all the cleaning jobs that needed doing over the next few days. We also decided on a work rota. As we were going to continue Mario's opening hours – 6 p.m. until midnight – until the busy summer season began, we decided that we could work in couples, one night on, one night off. Daytimes would be spent cleaning and removing much of the tack that sullied the bar. We'd made the decision that once the summer season got underway we should open for lunch as well but we would deal with that once the initial shock had subsided.

It was during this first meeting-session that one of the biggest shocks to our business partnership was revealed.

Joy had set about sweeping behind the bar amassing an impressive collection of bottle tops, cigarette ends and spent matches. Faith was just about to help herself to a Fanta Orange when suddenly she screamed, 'Daaaaaviiiiid!'

'What's wrong? What have you done?' We all fussed round her expecting our first use of the woefully inadequate First Aid box.

Faith, not bearing the most continental complexion at the best of times, had turned Arctic white. Her eyes were aghast with horror, her lips trembled.

I followed her frightened gaze to Joy's refuse collection anticipating a severed finger or a dead rat but there was nothing that you wouldn't expect to find behind a particularly grubby bar.

'Faith's got a phobia about matches,' muttered David, somewhat embarrassed.

There was a short period of silence while we waited for the punch line. None was forthcoming.

'Matches?' we both queried in unison. I couldn't contain a slight smile.

'It's not funny,' said Faith. 'I've always had it. If I see a match in the street, David has to go and get rid of it.'

David nodded in confirmation.

'Is it just burnt matches or any matches?' I asked half sarcastically.

'All matches... and matchboxes... and ashtrays.'

'Ashtrays?'

'Sometimes I don't have to see one, but if I think there's a match inside a matchbox or an ashtray I get a panic attack,' explained Faith. 'My brother's got a phobia about wet wood,' she added, as though this reduced the oddness of her own fear.

'That's going to be kind of awkward if you're working in a bar, isn't it?' said Joy.

'Everybody will have to make sure all the ashtrays are empty and check the floor before I come in,' said Faith.

'We'll have to tell people to use lighters instead of matches,' suggested David, keen to play down the potential seriousness of this revelation. 'We'll get some Smugglers lighters made up and give them out whenever we see someone lighting up.'

'Sell them you mean,' I interjected.

'Either way, we're going to have to make this a match-free zone,' he added.

I could see this was going to be an ongoing problem. I sneaked a glance at Joy. She raised her eyebrows and flared her nostrils and we carried on with our tasks without further discussion of the subject.

Bearing in mind Faith's match aversion, it was decided that on our respective shifts she would do the cooking and David would work out front. Similarly, I was to be the chef in our team with Joy using her outgoing nature to placate the customers out front. But, thankfully, these roles were not set in stone.

The following day, our routine was repeated with cleaning and shopping sessions during the daytime and cooking lessons with Mario for a few hours during the evening. It was obvious from the number of customers who poked their heads into the kitchen to say hello that Mario was a popular figure in the community. Knowing this merely added to the pressure. Understandably, we were going to be continually compared to the previous owners on all accounts, from the quality of food to the friendliness of service. I wondered how could we compete when Mario had almost two years' head start on making friends.

It still seemed surreal to be standing in a commercial kitchen surrounded by all manner of adult culinary equipment. The knives looked natural in Mario's huge mitts but felt cumbersome and awkward when I picked them up. The biggest blade I had ever used was a serrated bread knife. The largest in our set of black-handled weapons was the size of a cutlass.

Being the proud owner of a dozen matching condiment sets made me feel strangely uneasy. I was a drummer, a market worker. What authority did I have to be responsible for 12 condiment sets?

'Is all flicking easy,' Mario said, sensing my worry. He was tossing various ingredients into frying pans whilst simultaneously pushing buttons on the microwave and chopping greenery for the salad garnishes. 'Is all in the timing. You start with what takes longest and cook it in order. You just got to know what takes longest. No problem. No?' We nodded, unconvinced, dreading the time when Mario wasn't around to instruct us in 'a little bit of this and a lot more of that'. That day came sooner than we anticipated. A lot sooner.

The next morning we were a little taken aback to hear that Mario thought the time had come.

'OK. I go to Santa Cruz. You carry on. I back sometime today. Cheerio.' And he was gone.

Terror struck. We had flipped a coin and Joy and I were going to be first to fly solo with David and Faith on standby just in case we had to make an emergency landing.

'Shit,' said Joy succinctly as we watched Mario's car disappear along the shimmering tarmac. The mountains in the distance seemed to close in, the sea swelled up ready to swamp us in a deluge of incapacity.

'Right, well... I suppose I'll get shopping, you do the salad prep... do you think?' I drove off in our red Renault 5 that we had taken on long-term rental. Five minutes later I was back. 'What do we actually need?'

'I don't know, look in the fridge and see what we haven't got.'

I made a list and headed off again, returning after two hours with enough tomatoes to open a ketchup factory, four big boxes of what I thought were hamburgers but were in fact meatballs and enough toilet rolls to keep an army of little Labradors playful for years.

Joy in the meantime had managed to cut just the tip of one finger off and upon my return was standing pale-faced and wide-eyed with her hand under the cold-water tap.

'Had a bit of an accident,' she explained unnecessarily. Splashes of blood on the table gave the game away.

The cut wasn't as bad as she feared and soon the flow stopped, although Joy's usually dark complexion was still several hours away.

Despite an early start, we were still chopping meat and preparing the bar at 5.45 p.m., 15 minutes before our advertised opening time.

'You carry on in here, I'll stick some music on and put the chairs outside,' said Joy. I would have been happy drying the same pan for the rest of the night if it meant putting off baring ourselves to the public for the first time.

At 6.05 p.m. the sound system announced that REM were losing their religion. I was losing my nerve even quicker. By 6.25 p.m. we hadn't had a single customer and I was beginning to think that this wasn't so bad after all. Then they arrived. Not one, not even one family, but one huge crowd descended upon us. Rather naively I had envisaged a comfortable gap between one customer's simple request and the next. At our present level of capability half an hour would have seemed fair. But that great legislator, Murphy, had other plans. Daylight disappeared as about 20 people surged through the wooden doors clamouring for our attention. I wanted to get back to my pan, but it was too late.

We both stood behind the bar, gulping audibly, as we faced the inspection committee.

'So, you're the new ones, are you,' boomed a thick Yorkshire accent. 'I hope you're not bloody well going to put the price of ale up!'

'Don't worry about that. We're not going to change much to start with.' I assumed that Mario and his partners were popular landlords and it was best not to veer too quickly from their style.

'You can change what you like s'long as you don't put the prices up,' countered Yorkshire. 'I'll have a pint of El Dorado and half a shandy for Eileen.'

Eileen was two feet behind, and two feet down, smiling shyly up from his elbow. Yorkshire could see I was a little shocked at her stature. 'She might be small but she's got a helluva voice. You want to get her singing here one night. I won't charge you much,' he winked.

'Yeah, I just might do that,' I lied, as Eileen tottered off, two hands steadying her glass of shandy. 'Who's next?' I asked the crowd as my confidence began to grow.

'Pina Colada and a Tequila Sunset.' The confidence ran for shelter.

'OK. What's in those exactly?' I asked the young couple in matching Coventry City football shirts.

'I don't know. You're the barman, pal. New to the job, are you? You won't last long here if you can't make a cocktail. Ask the bird over there,' he said, pointing at Joy.

I didn't want to make any enemies just yet so without fuss I asked Joy if she knew the ingredients. Joy had her head in the beer fridge looking for orange juice.

'There's a cocktail book down there on the bottom shelf. Check in there.'

I picked up the book and dozens of baby cockroaches scattered in all directions as the roof was lifted off their commune. With a knotted stomach, not wanting to draw attention to them, I turned round to face the couple and was just about to rest the book on the bar when I spotted two hairs sticking out from between the pages. Then the hairs started twitching. Before my brain could register why this book would contain dancing hairs, it suddenly became alive with scuttling roaches searching for an escape from their flying island. I tossed it on the floor and out of the corner of my eye saw a riot of roaches emerge from the pages.

'How about I fix you both the new house special? It's twice as strong and because it's our first night you can have two for the price of one.'

The Coventry team was eager so I filled two tall glasses with generous shots of whatever came to hand, namely Peach Schnapps, Triple Sec, Cherry Brandy and Galliano, topped up with a blast from each of the fizzy soft drinks – Sprite, Fanta Lemon, Fanta Orange, Coke, tonic water – and a squirt of spray cream to top it all off.

'There you go, two Naughty Normans, 500 pesetas for both.' They looked awful. The next time Coventry came to the bar, he ordered two pints of lager.

Then came the first food order.

'Joe, two cheeseburgers, chips and salad and one pork chops, chips and salad. Table five.'

I counted up to table five to see if they looked like the type who'd complain if poisoned. They did. It was a silent grey-haired couple sitting with a heavily mascaraed girl of maybe 13 or 14. Both adults were sitting so unnaturally still, they seemed to be demonstrating to the girl how to sit up correctly at the table.

Glad to be out of the spotlight, I threw two chops and two burgers onto the hot plate and with a woof of propane ignition and the whiff of singed hand-hair, the first meal that anybody had paid me to prepare was on its way. Whilst the meat hissed, salad garnishes were decoratively arranged and the frozen chips were placed into the basket ready to be lowered to their crispy death. Easy, I thought. Then the power went out. The diners let out a communal groan.

All the trip switches behind the bar were still up so I ventured outside. The electricity in the Altamira hotel was still working and inland I could see a cluster of lights blinking against the dark backdrop of the Adeje mountain range.

Fortunately Mario was on his way into Smugglers to see how we were doing. 'Follow me,' he laughed.

We walked in darkness along the outer footpath that circled the complex. At the far side, near our back garden, was a dull grey electricity box. Either its doors had been removed or the utility company hadn't deemed it necessary to conceal the master trip switches for the whole complex. Mario flicked the main one back up and immediately El Beril came to life again.

'Flicking island,' he muttered. A wry smile suggested he found it amusing now this was no longer his problem.

'Does that happen often?' I asked.

'Depends. Sometimes not for a week, other times it pops all night.'

He'd conveniently forgotten to mention this defect when he sold us the business.

Back in the kitchen I had to wait for the chip fryers to heat up again.

Joy popped her head round the wall.

'Two half chicken and chips, one no salad, and two chicken in wines, chips no salad.'

The dreaded chicken in wines! When Mario had showed us how to make this creamy dish, his instructions were rather vague. A bit of this, a pinch of that, some of these, not too many of those. I suspect that it was his own recipe and he was reluctant to give away the exact ingredients, even to Joy and me who were now supposed to recreate it.

It's just a matter of timing, I told myself, trying to quell the nerves. I worked out which meal would take the longest to cook and began the preparation. This happened to be the chicken in wines. I tenderised the chicken fillets, coated them in flour and flopped them into a frying pan with a knob of butter. While they were gently cooking, using a large pair of dressmaking scissors, I cut a pre-roasted chicken in half and put the two parts in the microwave.

Turning round to face the hot plate, I flipped over the meat, and turned the chicken fillets in the pan.

'Steak medium to well, Canarians and salad, gammon and egg, chips and salad,' came a voice from over my shoulder.

I had stuck a large sheet of 'write and wipe' onto the huge fridge doors and added this order to the previous two. Now which would take longer between those two, I wondered. I spun round as the aroma of burning chicken filled the air.

The fillets had fastened themselves to the base of the frying pan and were releasing plumes of smoke into the extractor hood above. Damn. Peeling them off, I decided there was no chance of a resurrection and flung them bin-wards. One landed in the dustbin, the other hit the tiled wall and made a slow descent leaving a trail of burnt butter.

I started again with the tenderising, a little more forceful with the hammer this time. I dipped them in flour and tossed them into a new pan with more butter. The electricity went off again. There was another group groan.

'Mario!' I shouted. I knew he was at the bar loving every minute of his freedom from such dilemmas.

'I'm going,' I could hear him chuckling.

Within minutes the power was back on and the customers cheered. Once more I had to wait for the fryers to heat up. I thought about phoning David and Faith but decided against it. We had to get used to dealing with this kind of problem. It was already beginning to sink in that this island was no smooth-running machine.

'Two steaks, rare, chips and salad.'

I hadn't even started the first steak yet! In the meantime I had slammed our hotel reception-type bell to let Joy know there was an order ready. Try as she might Joy couldn't arrange the large oval dinner plates so three could be carried at the same time. She rested one on her left wrist and held another in the same hand but couldn't find the right balance.

'Come back for the other one,' I said, watching her struggle. It had seemed so simple when Mario managed to carry five at a time. Mind you, he did have hands like a couple of JCB buckets and thankfully Joy didn't.

Out with the hammer again, I bashed all three steaks and chucked them amongst the pork chops and burgers. I turned the chicken in the pan and turned the microwave on for the half chickens. The chips were plunged into the fryer, spluttering and spitting burning oil onto my hands and forearms.

More garnishes were needed so I laid more plates onto the table and grabbed handfuls of tomato, cucumber and onion slices and chopped lettuce, dumping a pile onto each plate as the aroma of burnt chicken filled the air again.

I snatched the pan from the heat and decided that this time they would have to be resuscitated so added some white wine, crushed garlic and sliced mushrooms and replaced the pan over the blue flame.

The first order was nearly ready so slicing two burger buns in half, drawing only a little blood from my left palm, the buns were added to the hot plate. The microwave dinged and I felt to see if the chickens were hot. They were – painfully. The wine for the chicken dish was bubbling away and I added the cream and black pepper. Slices of cheese were slapped onto the now-shrivelling burgers. The buns started smoking. I picked them off the hot plate, burning fingertips in the process and hurled them bin-wards. One missed completely and rolled out of the kitchen into the main customer area. I noticed several moments later that someone had discreetly kicked it back in.

'Half a chicken, chicken burger, mixed grill, two chicken in wines, all with chips and salad, oh, and a tuna salad. How you doing in here?'

I raised two smoked eyebrows, a blooded palm and formed charred fingertips into a reversed victory sign.

'Is that pork chop supposed to be on fire?' Joy asked casually as the aroma of burnt pig filled the air for a change.

I turned the microwave on and before the half chicken had time to complete its first twirl darkness descended once again.

This time Mario asked me to follow him again. He reached behind the box for a short plank of wood and wedged it underneath the switch. 'Now try and flicking pop,' he warned the box. 'Sometimes you just got to force the issue. But remember to hide the stick when you finished otherwise the bastards cut you off for good.'

Unsurprisingly the power remained on for the rest of the night and by 11 p.m. I had sent out all 32 orders. Some people had to wait half an hour, some two hours. Fortunately Joy had a knack of making light of my inadequacy and the customers displayed that true British spirit of pulling together in a crisis. They knew it was our first night and they knew that we hadn't a clue what we were doing. One customer, having sat patiently starving for an hour and a half whilst I fried, burnt, fried, burnt and fried again a simple plate of egg and chips even brought his own plate back into the kitchen and proceeded to wash up.

'You'll soon get the hang of it,' he said sympathetically as another basketful of blackened chips was dumped into the bin.

By 1.30 a.m., the dishes were washed, work surfaces wiped down and the gas rings and deep fat fryer were checked over and over again to make sure that they wouldn't contribute to an early bath for our catering career. I estimated the meat we would need to defrost for the next day and scanned the shelves to compile a shopping list.

The terrace had emptied except for two teenage lads attempting to impress the daughter from table five with their pool prowess. Her parents had left her with strict instructions to follow them across the car park to the hotel before midnight. With shoulders pressed back and pubescent chest thrust forward, she was obviously in no need of any posture advice and was lapping up the attention of the two pool sharks.

Inside, Joy had her elbows on the bar, her head cupped in her hands as a couple kept her 'entertained'. I switched off the kitchen light and went to join her for a much-needed nightcap.

After pouring, drinking and pouring another pint of Dorada, Joy, whose eyes had long since glazed over, introduced me to the couple.

'Joe, this is Betty and Eric. They have a guesthouse in Blackpool,' she said with feigned interest.

I shook hands with them. Betty's eyes were also glazed, but not through boredom. Her blonde beehive hairpiece had flopped to one side revealing grey strands. Eric rolled his head and attempted to say something but closed his mouth again and continued with the lolling. Betty tried to get me up to speed with the conversation.

'I was just saying to Joan,' she nodded her beehive at Joy, 'how we know what it's like when you've done a long day and you just want a drink by yourselves but you can't get rid of the last people in the bar and they keep on talking to you like you've nothing better to do and no home to go to and you can't get a word in so you're stuck there listening and nodding and asleep on your feet, just wishing they'd go away.'

I looked at Joy and then back at the two last people in the bar, nodding as Betty continued.

'We get it all the time, and we'd never do it to anyone else. We know how you feel, isn't that right, Eric? Eric!' She jolted him with a sharp elbow to the ribs. Eric tried to respond, then tried to look at his wife but failed on both accounts and contented himself with some more general lolling.

'We'll just have one more for the road. Cointreau and tonic and whisky and water.' Betty waved a lipstick-smeared brandy glass at me. Every finger was decorated with gold and a spectrum of glimmering stones.

I'd never met a Blackpool landlady before but Betty seemed to epitomise the fading holiday town – distastefully decorated, depressing and dated. In the conversation that followed, it emerged that most of her family seemed to have either ripped her off or else befallen some tragic consequence after having spent time living and working in the guest house, or hotel as Betty preferred to call it. There were suicides, muggings and attempted murders galore, not to mention all kinds of infidelity. I made a mental note never to visit Blackpool's version of the Bates Motel.

Eric, in a moment of extreme swaying, toppled backwards off his stool narrowly missing the edge of a table.

'I think he's had enough now,' said Betty as if this was her husband's equivalent of fetching his coat.

Whilst Joy balanced the money against the till reading, I washed the remaining glasses and began to sweep and mop.

'The reading might be a bit out,' I shouted. 'I think I cocked it up when I came out for a break.' Indeed the till was out, by exactly one-hundred-and-fifty-million pesetas. 'A simple error due to an over-sensitive "zero" button,' I explained, but we both knew it was human error.

We switched off the lights and stood in the doorway surveying *our* bar. All the furniture, the upholstery, the ceiling fans, the bar pumps, the bottles, the kitchen equipment, the washing machine, the urinals. I'd never owned a urinal before. It felt good.

But it still hadn't fully sunk in that this was our business, and it was entirely up to the four of us whether we succeeded or failed. Last week we were minions of the fish market, this week we had entered the world of entrepreneurs. We had been brave enough to trade a comfortable, albeit uninspiring, life for a 'new improved' model in a land of eternal spring. We wanted to tell somebody but at 3 a.m. as we walked home hand-in-hand all was silent.

Joy went straight to bed whilst I sat on the patio, beer in hand gazing at the most vivid sky I had ever seen. With no light pollution, the velvet black was awash with blinking stars. It seemed infinitely clearer, as though we had been looking at it through dirty glasses in England. This clarity extended further though. We had now chosen a path and were actually on it rather than dreaming about it. This was a success on its own.

Yes, we had made mistakes, some more than others, and yes, there was still a mountain to climb before we knew what we were doing but we had made a start. Result – 32 people fed, zero poisoned.

My mind was whirring with thoughts of what had gone on that night and what we had to do tomorrow. As I made a mental list, my bottle of beer began to slowly tilt in my lap and the luminosity above began to fade. Within seconds I was asleep. Even the last drop of icy beer running down my leg was not enough to wake me.

I must have come round enough to take myself off to bed at some stage because the alarm stirred us both to life. For a moment my brain clicked into autopilot, preparing to go through the rituals of a normal market day: reluctantly pushing off the thick quilt followed by a rapid dash to the cold bathroom; standing at the sink with my hands in hot water to warm up; flattening down my errant hair; piling on layer upon layer of warm clothes before unwillingly leaving the relative shelter of the house and dashing out into the pouring rain; watching in disgust as the first bus of the day pulled away from the bus stop.

Only there was no quilt. In fact, there were no bedclothes at all. They had been kicked off the bed during the night. This chink in the chain was enough to create a rapid appraisal of the surroundings and the elation of last night was replaced with the heavy heart of knowing there was another long and stressful day ahead of us.

CHAPTER 5

David and Faith were drinking coffee at the bar when we arrived at 8.30 the following morning. 'Sorry we're late,' I said, 'Long night.'

'How did it go?' asked Faith. We filled them in on the problems with the electricity and the difficulty of timing the food right. They listened intently, the fact that we had succeeded of sorts merely added to the stress they were facing on their first night.

'It wasn't as bad as I thought it'd be,' I lied. 'You'll be fine. How's Mal, by the way?'

'He's hiding in the wardrobe, won't come out,' said David.

'He's in a bad way, poor thing,' added Faith. 'We shouldn't have made him come.'

'I bet he's hot in that fur coat,' I said. 'You'll have to shave him.'

'He's getting rid of it himself,' said David. 'He left half his hair in the cage at the airport.' It seemed we weren't the only ones to be anxious about the move. According to Faith, Mal was a victim of stress-related alopecia and was currently quivering behind David's shoes in their wardrobe, unable to cope with the challenge of a new beginning. No prizes for guessing which parent he took after there.

Whether it was down to the constant smell of burning food and the inordinate amount of time it took for said food to be passed to waiting tables or merely a coincidence, the second night was worryingly quiet. Worrying on a financial basis but a blessing for David and Faith, who had a mere 18 meals ordered and only a small crowd of drinkers but at least their first night passed without incident.

We had listed a number of jobs that urgently needed doing to improve the overall look of the place and allocated ourselves the various tasks. On the fourth day, whilst David and Faith carried on with the daily chores of shopping, preparing food and readying the bar, Joy and I began the first of these, cleaning up the bar terrace. After all, it *was* the first thing that potential customers judged us on. Even though we had the monopoly on British food and drink within a two-mile radius, the present state of the exterior would still put some people off.

Only four days into our illustrious careers as catering entrepreneurs and Joy and I could be found on all fours, dressed in yellow Marigolds, scrubbing the outside floor tiles. Even though it was barely mid-morning the heat sapped all our energy within minutes of toil. The sun had risen just high enough to pull back the shadows from the Smugglers' terrace. Beads of sweat dripped onto the small mosaic tiles as we frantically brushed. The original speckled white pattern slowly emerged through beer stains, cigarette burns, splattered cockroaches and dried bits of food, but progress was painstakingly slow.

The 'energy spent to surface area cleaned' ratio was not impressive and after two-and-a-half hours we had only completed around two square metres. At this rate it was going to take days to restore all the tiles to something like their former glory. 'Why don't you ask the *technico* if you can borrow his floor machine?' suggested Patricia, the supermarket owner. She had been watching us with her arms folded for several minutes now that the morning rush for papers, milk and bread was over. 'That's what the rest of us do.'

Every residential complex has either one or a team of maintenance people. Owners of property on that complex pay community fees, which includes the wages for these *technico*s, as they're referred to. They're responsible for the communal garden areas, swimming pools, garages and general tidying duties. Like most of the Canarians their workday is divided between a 9.30-to-1.30 stint in the morning followed by a 4-to-7 shift in the afternoon. Outside of these hours, most are happy to forsake their siesta and lunchtime for the chance to earn a bit extra on private jobs for the owners. This can be anything from installing a new water heater to tending a private garden. Or in this case renting out one of the community machines for a small backhander.

I found Miguel, El Beril's *technico*, perched atop a ladder by the side of the swimming pool. The pool was split in two by a line of smooth grey boulders separating the larger adult area from the toddlers' pool.

There was nobody around and the temptation to break the glassy blue surface was immense. My baggy, cotton T-shirt clung like Lycra, I was covered in dust and I smelled of bleach. Full submersion in the cool, clean water was only a step away but I resisted.

Miguel was sawing through the branches of a young palm tree that was beginning to extend over the shallow end.

'*Hola,*' I shouted, shielding my eyes from the sun. He looked down, nodded indifferently, and continued chewing his gum. 'Have you got a machine for cleaning floors?' I asked.

Miguel shrugged his shoulders. '*Como?*'

'Machine... for floors?' I mimed holding onto the handles and pulling back and forth rapidly. Miguel turned his head slightly and raised an eyebrow. I continued the impression with renewed vigour until I realised that this looked somewhat lewd.

'No, no, no, no,' I said dismissing the notion with a flurry of hand-waving. Miguel had settled himself comfortably against the tree with his arms folded, awaiting the next act.

I crouched down and began to pat the rust-coloured tiles that surrounded the pool. 'The floor... floor... clean, here.' I smiled, though evidently I was not making things better. Miguel had stopped chewing. Both eyebrows were raised and I could see his grip on the saw had tightened.

An ageing German couple, each dressed in a white bathrobe, emerged from one of the poolside apartments and began to clamber over their garden fence revealing more wrinkled anatomy than I would have preferred to see at this time in the morning. They obviously knew Miguel and waved a cheery greeting. Miguel seemed genuinely pleased to see somebody he knew. He garbled something in Spanish and the Germans nodded and smiled politely. Their lack of response suggested they hadn't the full grasp of what he said.

'Hello,' they said in unison, nodding as Miguel pointed towards me. '*Ja, ja, ja.*' The man leaned towards me, his face so close to mine that I was engulfed in garlic with every exhalation. '*Guten morg n.* I help, *ja?*' He shouted as though volume would compensate for any disparity in our respective languages.

'I'm trying to ask Miguel for the floor cleaner.'

'*Ja.*' The man continued to share his breath.

'Floor cleaner? Cleaner de floor?' I continued.

'*Ja.*' He blinked and cocked his head to one side.

'Cleaner. Machine. Vroom vroom.'

'Ah so. *Mayi na.*' He raised an index finger as a declaration of under-standing then turned back to Miguel and curled his fingers round an imagi-nary steering wheel. '*Auto, auto,*' he barked, turning the wheel from left to right.

'No, no, not *auto,*' I intervened, grabbing the invisible steering wheel for some unknown reason.

He stopped. '*Nein, nein, nicht auto,*' he said, wagging a finger at Miguel as if it was completely his misunderstanding.

I decided to bypass the un-hired help. 'I have the bar,' I said slowly, rais-ing an imaginary drink to my mouth to help with the explanation. 'I want you...' I continued, pointing a finger first at myself and then at Miguel, '...give me...' I patted my chest, and fell into the trap of my first mime again. '*Si?*'

By now Miguel had descended the ladder and was scuttling off in the opposite direction glancing over his shoulder as he retreated. I wandered back to the bar dispirited, leaving the Germans to debate my intent between themselves.

'He's a bit strange, isn't he?' I asked Patricia. 'He just ran off.'

'He's normally fine,' she replied. 'I'll go and see if I can find him.'

Five minutes later Patricia returned, pulling the rotating floor cleaner behind her. She was doing her best to conceal a smile. 'You want to watch him,' she said to Joy. 'Miguel said he made a pass at him.'

They both looked at me. 'Weirdo,' I murmured. 'I just wanted to borrow the machine.'

Attaining at least a basic grasp of the Spanish language to avoid subse-quent embarrassments was just one of the things that I had yet to learn.

Not allowing well-intentioned locals to blow up the bar was another.

Frank was a dour truck driver from Oldham who had brought his kids to Tenerife after separating from his wife. At 49 he had taken early retirement and bought one of the first apartments on El Beril. Along with most of the English-speaking expats – and I'm sure other nationalities as well – he got easily bored. Being bored abroad is a mischievous combination, one that will eventually drive most people to seek desperately and without conscience anything to give them a purpose for being. Drink usually provides the fluidity necessary to find out about each other's business and thus discover that purpose.

We had a standard team of barflies, eager to occupy the tedious sunny hours with other people's concerns. They worked on a rigid two-two formation: Frank would hold the left wing next to the Dorada pump; Al, an alcoholic from Liverpool with a mysteriously large amount of cash and an equal quantity of razor-sharp wit, would provide a constant flow of banter for him to head at whatever target happened to have been chosen that day. At the back, Frank's son Danny would lob the odd remark over his dad's shoulder or pass it along to his sister Sam to dribble with for a while until the two attackers took control.

The two kids had tried a term in a local school when they first arrived but didn't like it and hadn't been back since. 'They know enough already, couple of wise-arses,' Frank would argue when the subject was broached. Since their brief affair with education they spent much of their time with their dad which, when not fishing, was more often than not on a Smugglers bar stool.

Danny probably knew more than us about running the bar, from cocktail recipes to how to change a barrel. Over the first few nights the 13-year-old would often help Joy or Faith out in times of crisis. ''Undred 'n' fifty pesetas,' he would demand from customers, his eyes barely level with the black painted bar-top. Whereas the two girls had been scared out of changing barrels by Frank: 'Don't lean over it. Knew a man in England who got his head taken clear off.' Danny would be only too happy to oblige.

As one of the original El Berilians, Frank considered himself to be a self-appointed troubleshooter dealing with a variety of problems that befell the other English residents. He wouldn't, however, help the foreigners as he called them. The Germans, French, Italians and Spanish were part of the problem and ironically, Frank's colonialist policy would have been to shoot them all if they didn't go back to their own country. Racist he may have been, but if you had a problem with your car or needed some DIY doing, Frank was your man, though the results were not always positive.

Two tall tanks housed in a flimsy metal cabinet on the terrace fed propane gas through the exterior wall, along the length of the restaurant and into the kitchen. This routing left a lot to be desired as the slightest leak combined with a casually discarded cigarette could have seen a drastic re-positioning of the Smugglers Tavern.

There was a safety device in place, which cut the gas off inside the cabinet if there was a fire or some other disagreeable disturbance in the flow. A week after the electricity supply was restored with a plank of wood, the shut-off valve jammed shut after one too many flaming chicken breasts. We called out the gas engineer on the Tuesday morning but by Wednesday lunchtime they still hadn't arrived. This meant that only microwave meals and salads could be served and it wasn't proving too popular with the regulars.

'All you need to do is bypass the valve,' suggested Frank knowingly, and in spite of our voiced doubts, he finally managed to separate the safety feature from the top of the gas canister.

'Right, try lighting it,' he shouted from what I noticed was a fair distance. With visions of a propane bottle shooting into the facing hotel like a rocket, I clicked the electronic lighter and watched, relieved as a pretty blue flame danced around the ring.

'Seems to be alright,' I shouted, just before a short, sharp and loud bang blew the top off the gas cabinet.

Frank was struggling to shut the propane off as it filled the air with flammable fumes. Several people came running to investigate the explosion, including Patricia who was holding a cigarette. 'PUT THAT FUCKING THING OUT,' shouted Frank waving a spanner at her. It was the most animated I ever saw him.

'What happened?' I enquired when it seemed that we, and the surrounding buildings, were out of danger.

'I don't think it'll work without that valve,' he replied sagely.

We decided that brandies were in order and celebrated that at least we were still alive.

The bar was beginning to look a little happier even if our power situation was not. The frosted 'mock fishing float' glass lamps turned out to be not frosted at all, merely dust-entrenched. Replacing dozens of light bulbs added to the brightness and the increase in luminosity was astounding. Combined with brand new tablecloths and a major dustathon the Smugglers Tavern no longer resembled a dingy taproom. It was at last beginning to look like a restaurant.

Chris Rea taunted us with 'On the Beach', as we paused to admire the way the bar was looking. Then suddenly he fell silent. The fans slowed to a halt and the mercury in the bar thermometer instantly journeyed north.

I stuck my head out of the bar, as the other business owners were doing. 'It's not just us then?' I asked Robin, Patricia's daughter.

'No, we're all off. The hotel's still on though. Its generator hasn't kicked in.'

There was not much we could do in the heat. At the far side of the bar, the kitchen received little daylight through the open doorway and had been plunged into darkness. Fortunately all the prep had been completed and put away, but with the fridges off any food would soon go off in this heat.

We sat outside with tepid beers. The cooler soon reverted to a heater without electricity. Half an hour passed and still the electricity didn't come back on. We knew it wasn't the old box at the back of the complex as Mario had managed to get the electricity company to fix the problem.

'Not paid your bill?' a voice asked from up above.

'You waiting for it to come back on?' grinned another man leaning over the railings at street level. We nodded.

'They'll be waiting a long time then, John,' sighed the first man.

'Aye, John. A very long time.' The two Johns nodded their heads pityingly. They obviously required some coaxing to share their secret.

'Is there something you know that we don't?' I asked, squinting in the sun. Thick gold chains rested on tanned chests. Both had silver hair, combed back away from identical Ray-Bans. Although each had a reasonable physique, I guessed they must have been in their 60s.

'You've been cut off,' said the shorter John.

'Aye, snipped,' dittoed the other.

'Not just you. Everybody. Everybody's been cut off. Apart from us, that is,' continued John One.

'We're alright though, aren't we, John?' added John Two.

'Are you going to buy us a beer then?' John One led the taller one down the middle set of stairs.

Apparently, the unfinished apartments at the top of the complex were the problem. In Tenerife, the builder is obliged to provide electricity and water until the complex is officially finished and handed over to the community, by which time the responsibility is passed to the individual owners. Our builder had decided that he had finished all the work that he was going to do and informed the electricity company who duly noted that nobody else had applied to take over the electricity account and promptly pulled the plug. Everybody on the complex was affected apart from those who had found out about the need to apply for a private supply and had already had individual meters installed. Our two jovial Johns had heard about the new requirements by chance and were two of very few on the complex who had not been plunged into darkness. For want of anything better to do they were now wandering through the complex gloating at everybody they could find.

'It's a bit serious, isn't it,' said John One. 'I mean, a bar without electricity? What can you do? Become a salad bar?'

'Aye, a salad bar. Good one, John. Salad and water – warm water mind.' They both set about laughing. This was getting us nowhere apart from feeling more irritated by the two clowns.

'What do you suggest?' I asked, interrupting their mirth.

'Dunno really. You should have gone and got your own meter,' said John One.

'You should have got your own,' repeated John Two.

'Nobody told us we had to,' said Joy.

'They won't have done. You have to go and find out,' said John One.

'Did you not find out?' John Two sucked through his teeth noisily and shook his head. The other John stood with his hands on his hips confrontationally.

'When did you two know about this then?' I asked.

'We've known for ages,' said John One.

'A long time,' affirmed the other.

'Well, why didn't you tell anybody else?' said Joy, beginning to get annoyed.

'That's not my problem,' he replied. 'It's not my fault if you don't shag the right people eh?' He nudged Joy and winked knowingly.

'What are we going to do then?' I asked Joy in an attempt to cut the two Johns out of the conversation.

'Have you got a long cable?' interrupted John One.

'How long?' I asked. I knew several extension leads were snaked underneath the bench seats throughout the bar. The number and location of power points had proved to be woefully inadequate.

'Well, if you can find a long enough cable to stretch from my apartment to here, you can feed off our electric until you get your meter installed.'

I was surprised by their sudden show of generosity. 'You wouldn't mind?'

'We're happy to help out, aren't we, John?' said John Two.

'Mind you, you don't get nothing for free in this life,' said John One. 'You can pay both electric bills while you're using ours and buy us the odd beer every now and then.'

'Can't say fairer than that, John,' agreed John Two.

We had no other choice than to agree to their deal. Fortunately John One's place was one of the closest apartments to the bar. We strung a succession of cables together across the roof tiles of three other buildings and ran them down into the commercial area ready to be plugged in. At least we could power up enough equipment to stay open.

But DIY has never been one of my strong points. Give me a flat-pack for an eight-foot-high wardrobe and I'll build you a five-foot-high dog kennel with a skylight and trapdoor. Add in a flash of distraction and the surrounding area becomes a danger zone. Thus, when the final piece of cable was dragged to just outside the bar doors for me to wire it into an extension box, I somewhat foolishly overlooked a rudimentary aspect of working with electricity. It's best to dispense with the current first.

'What you doing, Joe?' asked Justin, suddenly vocalising his presence behind me.

'Hi, Justin,' I said, 'didn't hear you arrive.' Nobody ever heard Justin coming. He was one of those children who suddenly appear at the crucial point of concentration like an apparition sent to test your resolve. His family owned one of the apartments at the Altamira where they spent weeks, even months at a time. Justin didn't seem to be lacking in education despite his forced absence. He was intelligent to the point of genius, constantly pushing his bottle-bottom glasses up his freckled nose as he rushed to explain how something worked. However, what he scored in intellect he lost in physical coordination. His mind always seemed to be three minutes ahead of his actions, making concentration on what he was doing a major problem. Not a night would go by when Justin wouldn't either break, or cause to break, a glass, plate, ashtray or plastic chair. The sound of shattering glass would usually be followed by a cry of 'Justin!' from his beleaguered parents.

I unscrewed the plug. 'What are you up to, Justin?' I began, and grabbed the bare wires. It felt like a shark had just bitten my arm and was trying to yank it from my shoulder. I wanted to let go but my hand wouldn't unclench. Justin was the only one around to share my eye opener but just stared on impassively. Instinctively I fell backwards and the cable slid from my grip.

For a moment I lay staring at the big blue, startled by the shock and by my own stupidity. 'We're going to the beach,' said Justin standing over me. My right arm and shoulder tingled with a dull ache. The same performance on a wet day in Bolton would probably have killed me. I thanked Tenerife for being so dry in June.

'That'll be nice,' I said from the floor.

'Did you just get an electric shock?' he asked after a while.

'Yes.'

'You should have turned the power off.'

'I know.'

'See you later then,' he said and skipped off.

'Yes, see you later, Justin.' I got to my feet just as John One appeared.

'Is it working?' he shouted from the top of the stairs.

'Erm... do you think you could unplug it at your end?' I asked.

Fortunately the connection proceeded without my body becoming an integral link again and we managed to power up the beer and mixer coolers, one bar fridge, a random selection of house lights, the kitchen fridge and the freezer. All the ice cream was ruined, leaving a sickly pool of meltdown on the bottom shelf of the display cabinet. Everything else was transferred into the kitchen chest freezer or the tiny freezer compartments in our own homes.

Apart from the financial loss of orange sorbets et al, our dining patronage understandably waned as all we could tempt them with were salads of various guises – tuna, prawn, seafood (tuna and prawn), cheese, ham, ploughman's (cheese and ham) and the Smugglers Special House Salad (a crafty combination of tuna, prawn, cheese and ham). There weren't many takers over the compulsory 'healthy eating' nights.

We had to put up with four weeks without a regular electricity supply, despite constant pleas at the electricity company's counter. Our business life had now invaded our only sanctuary. Lasagne, shepherd's pies and huge trays of curry had to be cooked in our apartments and hauled to the bar in time for evening meals – just to provide a bit of variety.

During our down time, the two Johns milked their 'odd beer' for all it was worth. They spent an inordinate amount of time sitting at the bar buying drinks for new holidaymakers, female ones in particular. It mattered not if the husbands were with their wives. The two Johns assumed that because they themselves were residents they were automatically more appealing.

It can't be denied that there exists a certain amount of disdain for the

'Billys' – as holidaymakers were affectionately known by the residents. We as newcomers had yet to adopt that arrogance but it was all too plain to see in the more seasoned expats.

Just as the two Johns tried to impress on the new customers that they were frequenting *their* bar, so it was with the island in general. Whether in Las Americas or in the secluded villages like La Caleta, the expats treated the island as if it was their own, making it perfectly obvious that holiday-makers were naive and ignorant in the ways of *their* land and were fair game to be parodied.

'*Dos El Dorads por favor,*' those brave enough to make the effort with the local language would ask at our bar.

'*Dos Dorads* ? You're not asking for a TV programme you know,' mocked John One. 'You mean Dorada. It's not *dr ad* , it's Dorada. *Dos* Doradas *por favor*. If you're going to speak the language, speak it properly.' This was from a man whose Spanish vocabulary came to a spluttering halt after exhausting his knowledge on two beers, a hamburger and shouting 'oy, *gap a*' (oy, beautiful) at anything with smooth legs and a pulse.

Mind you, our own attempts at launching into the local lingo had not altogether harvested the desired results. All of the delivery companies were Spanish and rather than call them all 'Manuel', as many of the expats did, we gave them nicknames: Chop delivered the meat; Captain Birdseye brought the frozen fish; Crusty took our bread order; Marine Boy dropped off the bottled water; Popeye was our soft drinks man; and Bill and Ben, two rotund beer truck drivers, delivered the barrels of Dorada.

It soon became apparent that learning the numbers was essential if we wanted to order the correct quantities. Miming 60 bottles of water was not only time consuming but also carried something of a margin of error. More often than not we got it right but once or twice, to our cost, we didn't.

Flushed with the success of placing an order for extra beer barrels over the phone for the first time, I decided that it would save a lot of time getting the cash and carry to deliver what we needed rather than going on our daily two-hour shopping trip. It was to be a lesson in realising my own limitations after I inadvertently ordered *qi nientos* (500) packs of toilet rolls instead of *qi nce* (15), *dc e* (12) bottles of Johnny Walker instead of *ds* (2) and only *uno* (1) frozen chicken fillet instead of *once* (11). On top of all that the flour was self-raising instead of plain, the tuna arrived in what seemed like one-ton containers rather than the usual one-serving cans that we preferred and the lettuce looked like it had already been eaten once. It proved too difficult to get across our grievances to the teenager who was neither interested nor willing to listen to our pained complaining. Our lack of Spanish language ability was judged as a sign of stupidity and we were treated as though we had no idea what we were doing – which wasn't altogether untrue.

This widespread contempt was surprising, particularly from the business owners who relied on the swarm of British visitors to keep their tills ringing. In all aspects the holiday-Brit abroad was looked down upon even by their expat counterparts. An attitude prevailed whereby it didn't matter if you upset one lot of tourists one week as the following week a planeload of new arrivals would be ripe for the picking. Why pull out all the stops to be friendly and courteous if you could get by with the barest of service?

There were literally hundreds of bars in Tenerife all competing with each other. Most relied on advertising the lowest price for a pint of beer, a vicious circle that led to some bars making absolutely no profit on the beer but compensating by hiking up the price of the soft drinks to an extortionate level. The constantly busy bars kept the prices moderate but relied on word of mouth about their hospitality. It was a path that we were determined to follow.

We did wonder if some of the holidaymakers had booked their brains on a later flight. This was most evident in the standard of driving.

The locals have honed a specific set of skills that enable motorists to neatly mesh into organised chaos – use the horn instead of the brakes; park where it's most convenient for yourself; ignore such inconveniences as pedestrian crossings, other people's driveways and cars already occupying the desired space; and don't attempt to use your indicators except after completing a turn.

Unfortunately this can appear a tad intimidating if you're used to the relatively synchronised skills of Britain's road users.

Worse still, the majority of new arrivals are dumped onto the bedlam of Tenerife's road network on the same day – either Tuesday or Friday. Mingle these road virgins with Tenerifian boy racers in souped-up Seat Ibizas, taxi drivers who have no regard for any vehicle that is not a white Mercedes and pop-pop scooter boys weaving in and out of traffic on their squealing mobile hairdryers and you can see why two weeks in Playa de las Americas can easily become two weeks in Plaster of Paris.

Having been foolishly thrust off in their rented dodgems with no more than a 'Welcome to Tenerife' paper placemat to guide them, holidaymakers soon cause chaos on the TF1 motorway as they slow down to an almost dead halt while they squint at the road signs.

'I don't know where we are, Roy.'

'Find *Cambio de Sentido* [Change of Direction] on the map. I think we must be near there. We keep passing signs for it.'

Even the 'safe' drivers cause confusion in this predictably erratic environment, as normal manoeuvres are often the least expected. On roundabouts, you would often see a rental car circling repeatedly whilst the driver, his face pressed close to the windscreen, searches in vain for some clue as to how to safely exit the demonic carousel.

One day I followed a car on my way back from the cash and carry. The first thing that struck me was the fact that either there were no seats in the car or its inhabitants must have both been less than four feet tall. For a good three kilometres their speed remained fixed at 35 kph regardless of what obstacles presented themselves. There was not the faintest hint of acknowledgement for the give way signs. No concessions were granted for individuals already on pedestrian crossings and there was no change of pace or prior suggestion that a violent swerve was about to take place. It was as though the car was programmed to travel at 35 kph in whatever direction the munchkins pointed it until it met an impenetrable obstacle or ran out of fuel.

Several times they must have thought they had reached their destination and made to turn into an entranceway only to veer back into the middle of the road having gone off the idea. An obligatory blast of the horn fell on deaf ears. They had probably grown immune to the sound of irritated drivers tooting their displeasure.

Finally they disappeared through a gap in a wall and all seemed safe until a moment later when only my evasive action prevented them from hitting me side-on as they suddenly sprang out from another gap. With them now bearing down on me in the rear-view mirror, fear overcame my feelings of curiosity and amazement and I accelerated out of reach. I glanced back just in time to see them swing round a corner and proceed in the wrong direction up a one-way street, off to terrorise some other unfortunate soul who had risked taking to the streets on a Tuesday or Friday.

CHAPTER 6

Having successfully reconnected to the electricity supply we were now required, not altogether unjustly, to arrange some means of paying for it. A transfer to pay the first instalment then a standing order for subsequent bills was the obvious solution and one favoured by the electricity company. However, because we had three separate accounts with the bank (personal accounts for David and me, plus a joint business account for the Smugglers) there would have to be some shuffling of funds between the three before we could make the initial payment.

At the best of times the dealings with our bank had not been totally satisfactory and we were loathe to trust them with something as complicated as making a transfer and setting up a standing order.

It was a mystery as to how the bank was so inept. When you employ a gardener you quite reasonably expect him to look after your garden; when you pay a cleaner you expect them to take care of your dusting. But when we trusted our finances with a bank, the one thing that they seemed incapable of doing properly was looking after our money, although it has to be said, they were very proficient at furnishing us with free gifts of kitchenware and bombarding us with generous offers of credit.

To date there had been only one occasion when a statement had arrived and not revealed that some fortunate stranger had benefited from an involuntary charitable gesture from our account.

Our branch was is in Los Cristianos. With the arrival of tourism, this sleepy fishing village had been hauled out of bed and re-dressed from top to bottom in hotels, apartments, souvenir shops and banks.

As was the norm, I took my place in a queue that started just outside the adjoining cake shop. I wanted to explain that I was not a charity and just because I had been seen making polite conversation with other account holders in the queue, we had not yet reached that cosy stage of friendship whereby my funds were freely available to all and sundry.

There were two counters at the branch but as the queue inched forward

I could see that, as was customary, only one was in use. Behind the other sat a stern-looking madam, inattentively flicking through a bulging wad of 10,000-peseta notes. Occasionally she glanced up and from over horn-rimmed glasses cast a lofty look of contempt over us all.

The man at the front of the queue had emptied the contents of one of several large brown envelopes onto the counter. The clerk set about sorting the notes into separate piles, meticulously making sure they were all face-up. We were in for an exceptionally long wait.

To pass the time I decided to write down the precise details of what I hoped to achieve from this particular visit. I drew pictures showing little stickmen happily passing money to one another. From these I felt sure that there could be no doubt that I required money to be transferred from account A to account B and then to the electricity company. I knew that if this actually occurred it would be a minor miracle and I, along with my little stickmen, would be extremely joyous.

After 40 minutes of slow shuffling, I gave the piece of paper to the girl. She turned it around in her hands and without a glimmer of personality passed it back informing me that I had to join another queue to process a transfer. To save the trouble I suggested she just withdraw the money from account A and then deposit it back into account B. We stood eye to eye for a while whilst I waited for the logic to register. It finally clunked into place. Hesitantly she filled out a form, pondered over it for a while, screwed it up and filled out a different one before asking for my signature.

I then queued to see the assistant manager to find out why I had been chosen to pay my brother's health insurance, my stepfather's phone bill and a complete stranger's monthly subscription to *National Geog aphic* magazine.

'They didn't have enough money in them,' he explained. 'To avoid them going overdrawn we transferred the money from your account.' He sat back and smoothed down his tie, content that this was a perfectly logical solution to the problem.

'But that was my money!' I said, exasperated.

'But you know them,' he countered.

After I explained that it was totally unacceptable, completely immoral and probably illegal, he begrudgingly agreed to put the money back and promised, with a tone that suggested he thought I was being a little selfish, that it wouldn't happen again. We both knew that it most certainly would.

By way of an apology for our near incineration, Frank offered to take the four of us out on his boat. When he wasn't tampering with gas supplies or threatening to shoot the locals, he could usually be spotted bobbing several hundred yards out at sea with a fishing rod in one hand and cool beer in the other. He admitted that he wasn't a people person and even back in the UK he much preferred the companionship of dead carp.

David and Faith had to decline the offer as it was their night on duty. Danny and Sam were staying with friends and Al was recovering from a three-day bender in his apartment.

The marina of Puerto Colon has often been termed as Tenerife's secret, though how multi-million pounds worth of flashy steel and sail, the majority skippered by a bunch of raucous nouveau riche, can remain a secret is anybody's guess.

Tenerife's yacht-erati shared their berth with an array of excursion boats varying in size and comfort from the latest catamaran to converted fishing boats with on-board menageries. There were bright yellow glass-bottom boats, fiery red speedboats, replica schooners and a dozen or so serious ocean-going yachts.

The rattling and chinking of masts brought forth similar feelings that I had about airports. This was a port of fantasy. From here, lifetime adventures would begin, culminating in a step ashore on any exotic coastline that took the fancy.

As with planes, the mystery of propulsion added to the intrigue. How could these tiny vessels, reliant on the direction of wind and speed of current, be navigated precisely in the vastness of the ocean? Boating was shrouded in its own language, its own culture, its own sights, sounds and smells. If you weren't in the club, it was unfathomable.

The tourist industry too had always held an air of mystique. I was always mesmerised on family holidays when we were ushered in to our tourist world. The British reps in their matching uniforms seemed as alien as the land we were visiting. *What were their lives like? How il d they spend their time off?W here would hey g on hol idy ?*

The holiday would run seamlessly from buffet breakfast through games and activities, afternoon excursions and themed dinners. It was just a fortnight for us, but in a whole new world created just for enjoyment.

Even long after I had tagged along on my last holiday with my parents, I still remained in awe of holiday resorts and the parallel world they represented.

Without realising it I had crossed over into this surrealism when we took over the Smugglers Tavern. No longer would resorts or hotels be exciting and mysterious. I had stepped across the line and seen the mysteries, been part of the set up. I had already stepped through the back doors, the trade entrance of the Altamira, spoken to the reps when they were off duty and met performers without their makeup. For me the mystery was gone forever. But possibly I was now the focus of that same sense of wonder in some of our own customers.

Frank was about to enlighten Joy and me about the mysteries of the fishing world, a seemingly sad, sullen population of loners who would much rather sit in the rain staring at ripples than join the real world.

He was almost ecstatic in his enthusiasm. Well, at least as ecstatic as Frank could be.

'Best thing in the world,' he droned in a monotone as we bounced along the pontoon towards a row of sleek and shiny motor cruisers. Smoked glass windows punctuated the fluorescent white hulls like Ray-Bans on a Hollywood film set.

This was a shock. Could it be that Frank's dress-down demeanour was a disguise? Was he a secret millionaire living the idle life? His drinking partner Al had hinted that Frank was a secretive soul who liked to keep some things to himself. Was this his mystery solved?

No, was the answer. 'Flash bastards,' he muttered as he placed a cool box, plastic bag and petrol can underneath the upturned bow of one of the mega-cruisers. In the shadows, between this and another similarly showy boat, was an eight-foot motorboat. It was the colour of an old beige bathtub and rocked from side to side in the wake like a demented, trapped animal. It could barely accommodate the two thin wooden benches. In between lay empty beer cans, more carrier bags and an assortment of fishing tackle. Frank was certainly not from the old school of seamanship. Shipshape and Bristol fashion were clearly absent from his nautical vocabulary.

After bailing out a small puddle he yanked on the starter rope and fired the bathtub into life. I had never been particularly good travelling on water, or rather my insides hadn't. The outside was more than happy with the exfoliating sea spray, sun on skin and breeze through hair. Fortunately, as we set off, the sea was remarkably calm.

'It's still,' I noted, content that even my weak stomach could hack this millpond.

'We've not left the harbour yet,' said Frank. 'It'll be a bit choppier out there.'

Sure enough, as soon as we passed the harbour walls the boat began to lunge at the oncoming waves. Joy and I lurched back and forth on our bench like Muslims at prayer.

'It's not too bad,' said Frank.

By the time Puerto Colon was bobbing on the horizon, I was not feeling my best. I scanned our surroundings; further west over the great watery expanse lay the Americas, shorewards Tenerife's southwest coast played hide and seek behind the swell. Beneath us lay the very creatures that I was so keen to escape from in Bolton.

Frank cut the engine and opened the cool box. 'First things first,' he said taking out three cool cans of beer. We sat in silence for a while drinking Dorada. The ocean clapped time against the side of the boat, a rhythmic accompaniment to our synchronised swaying.

'So how's it going with the bar?' Frank broke the hypnotic spell.

'OK, so far,' I said. 'Most of the regulars seem nice.'

'Aye, well don't believe what anybody says, they're a bunch of two-faced bastards. Kiss your ass in the morning and stab your back in the afternoon.'

'Why? Who's like that,' asked Joy.

'All of them,' said Frank. 'The two Johns are the worst.'

'They've been alright so far,' I said. 'They were good to help us out with the electricity.'

'Aye, and they won't let you forget it. They're nasty little gits, especially little John. Don't get too friendly with him.'

'We'll bear it in mind.'

'Same goes for Patricia. She might seem OK but she'll be saying differently behind you back. Watch what you say to her.'

'What about Al?' I asked.

'Al's OK. Pain in the arse when he's pissed but he's OK on the wagon. It might seem like a tight-knit community but believe me, they're all stabbing each other in the back behind closed doors. They're bored. Fucked off and bored, that's their problem.'

'And you?' asked Joy. 'What do they think of you?'

'I call a spade a spade. If they don't like it they can fuck right off. It's no skin off my nose. They probably think I'm a common piece of shit, maybe I am, but at least I don't try to hide it.'

'Why did you come here?' said Joy. 'You don't seem so happy.'

'Don't let this miserable face fool you. I like the sun and I like my fishing and that's all I need. I wouldn't go back to England now if you paid me. Too much rain, too much bad news on the telly, too many foreigners and too much tax. You can't make a living in the UK now, you just work to pay the taxman. Plus Shark Bait would want some more money off me.' He could see we were puzzled. 'Shark Bait... the ex-missus.'

'So you're hiding from her then?' asked Joy.

'No, she knows where I am but she can't get anything from me if I stay here.'

'Why did you split up?' Joy persevered.

'Let's just say a difference of direction,' he answered, throwing back the last of his beer. 'Anyways, come on. We're not here to fucking gossip, let's fish.'

The beer had helped to quell the seasickness momentarily and Frank handed me a rod baited with semi-frozen prawns. The nausea soon returned though as he reached into a bag beneath where he was sat and threw a handful of reeking *Cebns a* into the water.

'What the hell is that?' I said holding my nose.

'Anchovies, sardines and tuna mixed with biscuits,' he said. 'The fish love it.' He extended a handful of the mush towards me. 'Here, want to try it?'

I had only fished once before. It was with some school friends at a duck pond in Howard Park. That outing had merely resulted in an extreme bout of apathy and a telling off from the park keeper after nearly lassoing a mallard with an errant cast.

Thankfully, in the absence of webbed obstacles, I managed to cast my line without any immediate threat to Joy, Frank or myself. The bright floats played peacefully on the surface of the ocean whilst Frank and I watched them like protective parents. Joy had already lost interest in her line and had reclined as much as Frank's boat would allow. The sky was an unblemished canvas of vivid blue, reflecting its glory in the vast ocean.

Suddenly my reel began whirring. 'Got one, you bastard,' Frank shouted. He put down his rod and turned his attention to mine. 'Give it a jerk and start reeling it in,' he said. The fish didn't put up much of a fight, presumably saving its energy for face-to-face combat. It broke the surface a couple of metres from the boat. I lifted the line and it swung in towards Frank's face, missing by inches.

Now don't believe every rubber-suited wet-head who boasts of the unspoilt beauty that lies beneath the waves. There are some damn ugly creatures living down there. Let's face it, sea cucumbers, weeverfish and moray eels are not going to win any underwater beauty pageants. These unsightly monsters understandably spend much of their time hiding their afflictions in dark caves or camouflaged against the seabed until some scuba diver starts adding to their misery with a spear gun.

I'm not saying that the undersea world doesn't have its fair share of fetching characters. The unjustly named Bastard Grunt has a certain cutesy appeal with its delicate shade of pink whilst large gangs of Turkish Wrasse with Day-Glo blue decorate the water like hand-painted ornaments.

But it's the downright hideous that elicit most gasps and I had one of their brethren dangling by the lip. Back on the market this was not a fish that would have sold at three for a fiver, even ten for a fiver. Its brown and white body was mottled with a profusion of tiny warts and its dorsal fin was clearly designed to be left alone by the sensible.

'Fuck!' muttered Frank. 'It's a twatting scorpion fish.'

Anything prefixed with the word 'scorpion' – or 'twatting' for that matter – did not sound like it should be encouraged to share my personal space. 'What do I do with it?' I held the rod at arm's length, which sent it swinging in an even larger circle amongst us. Joy was awoken by the commotion and sat up just as the spiky brown creature headed straight between her eyes. She flicked her head to one side, narrowly avoiding a more intimate introduction and the fish spun wildly past, opening and closing its mouth in a dizzy protest. After completing a couple of circular tours, causing all three of us to duck consecutively, Frank seized his moment and grabbed the rod, lowering the fish back into its more familiar surroundings with a small splash. He reached and cut the line, releasing it, and us, from the unpleasant encounter.

I was thankful that the next half hour was spent fruitlessly, but by now the combined stink of oily fish, petrol and sun tan cream was adding to the roller coaster ride that my stomach had to endure.

Frank could see the telltale green tinge and reeled in the lines. 'We'll find somewhere sheltered,' he said pointing the bathtub shorewards.

El Beril came into sight as we neared the coastline. The terracotta roofing looked like a red oasis in a desert of grey and black rock. To see the resort detached and in its entirety allowed a degree of pondering. Living in a coastal community where the sun always shines has to be considered fortunate in anybody's eyes. We may have been in heavy debt but this burden remained on dry land. From our current vantage point the days of market toil were two-dimensional, like photographs in an album.

To the left of El Beril lay the Altamira and further left still was a similar structure but in skeleton form. This was intended to be the sister hotel of the Altamira until lack of promoter's funds aborted any hopes of a sibling.

We jerked on past the hippy commune where a dozen tepees punctuated the cacti-infested slopes. The reward for living in such prickly surroundings was Spaghetti Beach, a rare stretch of golden sand, popular with nudists.

It gained its name through an opportune chef operating a totally illegal, but nevertheless popular, beachside eatery. Of Italian descent, naturally spaghetti was on the menu. Unnaturally and rather off-putting, the spaghetti was delivered to your table by the chef himself wearing nothing more than a congenial smile and wayward splashes of bolognese sauce. Personally I thought it was taking al fresco cuisine a little too far but, judging from the often full wooden benches, many disagreed.

A few minutes further north along the coast we turned inland and headed for a rocky promontory occupied by a solitary villa. We motored around the headland and into the concealed entrance of a small horseshoe cove.

A cluster of buildings hugged the rocks and shingle to the right. Weatherworn green and blue doors marked cave residences dug into the volcanic rock three metres above the frothing surf. Half a dozen white, three-storey houses cluttered the shoreline; a contained community seemingly designed by a random school of planning.

The largest structure formed a crumbling backdrop along the entire length of shiny black shingle. Through the open side doors I could see bunches of green bananas stacked high in wooden crates, presumably harvested from the plantation that swathed a channel through a black, rocky gully behind the village like a green glacier.

Frank tethered the boat to a faded pink buoy, one of half a dozen that had been anchored to the seabed. The water was so clear it was possible to trace the rope all the way to the sandy bottom although it was difficult to gauge the depth.

'*El Puertito*,' announced Frank. 'It's a bit calmer here. You'll feel better if you have a swim.'

Joy and I jumped overboard, startled by how cold the ocean was on such a warm day. Almost immediately the nausea disappeared. Frank passed down two beers as we treaded water. A sun-wizened old man sat on a slipway inspecting the cork floats on a bright blue fishing net. He looked up at the intrusion and stared for a discomforting length of time before focusing once more on his task.

This was a side of Tenerife that we hadn't seen before. A side as yet untouched by the tourist trade. But a dumper-full of imported sand and one or two bars or restaurants would surely already be in the plans of a canny developer and it would only be a matter of time before the foreign invasion claimed yet another patch of Canarian life.

While Frank happily fished off the side of his boat, Joy and I swam ashore. Next to the slipway a small *tasca* had just opened its doors. A few old boys eyed us suspiciously as they took their places on the sea-facing veranda underneath a blue hand-painted sign that had faded in the sun. The words *Bar Pepe y Lola* were just visible. Even in this intrinsically appealing cove there were no obvious efforts to attract custom. Two beers were pushed towards us without a word spoken or eye contact made. The chairs and tables were of untreated wood that would have greatly benefited from a sheet of sandpaper. Despite the rawness this lack of grace and pretension was refreshing after so many hours forging fake hospitality at the Smugglers.

The sullenness, although disconcerting at first, meant that we could relax without that intrinsically British trait of needing to be approved by complete strangers who for all you knew could have been cannibalistic psychopaths and other ne'er-do-wells.

This UK habit seems exaggerated when surrounded by a culture for which unnecessary social deportment is considered an affliction rather than an asset.

I had only been on the island for two weeks but had already become aware of just how many times the Brits bandy around pleases and thank yous compared with the Canarians. They're thrown like confetti at a wedding; not as an expression of gratitude, more as a signal that a particular encounter has come to an end.

Take, for example, being seated at a restaurant. The waiter seats Mr and Mrs Brit – if it's a reasonably salubrious joint – and they *thank* him.

He hands them the menu.

'*Thank you*,' they beam graciously.

'Would you like a drink?'

'A bottle of house red *please*,' they reply, adding a *'thank you'* as he wanders off to do, what is after all, his job. He produces the bottle and allows them a sample.

'That's fine *thank you*,' they nod agreeably.

He then proceeds to fill their glasses and again they *thank* him.

A variation of the same conversation then resumes with the ordering and receiving of food. And again with the charade of paying the bill. By the end of a three-course meal, the Brits may have graciously thanked the waiter an average of 15 times.

My argument isn't one against politeness. My mother brought me up to observe manners; not to wipe your nose on your (or anybody else's) sleeve, always to say please and thank you when snatching other children's toys, that kind of thing, but there are extremes. The Canarians, with their economical and abrupt demands, seem to be at the other end of the scale.

'Cerveza!' they bark, proceeding to slap money on the bar top and chug the contents without another murmur. This, to a Brit, seems rude. To them it's not. It's just an example of a successful interaction. Once, when local Canarians absent-mindedly stumbled into the Smugglers, they asked why *I* was thanking *them* when they were the ones being given the service. It was a fair point but it's a habit that is hard to curtail.

We returned home as the sun began its steady decline behind La Gomera, turning the mountains a glowing orange and laying huge shadows in the ravines. 'Look, over there,' shouted Frank suddenly. We veered away from our coast-hugging route and headed further out to sea.

'What is it?' asked Joy.

'You'll see,' he replied.

In the failing light we couldn't see anything unusual. Then all of a sudden a shadow appeared under the water next to our boat. 'Down there.' Frank pointed. The shadow broke the surface just six feet away from our boat mirroring our speed and direction exactly.

'Dolphins,' said Frank calmly. Another grey fin broke the surface a little further away, then another, and another. In seconds we were in the midst of a group of 15 to 20 dolphins, all racing our boat.

Joy and I were stunned. To be this close to a pod of dolphins in their natural surroundings seemed surreal. What made it all the more astounding was the interaction. They seemed to be toying with us, almost as curious about us as we were of them. One was almost close enough to touch but as I reached out it sped forwards, leaping from the water ahead of us. Frank cut the engine and we drifted for a while as the dolphins submerged one by one and disappeared into the blue. The performance had ended, but the show had not.

Minutes had passed since we resumed our journey inland when a fish shot out of the water in front of us and flew inches above the waves before splashing down a hundred yards further on.

'Did you see that?' I said.

'Flying fish,' said Frank, unimpressed. 'You see loads of them out here.' We approached the sparkling lights of the harbour in contemplative silence. I felt like a traveller more than a migrant worker, completely absorbed by the sights and sounds I had just seen; the mysterious creatures, the soporific swaying, the warm night breeze, the clinking of masts and ropes as we glided towards our mooring. I had temporarily forgotten our reason for being here. It was the first time since arriving that I felt like a tourist.

Frank's boat excursion and the indifferent behaviour of Lola and Pepe had provided a reminder that we were overseas, even though at times it seemed like an imported little Britain full of patrons who thought that abroad was any sunny place bedecked in red, white and blue where the locals couldn't talk properly.

Although the boat ride did not attain the level of luxury that we had quietly hoped for, it did provide a welcome break in our routine, something that we were always grateful for.

You could only endure chopping so many cucumbers and onions and washing so much lettuce before boredom took a hold and you imaginatively tried to find more interesting ways of dealing with vegetables, usually leading to a brief but hurried excursion to the local casualty unit.

On one such occasion at the hospital I had been bleeding patiently for over an hour after insisting that I did not need to be kept overnight and plugged in to every drip that they could bill my insurance company for. Eventually the receptionist led me to a treatment room and disappeared, presumably to try and prise a doctor from the hospital bar. The array of shiny tools was fascinating and I wondered which ones would be used to cure me of my ailment. Hopefully not the large coal shuttle look-alike. That must have been for gathering up spilt innards or scooping out the brain in medical conditions deemed a little more serious than my own.

Eventually a man of the green cloth was pushed into the room and I proudly revealed my affliction. Blood was still seeping through the checked tea towel that was tightly bound around my hand. I had gashed my palm attempting to model a carrot into the shape of a delicate orchid with an eight-inch bread knife when my hand slipped and I dripped blood on the floor, muttering expletives all the way to the cold tap.

The medical man peered at my hand and gazed inquisitively around the room. It was at this point that I had the uncomfortable feeling that this was all a bit unfamiliar to him. He picked up a brown glass bottle, scanned the label and liberally scattered the contents over my wound. We both waited a moment, he a little more curious than me to see what reaction I would have to this liquid. I was relieved when no more than a vague tingling occurred, but I sensed disappointment and surprise from him. Next, he dabbed at my hand with an unnecessarily large wad of cotton wool and told me to hold it there while he went off in search of needle and thread.

We have all heard those news reports of phoney doctors performing intricate surgical procedures on unsuspecting patients, well I was beginning to think that this man was no more of a doctor than I was. To flee or not to flee battled in my mind, but before I could run for it, he returned looking very excited.

Being English and therefore not wishing to appear rude, I tried to think of a polite way of asking him if he was actually associated, in any way, shape or form whatsoever, to the medical profession.

'Have you been busy today?' I lightly enquired.

'No not really. A splinter, couple of broken legs and… how you say… a bad joint.'

He could have been either a medic or a carpenter. Time would tell.

'Da-da! Finished,' he announced before taking a step back to admire his own craftsmanship. It wasn't the neatest seam that I had ever witnessed but at least my blood had stopped deserting me.

Before I could thank him, he disappeared into the corridor and returned with someone to whom he seemed eager to show his handiwork.

'Good,' the stranger said, nodding his head in surprise.

The man who had treated me beamed from ear to ear.

See? I could be a doctor, his expression seemed to suggest.

My hand was fine, although it has an irregular scar meandering across it. I don't know to this day if he was a genuine medic or not but I'm sure I've since seen him driving a Dorada lorry.

I was rather pleased that there was a man peering into my fridge oinking at me. It broke the monotony of my early morning prep.

'I think he's Magyar,' explained Joy as though the man rummaging through the fridge whilst doing animal impressions was displaying a trait that was clearly Hungarian. It was obvious that something swine-related was required so I dangled a piece of bacon in front of him. He shook his head vigorously and continued to peel all the lids from the Tupperware containers.

'Ham?' I offered.

'Yah. Ham!' he repeated clasping both my shoulders in an alarming show of cross-cultural bonding. I feared he was going to kiss me.

'Ham with…' And so began act two scene one as he continued to forage for an accompaniment. As he continued to seek out ingredients, I spied through to the public area and could see we were in for our daily dose of Friedhelm.

Running a bar/restaurant obviously involves being in the company of all sorts of characters from many different walks of life. Some you could quite happily spend time with, others you would avoid like the plague. Joy had the fortunate knack of making people from both groups feel like they were all her favourite customers. All except one. It wasn't that we particularly disliked Friedhelm, he was harmless enough, it was just that we had no time for him. To everybody else this was clearly evident but Friedhelm had such thick skin that our indifference went, at least apparently, unnoticed.

He had the appearance of a disgruntled hound dog. Saddlebag jowls tugged at bloodshot eyes and dragged the corners of his mouth into a permanent frown. A retired insurance officer, he liked to pass the time of day describing the various ailments that had befallen him that day. Every sentence would be punctuated by a dramatic gasp for air, and because of his limited knowledge of English his riveting stories could rasp on for hours.

Fortunately we had discovered that a second party wasn't entirely necessary to partake in one of Friedhelm's conversations and if you quietly removed yourself from the proceedings he would happily continue moaning to himself, unhindered by the lack of audience.

His second favourite topic was sex, or rather recounting in vivid details his latest exploits at the local brothel. Although we didn't understand what he was saying most of the time, the constant references to 'fucky-fucky' and the faint glimmer of mischief buried deep in those sunken eyes enabled us to get the gist.

The only time we would see him smile is when he would amuse himself with lewd jokes. Although completely wasted on us, Friedhelm would chuckle himself into a gargling bout of phlegmatic coughing that could only be brought under control by chain smoking three or four foul-smelling Krugers.

It has to be said though that he was one of our most loyal patrons despite our negative hospitality. Every single day he would drag his decrepit body to the same table by the window and struggle for breath as we poured him the first of many large beers.

'Big problem,' he croaked, pointing to various parts of his anatomy. The loose flaps of his cheeks wobbled as he shook his head in self-pity.

'You're the big problem,' muttered Frank from his bar throne.

'Gammon and chips for Suicide Sid,' shouted Joy from around the doorframe. She reminded me that Friedhelm liked his fried egg hard, his onion chopped fine, his chips burnt and his salad served with sugar.

In the meantime my Hungarian companion was motioning at me with an egg in each hand, reminiscent of the Swedish chef from the Muppets. I smiled obligingly and set about Friedhelm's meal.

The Hungarian had found himself a pan and spatula and was quite happily standing beside me preparing himself a ham and mushroom omelette. Why couldn't all of our patrons be this helpful? He even washed the pan afterwards, and left a tip. I think we had found the perfect customer.

Joy was frothing the head of Friedhelm's third pint, he insisted on half liquid and half foam, a request that was fine by us as we could charge full price for what was essentially a half pint. The Germans were most impressed to see us making the effort to accommodate their preferences instead of pulling a pint the British way. If the Brits could lift the glass off the bar without spilling any then it wasn't a full measure and they usually let us know in no uncertain terms.

Our Dorada pump was exceptionally good at German-style pints as it was prone to the odd asthma attack, which would see it wheeze up more air than beer. Occasionally it would be having an extremely bad bout and you could end up with a pot of froth with a token inch of beer hiding at the bottom. These we would pour into a jug in the waist-level fridge under the bar top and serve later when our customers' attention was more blurred. That's if the cockroaches didn't find the beer first.

Roaches are rather partial to a bit of the amber nectar as we often found out after leaving half-finished drinks on the outside tables overnight. When we came to clean up, it was like the morning after a roach rave with lots of the drunken beasties up-ended in their favourite tipple.

'Reserving' the beer was one of the few economies that we played on customers to cut down costs. Many other bars have a larger array of drink scams. Some barmen when asked for a spirit would discreetly dip the rim of the glass in a hidden saucer of whisky, gin or vodka and fill the glass with ice and a mixer. The only alcoholic content was on the edge of the rim but the taste would be there at least until half the drink had been consumed, by which time it was not worth complaining about.

I decided to bring out Friedhelm's offering as I could see Joy was busy at the bar, but as I was lifting the plate, the egg slipped onto the floor. Luckily it bounced as I'd cooked it to our German customer's preference. To fry another would have meant the rest of the food going cold, besides which I had to count our empty beer barrels before the beer men came and nicked a few, charging us extra on the non-returns and pocketing the money themselves.

I scooped the egg off the terracotta tiles and dusted it down with the edge of my apron. At the bar stood a couple of men that I hadn't seen before. They had the deeper tan of residents, appeared more confident and purposeful than holidaymakers, and there was something too cocksure about their manner. After placing the plate in front of Friedhelm I went behind the bar to get a closer look.

One had a scar running from just below his left eye to the corner of his mouth whilst the other looked old enough to be his father and wore a cocky smirk across a boxer's face. Joy was chatting to them; 'This is Joe, my other half,' she said throwing an anxious glance my way. The younger of the two nodded whilst the other ignored me and looked round the bar.

'This your gaff then?' asks the older one in a nicotine-raked London accent. He continued to survey the premises.

'Well, ours and my brother's actually,' I replied, figuring there was strength in numbers.

'Nice place,' he rasped nodding. 'Make much money?' I could feel the younger one's eyes boring into me.

'We get by,' I said. 'Are you staying round here?' I quickly added in an attempt to steer them away from that line of enquiry.

'Might be. It depends.'

They were both staring silently at me now. I picked up a clean glass, pretended to notice a mark and put it in the sink.

A moment passed before the elder one spoke again.

'See you later then,' he smiled insincerely. They both turned to Joy who was nervously shining a little circle on the dark wooden bar top.

'Nice to meet you, Joy.' The younger one broke his silence and lifted her hand, keeping his eyes fixed firmly on mine whilst placing a kiss on the back of Joy's fingers.

'Did they pay?' I asked Joy nervously after they left.

'Did they pay! We've just had a visit from the Godfather and you want to know if they've paid!'

'Who were they?'

'The older one was Ron and the younger one was his son, Micky.'

'Well what did they want?'

'They didn't say. They just said they wanted to move in somewhere and were looking for the right area.'

The words 'move in' slammed the panic button shutting off the valve to my heart and releasing a flow of emergency expletives.

'I'll tell you what they want,' said Frank. He'd been sipping quietly on a beer at the far end of the bar. 'They want shooting. If you don't shoot them they'll be back here demanding money. It happens all the time in Las Americas. I'm telling you, get 'em shot... fucking *bnid ds* . It's "The Firm", the East End mafia. It's like herpes, once you've got it, you can never get rid of it.'

We were in trouble. Big trouble. In my mind, troops of fishmongers had assembled for inspection. We had heard of protection money being paid to some of the gangsters who ran Las Americas but had always thought we were safe up here out of the way.

I wandered back to the kitchen, ignoring Friedhelm's glass-waving appeal for another drink. Like lambs to the slaughter, I thought. I wondered how much we were going to have to pay to retain all of our limbs.

I spent most of the afternoon obsessively drying my comforter, a big-enough-to-hide-in metal saucepan. I toyed with the idea of refusing to pay but as soon as I heard Joy acknowledging anyone's arrival my hand was already in my wallet. It felt like the beginning of the end.

CHAPTER 7

The busy summer season was upon us and the decision was made that next week we would open for breakfast and lunch as well as evening meals. In light of this, the last thing we needed was an added hassle but naturally we got one. Our apartment had been sold and we had three weeks to find somewhere else to live.

Other news to reach us confirmed that an East End gang from London were doing the rounds, targeting British bars in the south. We called a meeting to discuss what to do when Ron and Micky came back.

'We're not paying them,' said David. 'Give in to them once and they'll just want more next time.'

'So what do we do? If we say no they'll smash the place up and we'll lose business, plus we'll have to pay the cost of repairing things,' I argued.

'The police?' suggested Joy.

'Well you're not legal and we still haven't got an opening licence so I don't think we want to involve them,' I said.

'Look, we're assuming they're going to come. They might not. We're away from the main drag. They might not come up here,' said David.

'They've already been in,' revealed Joy. We hadn't told David and Faith about our visit. There was no point in worrying them if it proved to be nothing.

'Ah,' said David.

'Ah,' said Faith.

We decided that there was nothing that we could do. If we were going to be approached for extortion money we'd have to pay. It was not a particularly pleasing prospect but one that was better than having a beer barrel delivered through the window.

Ron and Micky were conspicuous by their absence over the next few days, serving to heighten the suspense, although we did have our fair share of alternative dubious characters frequenting the bar. Some were daunting, some just plain demented.

We assumed that the King of the Canary Islands was one of the wigwam residents from Spaghetti Beach but we had no proof. Just like we had no proof that he wasn't the King of the Canary Islands. He said he was, insisting that it was for this reason that he never paid for anything on the island.

By this stage we had put up with his renditions of songs from the musicals, hoping that once he had finished half a chicken and chips he would move on. Alas, he knew every verse that Rogers and Hammerstein had ever bickered over. In between mouthfuls of food, flourishing gestures would accompany his recital.

'Can you keep it down a bit?' I asked.

'Gonna vash zat man right outta my hair…' he continued, a chicken wing finding unexpected flight as he swiped it over his head.

'Come on, either keep it down or you'll have to go.'

He continued to 'vash dat man's hair' in a stage whisper.

I headed back to the kitchen and smiled apologetically at the bemused family of Germans on table four as a rousing chorus trailed after me.

He bowed deeply but on hearing no applause shrugged, sat down and continued gnawing on the chicken carcass, humming to himself.

Joy went out to collect his plate and deliver his bill.

'Did you like my show?' he asked, grinning inanely.

'Yes, very good,' said Joy trying not to make eye contact. '850 pesetas please.'

The man frowned.

'You want that I pay?' he protested. He raised his hands in disbelief towards the other diners sat outside. 'But I give you songs. *You* must pay *me*.' Beneath the serious expression, playfulness surfaced but Joy had people to serve and had no time for games.

'Come on, pay up. I haven't got time for this.' She extended an out-stretched palm.

'Pleased to meet you,' he said, shaking her hand. 'I am the King, the King of Canary Islands. And you are?'

'Batman. Now pay the bill.'

'But I am the King. I pay for nothing. All this is mine.' He had stood up and thrust his chin skywards in an attempt at looking regal but the mop of blonde surf hair, the cut off jeans and the lack of shoes belied his status.

'Pay!' Joy demanded.

'But…'

'Pay. Now!'

'Do you want me to sort him out, Joy?' Danny had heard the argument from behind the bar where he was cleaning glasses. His skinny frame barely came halfway up the doorway where he stood drying his hands on a tea towel.

'No, it's all right, Danny,' smiled Joy. 'He's just leaving.'

'Aha! Your husband,' said the King and bowed in Danny's direction.

Joy's resolution held firm and he thrust a crumpled note into her hand. After bidding everyone a fond farewell he disappeared up the steps singing more tunes from *South Pacific*.

He was to become a regular visitor and one who tried our patience but always knew when he had crossed the mark. Once, when he came in calm and ashen-faced suffering from the flu we found out his real name was Johan, a dropout from Germany. His father was an executive for a medical research company and his mother had died when he was fourteen. His father gave him a bundle of money with which to make something of himself. Johan was clearly not one to take fatherly advice.

That was the only time we saw his real self. Whether it was drugs, mischief or schizophrenia, he would always be the King after that visit. One day he turned up wearing a bin liner around his waist and a sawn-off five-litre water bottle on his head as a crown. It was, he said, a very important day for him. He had been King for ten years and he was celebrating. Instead of a bottle of Dorada he ordered a bottle of house wine and insisted we joined in his jubilee.

'To my kingdom… and my people,' he toasted.

If he sensed that we were getting tired of him he would pick himself up by the collar and lead himself out with a look of self-pity. Only once did we have to see him off ourselves.

He must have been drinking heavily as from the top of the stairs he pretended to pull down his zip as if to flash at customers that were coming or going. I don't think he would actually have gone so far but it wasn't exactly the maitre'd welcome that customers anticipated so we shooed him off with threats of the police. In due time he returned and apologised profusely, presenting Joy with a posy of dying bougainvillaea and a handful of bottle tops as a peace offering.

One thing that Mario and his partners didn't do was provide any kind of entertainment and for the busy summer season we needed a way of persuading people to spend more time in the bar. We were sending out a steady number of meals but then emptied early when the kitchen closed at 10pm when our customers would head for the bright lights of Las Americas in search of 'a good turn'.

Currently, the only night time distractions in our vicinity were provided by the sporadic 'cabaret' acts in the basement bar of the Altamira where star quality was never a priority. At best they were captivatingly crap, at worst, monumentally appalling. If it wasn't a bunch of overweight waiters attempting flamenco with all the fiery passion of damp matches, it was Derek and his dancing poodle – who nine times out of ten, didn't.

The handful of people who attended such 'extravaganzas' were either recreationally challenged or too lazy to venture more than a finger-click's distance away from the hotel bar. Sunshine and sangria were a potent partnership in anaesthetising even the most cynical of audiences.

We decided that a scouting mission was in order to see if we could offer a plausible alternative to Derek's uncooperative canine. It was either that or karaoke and we were all trying to hold out as long as possible before succumbing to such painful pleasures.

'Tina Turner, Rod Stewart and Neil Diamond'. For a newcomer to Tenerife an advertisement like this outside somewhere like the Mucky Bucket in Torviscas must have seemed a tad extraordinary. Free admission, beer at a pound a pint, three mega legends and bingo in the intervals. Where else could you find that?

On any given night, sandwiched between 'play your cards right' and 'spin the wheel', the likes of Elton John and Meatloaf could be found picking out the night's raffle ticket winner before bursting into 'I'm Still Standing' and 'Dead Ringer For Love' respectively.

You have to be extremely vigilant to avoid a collision with a major celebrity on the streets of Las Americas. While a selection of Elvis Presleys would be puffing and panting in full regalia en route to their next half-hour spot, turned-up collars and two-foot quiffs flapping up and down like a flock of crested eagles, Tina Turner would be stumbling along Avenida Rafael Puig, one hand holding down her wig, the other restraining a threatened breakout in the cleavage department.

We were tempted by the enthusiasm of a voice interacting with a crowd in a nearby bar. On closer inspection perhaps this wasn't the show for us. A six-foot transvestite with neck to wrist tattoos was trying to whip his audience into a frenzy. 'Everybody on the left shout "hoo", everybody on the right shout "hah".'

A bewildered table of pensioners who looked like they had just stepped off the wrong bus and a young family playing 'Connect Four', obviously felt neither inclined to shout 'hoo', nor indeed 'hah'. We moved on, opting instead for an Elvis bar that offered the bonus of food at this late hour.

The show hadn't started as an ageing waiter in sauce-stained black and whites motioned towards a table close to the strands of glitter dangling stage right. From here we had a perfect view of two urinals, and a vending machine offering heightened pleasure for only 500 pesetas. In hindsight our money would have been better spent there.

A plastic menu was thrust upon us listing such imaginative delights as egg and chips, sausage and chips, burger and chips. Each one was accompanied by a glossy photo for the benefit of those who had never eaten before.

The *menú d l il a* of prawn cocktail, half a chicken in mushroom sauce and a choice of ice cream would suffice and I gazed around for someone with whom I could share our opinion. Both waiters were now loitering round a table of giggling teenage girls and despite much eyebrow-raising, finger-extending and finally arm-waving, their attention would not be prised.

We were in no great rush as the real reason for a visit was to steal Elvis so we sat patiently until a shadow loomed over our table. A barely visible flick of the head signalled that our waiter was now prepared to take the order and I decided to attempt to utilise the nursery level knowledge of Spanish that I had managed to ingest.

'*Dos d los menús d l d a, por favor, y un med o litro d vino tinto,*' I offered jerkily.

'Prawn coat tail, half a chin with sores and I scream. Yes?'

There was a slight pause as we stared at each other.

'*Perdne ?*' I said somewhat baffled.

'What?' He flicked his head again.

'*Repitez s'il vous plait?*'

'*Como?*'

'I'm sorry?'

By some miracle we both glided back into our own languages and shaking his head, the waiter whisked away the menu.

In a worryingly short space of time, two prawn cocktails and a specimen jar of wine were, if not slammed, then sternly placed in front of us. The prawn cocktail comprised just that. A solitary prawn, friendless in a pink and white sea of stirred ketchup and mayonnaise.

The ensuing main course was covered in a sauce so thick and sticky that I feared plunging my knife and fork into it lest I was unable to pull them free again. However, I managed to persuade some of it to let go of the plate and just as I was lifting it to my mouth a tray of glittering jewels blocked its path. A representative from one of Asda's African branches had chosen this moment to show me a range of watches that they were apparently now stocking.

'Good price for you, Jimmy. Asda price. Give me five thousand, any watch. Good quality. OK, OK, my friend, four thousand. For you special price, three thousand and I give you a bag. Asda price. Two thousand, yes? Take two, one for your special lady.'

I fended him off with a stale bread roll that I hadn't ordered but was sure to be charged for and he wandered away to barter with himself at another table, a piece of my chicken dangling from beneath his tray.

Just at that point the lights dimmed and to an impressive fanfare of ear-piercing feedback, Elvis appeared on stage. Now correct me if I'm wrong but Elvis was tall, talented and dashing. The spectacle before us was dressed in extra-wide Bacofoil, was about four-foot-ten, 160 kilos and had a voice like George Formby on helium. The only thing that distinguished him as The King was that after every song, following a short bout of eye-crossing concentration, he would contort his mouth into what presumably was an Elvis sneer and mumble in the lowest falsetto that he could muster, 'Uh-huh. Thang-you, thang-you. You're all won'erful people. Uh-huh,' in a thinly veiled Scottish accent.

We persevered through the main course but our appetites for the food, and for this particular Elvis, had long since fled so decided to forego the ice cream.

We arrived at the next bar amidst quavering brass and a crescendo of key-boards. A man in over-tight, blue spandex trousers flamboyantly introduced the handful of punters in the audience to his beaming assistant. Undoubt-edly a dropout from the 'Delightful Debbie' School of Stage Assistants, the poor girl's feathered crown slipped over her eyes as she curtsied to the non-existent applause. She dutifully returned the compliment to her master who accepted the silent adoration with conceited charm.

Formalities over, both flourished into position. The girl manacled herself to an upright slab of black hardboard whilst *el maestro* dramatically threw his arms to the heavens and strode towards a spot some 20 feet away from her.

He withdrew three metal strips from a black velvet bag. We were to pre-sume they were knives but they looked more like crucifixes from year one's first metalwork project. Evidently he was going to hurl these primitive missiles at his trusting assistant but in case there was any doubt amongst the audience he went through three demonstrations, feigning acts of drunkenness, blindness and foolishness respectively in a bid to heighten the tension.

The only change in emotion seemed to be from his assistant whose toothy smile was beginning to wane as she tipped her head back, peering from beneath the band of plumage, which had come to rest on the bridge of her nose.

I have to admit that at this stage I was intrigued. Was the girl's life really going to be put at risk for the sake of half a dozen customers who seemed more interested in a large cockroach that was scuttling along the dirty tiled floor? It began to appear not.

I noticed that the man had discreetly shuffled to within six feet of his assistant during his mimes of ineptitude. The music turned to a drum roll and he asked the silent audience for complete quiet. The man's face took on a look of serious concern. By now we couldn't see the girl's face at all as the crown had managed to slip past her nose and was only being prevented from travelling further south by her resolutely puckered lips.

Gripping the knife between finger and thumb, the man drew his arm back and brought it sharply forward again leaning close enough to his target to be able to literally place the knife in the board. When all three objects were safely embedded he spun round, arms aloft and stamped a foot almost in time with the final cymbal crash. Neatly, it came down square on the cockroach for which he gained a trickle of applause.

Obviously money had exchanged hands for this performance, but who in their right mind would book such an act? Not us, that was for sure. After a fruitless search we decided that we were going to have to resort to the dreaded sing-a-long. The question was who to get to run it. We needed a compère and with the summer season a mere week away and all the best performers booked up we needed to act fast.

Another pub owner who had come to the bar one night to check us out recommended a friend who had just arrived on the island and was looking for work. She had her own gear and although it had been a while since she'd been on the circuit we were prepared to give her a try.

However, whilst the rest of Las Americas were regaled by the slippery patter of their own Graham Goldenthroat, Johnny D'Amour or Simon J.

Shinyshoes, our Delightful Debbie turned out to be a Dour Doreen.

Despite last minute protestations, particularly from David and Faith who absolutely detested any form of cheesy entertainment, table number five was dragged down the bar towards the kitchen to form a partnership with table number one. We decided against dangling tinsel as a backdrop and instead bought a huge piece of black cloth to force those sitting outside to watch the fun from within.

We have to admit that although ceiling fans were constantly in use, causing surface ripples on our patrons' pints, they only managed to circulate the hot air that was trapped inside. The heat in the bar area was occasionally overbearing, leading to an exodus to the outside seating, however it was nothing compared to the heat in the kitchen.

Sundays were the busiest nights for food with 100 people plus ordering a traditional roast beef dinner. The piece of topside delivered to accommodate this demand looked like a full quarter of a cow and the effort to just lift it into the oven when the kitchen thermometer read 140 was enough to guarantee a tidal wave of perspiration.

Mario had built up quite a following for his Sunday roasts with people coming from all over the south to get their helping of edible reminiscence. It was all that we served on a Sunday and made for a somewhat more relaxing shift in the kitchen, except for the washing-up.

Mario had installed a dishwasher, which we promptly uninstalled. It was proving just as efficient to wash by hand as the machine would take the best part of an hour to trudge through its cycle. Not only that, close inspection revealed that it was the home of probably the cleanest community of cockroaches anywhere in the western world. The damp, warm interior provided their perfect pied-á-terre, a veritable holiday camp of spindly beasties waiting to jump out from gleaming crockery.

Proportionally, the little things in life shouldn't scare the big things. But it happens. It was a common sight to see a bar load of adults fleeing from one side of the room to the other just to avoid being anywhere near a two-inch insect. Of course, the bug realises the terror it can cause. Why else would it chase people?

This cat and mouse game actually encourages the roach population to run amok amidst crowded areas. Just think of the power trip it must be on, scattering people like a motorbike in a ballroom.

It's believed that the cockroach is the only creature that could withstand a nuclear holocaust and thereby take over the world. If those aspirations were being considered, we were doing our utmost to rain on their parade.

One of our more common purchases was Raid. In the cash and carry it was the pharmaceutical equivalent of buying condoms. You hid a couple of cans between the beans and frozen chips before making your way sheepishly to the check-out.

If you had a can of Raid amidst your stock you might as well have stood up, raised one arm and admitted, 'Hello, we're the Smugglers Tavern and we have cockroaches.' Our bar was constantly the scene of an aromatic battle between Tetramethrin and Airwick. We'd spray the little buggers like it was napalm, despite the fact that only a little zap was actually required to send it into a frenzied break dance.

We also scattered several cockroach traps around the bar, kitchen and patio. These are not leg-grabbing bear snares but little black discs filled with an alluring chemical. The intention is to attract the bugs into the maze with the equivalent of a cockroach cream cake. Whilst in there, in the excitement of finding such a treat, they trample through a slow-acting poison which they then unwittingly tread back to roach HQ to contaminate all their friends and family. Consequently, not exactly being the most popular roach in the neighbourhood, they're sent to Coventry and die a lonely and miserable death in someone else's dishwasher. Or something like that.

Fortunately, the novelty factor of the Smugglers Tavern hosting a karaoke night had overcome our customers' aversion to heat exhaustion and the bar was packed.

At 10pm when the kitchen closed the karaoke bandwagon that we had all dreaded slipped into top gear. 'Right, I'm off,' announced Frank, slamming his empty glass on the bar top. 'I'm not listening to this shite.' Danny stayed behind, loyal to the end while his sister shrugged her shoulders, smiled and ran after Frank slipping an arm round his waist, happy to have her dad to herself for a while.

Maxi Belle – her stage name, obviously – was a large lady who would have looked more at home on a milking stool than on a makeshift stage. Her mouth was fixed in what looked like a cross between sheer terror and hysterical laughter. She wore a billowing lilac dress under which any number of small cars could have easily been parked. For a supposedly experienced artiste, and a large one at that, Maxi displayed a dazzling lack of stage presence.

'Yurr simply the best…' she sang in a heavy Blackburn accent as two kids played catch-a-ball at an ever-increasing pace right in front of her.

'Betturr than all the rest.' Her eyes belied the pasted smile as they flicked nervously back and forth to the children. Invariably the little ball went wayward, striking her in the middle of her forehead before disappearing beneath the many folds of her flowery frock.

'Beturr than… Gerroff!… anyone.' With one hand she swatted at the kids who, oblivious to her performance, were lifting the hem of her dress in search of the plastic ball.

'Have you found it?' asked a young mother as she bent forward to help in the hunt. Her micro miniskirt rode north revealing to the audience a pair of tiny pale blue knickers doing their best to accommodate the flabby white twins within. This in turn brought a spontaneous round of applause, both encouraging and surprising Maxi. To her credit, and in the best traditions of showbiz, she carried on with renewed vigour, bobbing and bending to sing past the expanding search party, some of whom had now joined her onstage.

Soon she was swamped. Muffled enquiries were booming through the PA:

'Start spreadin' the news…'

'It can't have gone far.'

'There it is!'

'I'm leaving t-day… Ow! Get your 'ands off me toe.'

'Sorry, love!'

'I wa-nna be a parrt of it…'

'Hey, hasn't she got big feet?'

'I like that nail varnish. Irene! Come and have a look at this nail varnish.'

Strangely, the ball never was found even after Maxi left the stage sobbing.

The karaoke started after our host had managed to compose herself and we had persuaded her not to hand in her resignation. A litter of miniature Spice Girls got up and stared open-mouthed at the screen for three minutes and twenty-five seconds before skipping back to proud parents under rapturous applause.

Several young lads tunelessly shouted the words to 'Wonderwall' for what seemed like a couple of days, until finally, after many other wannabees had demonstrated that they were clearly nevergonnabees, the big finale was provided by a short man in a well-worn suit who made his way unsteadily to the stage from a dark corner of the room.

In the bar we had often witnessed the sad sight of couples who, after many years of marriage, had simply run out of things to say to each other but who still fulfilled their social duties by sitting together for hours in complete silence.

'This is for my wife, Madge, whom I have loved dearly for 65 years.'

With alcohol inducing romantic memories of cavernous dance halls and the smell of Brylcreem, he proceeded to wring out a teary-eyed version of 'My Sweet Love And I'. The depth of his passion did little to compensate for the ear-slashing rendition of what was once probably an adequately tuneful ballad. At the point where it seemed no more emotion could be wrenched from the discordant song, he broke down and buried his head in the ample bosom of the embarrassed compère. Maxi Belle led him back to the source of his anguish.

'You silly old sod. You've had too much to drink,' said his wife, unmoved. 'Get your coat, we're goin'.'

Needless to say, two bouts of onstage blubbering would always put a bit of a dampener on what was supposed to be a night of family fun but the till had never stopped ringing as customers purchased the courage to appear in the spotlight, proof enough that it was worth having entertainment.

Another good point that came out of the evening was that Joy and I were offered another apartment. The bad point was that the lead came from Micky and Ron who had returned to the bar whilst we were in full swing.

CHAPTER 8

'Doing alright I see,' shouted Micky above the karaoke riot. His father had his back to the bar and was smiling to himself, evidently pleased with the crowded atmosphere.

'It's going all right,' I answered. 'We've not seen you around for a while.'

'No,' said Micky, 'we've been taking care of a little business. Thought we might have a little time off now, spend some time round here.'

'Have you bought somewhere on El Beril then,' I gulped.

'You could say that.' Father and son looked at each other and laughed.

'Whereabouts?'

'Down on the front, number 28. Nice place, or at least it will be after a bit of work.'

'That's Richard Forgreen's isn't it? I didn't know he wanted to sell it.'

Ron turned round. The smile had gone. 'Neither did he.'

Richard Forgreen was another of the original El Berilians, an estate agent who was rarely seen on the complex. Probably a wise move considering his less than shiny reputation. He and his family had been in the bar only once and even then he never seemed at ease, constantly looking over his shoulder.

'You and the missus still living at the back?' continued Ron. I figured Joy wouldn't have told them where we lived. I certainly hadn't. I was feeling uneasier by the second.

'For the time being. We're looking for somewhere else though so we'll probably be out of there soon.' The truth was, 'soon' was at the end of the week and still we hadn't been able to find anywhere.

'Why don't you ask Terry? He's looking to rent his out,' said Micky. 'We could be neighbours,' he added, smiling at Joy.

The thought of borrowing a cup of sugar from the local mafia wasn't overly appealing and for the time being we dismissed the idea.

The day before we were due to move we had resigned ourselves to not finding a new home. We had neither the time nor the energy to look round properly and had no option but to rent a holiday studio in the Altamira for the time being.

The view from our new home was jaw dropping. Double patio doors framed a tri-band of green lawn, turquoise sea and blue sky. However, the inside was not so agreeable. The small living room doubled as both bed-room and dining room. The bed had to be folded away every night to make room to sit down but the biggest problem were the sun's rays which loitered on the glass doors for most of the day. Inside, the temperature was stifling.

Although air-conditioning units were fitted in the hotel, they were never activated. The community of residents who owned several apartments had decided that the costs of such a luxury would weigh too heavily on their community bills. All units were controlled by the same master control so if one was switched off none of them functioned. It was like being back in the Smugglers kitchen.

What little available time we had for sleep was spent tossing and turning, trying to find a cool patch of pillow. Joy had taken to lying on the tiled floor in a bid to cool down. Even with the patio doors open, the breeze that circu-lated was only marginally cooler than the stuffy air we had trapped within, plus it was an open invitation to mosquitoes.

We were growing more exhausted by the day, averaging only a couple of hours' sleep a night. Our tempers were frayed and our quality of life had taken a serious downfall. Something had to give. After one week of living in a sauna, moving next to the mafia was beginning to sound like a preferable option.

By now the season was at its peak. Our mortgage repayments, added to the monthly amount we had agreed to pay back to Jack, meant that it was vital we maximised the potential of this busy period.

The summer routine was for one couple to prep and shop from 9 in the morning then open the doors for breakfast at 10.30 a.m. The same couple would then work until 1.30 p.m. before heading off for a siesta and handing over to the others who would then work alone until the other couple came back in at 6.30 p.m. The couple that started the day would also finish the day, locking up after the last person left which frequently was on the yawning side of 2 a.m. The rota would be reversed the following day. This meant that there were always four people working through the busiest period of 7 p.m. until 10 p.m. It also meant that I worked with Faith in the kitchen whilst David ran the bar and helped Joy on the waiting side.

Being thrown in at the deep end and all being equal partners resulted in the familiar 'too many chiefs, not enough Indians' scenario. Menial tasks were being overlooked whilst everybody was keen to apply their stamp on the surroundings.

In the backroom, Faith was in charge of the cooking whilst I took the orders, prepared the garnishes and accompaniments and washed up as we went along. By now we were regularly topping 80 meals a night in a four-hour slot. In the 140-degree heat, stress cracks were beginning to show.

Faith in particular was suffering. Inhaling chip fumes whilst leant over four super-hot gas rings and an industrial oven were visibly melting her work capacity. Orders were backing up on the board and Joy, who was undergoing a barrage of hassle from hungry patrons waiting to be fed, was exerting pressure. There was no time for small talk; the only conversations ran along the following lines:

Faith: 'Got two pork chops, a chicken in wine, two cheeseburgers and three mixed grills coming up. Fries ready?'

Me: 'Two minutes for the fries. Still waiting for an egg for the gammon.'

Faith: 'I can't slow these meals down. Speed up with the fries.'

Me: 'There's nothing I can do if the fryers are full. You know we can only do six portions at a time. I need that egg, the gammon's going cold.

Faith: 'I can't do everything at once. Send it without the egg.'

Joy: 'Where's the egg?'

Faith: 'I'm not doing it.'

Joy: 'You take it out then.'

Faith: 'I'm not the waitress.'

Joy: 'Exactly. You don't get the grief.'

Faith: 'Oh, you don't think working in here is grief? That's it. I'm not having this.'

And with that Faith would fling her apron to the floor and go on one of her regular walkabouts down to the sea leaving an ensemble of meat cuts shrinking on the hot plate. Invariably David would then abandon his bar duties and become stand-in chef until Faith reappeared a little cooler in body if not in temper.

Subsequent meetings led to the admission that Faith found the cooking too stressful and thus swapped roles with David.

However much she thought working in the engine room was the hardest job, being transferred to the front line brought no respite from the stress, particularly with our more boisterous customers.

Although our clientele still consisted of around 90% British, the German timeshare line selling units in the Altamira was working overtime to bring in fly-buys, cannon fodder for the salesmen who were enticed to Tenerife with free accommodation. As such, Faith had not only to learn the basics of the language but also intervene when some of the more embarrassing British patrons found it hilarious to perform goose step marches and make Pythonesque references to the war. Once or twice German customers were forced to leave before finishing their drinks. At times we were embarrassed to share a national identity.

'They started it,' the British contingency would argue.

'They were just having a drink,' we'd retort.

'No, they started it in 1939 in Poland. Serves them right.' This coming from a sunburnt skinhead in white vest and Union Jack shorts, young enough to have no personal experience of the war and old enough to know better than to exhibit his prejudices in front of his young offspring.

The diverse type of customers that frequented the bar was astounding. From the empty heads who thought they were in Spain and enquired about coach trips to Barcelona, to the sanctimonious older expats who bore the unmistakable hallmarks of British colonialism at its worst. They knew that 'abroad' wasn't part of England (yet) but was merely waiting to be educated in the superior ways of pallid supremacists.

We were forewarned about an inspection visit from a group of "swallows", expats who spend the winter months in more temperate climes such as Tenerife. One of their flock deemed it necessary to make a special trip to announce that he, and eight of his compatriots, would descend upon us the following day. 'We heard that the good old Smuggs had changed hands. We're coming down tomorrow to have a recce, check you're keeping up the standard.'

Sure enough, at 7.30 p.m. prompt the following night, a group of neatly groomed expats loitered around the entrance gazing disdainfully at the free and easy atmosphere in the bar. Two children no older than eight or nine stood on chairs behind the bar washing glasses. Danny was cleaning one of the glass table-tops, showering Glassex over a couple of diners at the next table.

We had inadvertently become a drop-off zone for parents who wanted a few hours on their own. 'I'm leaving Adam and Georgia here for a few hours while we go out for a meal. Let them have whatever they want and we'll sort it out later.'

Joy had instigated this trend by offering to provide 'work experience' to one young holidaymaker who had followed her round all week awestruck, and announced, with all the seriousness that a six-year-old talking about careers could muster, that she intended to be a waitress when she grew up.

Naturally this set a trend with other children. 'Can I help, can I help?' One week we had a supplementary staff of nine junior Smugglers cleaning tables, washing glasses and delivering a round of drinks – one at a time. In times of extreme business it was helpful to have extra glass collectors but sometimes it wasn't possible to get behind the bar without trampling on at least a couple of mini recruits.

'We have a table reserved for eight. Name's Connaught-Smith.' The man leaned into Joy as if facial proximity would overcome any possible confusion. He wore beige slacks, and a long-sleeved silk shirt topped with a gold cravat. The other members of the party were equally eccentrically attired. One lady wore what appeared to be a resting stoat around her neck.

They swept through the bar towards table one like a troupe of variety performers. One of the party made a show of running her finger along one of the tabletops and shared the result, aghast.

I watched through the kitchen doorway and offered a smile to each of them but they looked beyond me to check out the state of the kitchen. Luckily, we had decided on a blitz several days earlier and the tiles on the facing wall had returned from a greasy rust colour to their natural white. The plastic ketchup bottles were lined up in military fashion on a ridge just below the serving shelf, nozzles cleared of hardened sauce and bodies wiped of sticky surplus.

We didn't pretend to be a high-class restaurant. We were catering for the clientele who happened to be on hand, most notably package holidaymakers, timeshare fly-buys and loyal residents. There was no demand for haute cuisine, despite David's urge to extend his creative culinary skills further than fried or grilled, microwaved or mashed, and heated or chilled. On the odd occasion when he had satisfied his own artistic urges, pumpkin soup was sneered at in favour of prawn cocktail; chicken and chips were preferred over coq au vin, and crème brûlée was laughed off the menu when competing with apple pie and custard.

The expats clearly expected more as they surveyed the handheld blackboards that we employed as menus. 'Would you wipe this table before we start. It's filthy,' said Mr Cravat. 'It's like a greasy Joe's.' Joy resisted the temptation to tell them that it was 'Joe's'.

'Do you have a special of the day?' barked another.

'I think we've got one portion of home-made beef and mushroom pie and two portions of chicken curry,' answered Joy.

'No thanks,' replied the man, unimpressed. 'Well, would it be at all possible to order some drinks while we're browsing the menu?'

'Certainly,' smiled Joy.

'Right. Five gin and tonics, one without lemon, two without ice, all Gordons of course. One Pernod and lemonade, one dry Martini with a twist of lime, and a whisky with just a splash of water and definitely no ice. I shall send it back if you put ice anywhere near it.'

Joy's capacity to remember orders was infinite. However, behind the bar, Faith's was not.

'How am I going to remember all that? Write it down,' she complained. The bar was filling up quickly by that stage and Joy scribbled down the order for Faith and rushed off outside to greet some newcomers.

I was chopping more cucumber to deal with this unexpected rush when I noticed two men in shirt and tie and carrying briefcases on their way in.

Only yesterday we had heard that the supermarket had been the target of a work permit inspection. Thankfully Patricia, the only member of her family with work papers, was on shift at that time.

I rushed out of the kitchen, called two children out from behind the bar and grabbed Joy's elbow just as she was about to bring in an order. 'Grab a seat and act like a customer,' I hissed. 'I think the inspectors are here.'

Joy immediately sat at the nearest table and started to make small talk. Unfortunately it was a table of bemused Germans so she quickly sidled outside to a family of regulars whom we had got to know over the past week.

Faith was leaning over the bar. 'Joy. Joy!' she shouted. From behind the two officials I motioned with my head at the two men in front and opened my palms like a book. Faith's eyebrows launched into orbit. 'Can you take these drinks to table five for me?' she asked in a nervous high-pitched voice.

I could see Joy peering through the window as I delivered the drinks to table five.

'Could you send the young lady over now, we're ready to order.' said the Mr Cravat.

'I'll take it for you,' I said. 'She's just had to go outside for a minute.' I took their order and rushed into the kitchen, explaining to David what had happened.

The two at the bar ordered a drink and watched the comings and goings. The table of Germans near Joy were sitting in front of empty glasses and tried desperately to get her attention. Joy ignored their waving for as long as possible then snatched their glasses and took them to the customer side of the bar. She was sweating visibly as she asked Faith for two more beers, pretending they were for her. The two suits by her side stared at her.

'Err... can you put it on my bill please,' she smiled and returned outside, discreetly placing the beers in front of the Germans before sitting down again. One of them lit a cigarette and mimed that he needed an ashtray. All of the ashtrays were being used so she apologetically passed them an empty can of Diet Coke that was on the next table, motioning for them to drop their ash in the top. The Germans looked at the can, bemused.

Another table to whom Joy had given the menu were beckoning her over. 'I'll be there in a minute,' she waved and sank down in her seat, picking her nails.

We were all doing two jobs now. Faith and I were waiting tables and working the bar and trying to dissuade our junior helpers from furthering their work experience for the moment. David had to cook and provide his own accompaniments, as well as keep on top of the washing up.

The suits finished their drinks and stood up. They tried to catch the eye of Faith who was doing a better job of avoiding it. I decided we might as well get it over with so they would leave and approached them, removing my sweat-stained apron in a token gesture to look businesslike. The taller and more sullen one raised two fingers and waved them over the empty glasses. They wanted another beer! 'How long does it take to see who's working and who's not,' I thought.

By now, Joy had slid as far down in her chair as she could without lying on the floor and was the focus of all the table's around her. Faith and I were doing our best to take and deliver orders and explain to people that Joy was on her break. Faith was just on the verge of hysteria when Patricia walked in.

'Are you on strike?'

'Work inspectors,' whispered Joy, jabbing a finger towards the bar.

Patricia laughed and went inside. She returned a moment later with the two suits. 'Alejandro and Raul,' she said introducing each one. 'They're in my Jehovah's Witnesses congregation. They've been pioneering round here, that's why they're dressed up. You're safe.'

Joy sunk a little further. She was safe for now but the false alarm fuelled the growing insecurity of working illegally. Our *g storia* had repeatedly warned us that it was only a matter of time before we would be visited.

By the time Joy returned the expats had grown agitated.

'Why your boss lets you take a break whilst you're so busy I'll never know. It's just not on. We had to wait 40 minutes for our food. And the cleanliness... well, what can you say? It's just not good enough.'

Joy smiled. 'I'm sorry to hear that. I guess we're not up to the high standards to which you're obviously accustomed. Perhaps you should try Mc-Donalds. I hear they're very good.' We never saw them again, surprisingly.

The scare with the officials strengthened our resolve to make Joy legal and we made another appointment to see Julie, our *g storia*.

The appointment was at 4 p.m., which gave us just enough time after finishing our morning shift to move our belongings from the studio into Terry's. It was a two-bedroom apartment at the bottom of El Beril near the sea, one of the few homes on the complex that had an upstairs and downstairs plus a small lawn in front. Compared to the studio we had been boiled in for the last week it was cool luxury. Terry informed us that we could have it for as long as we wanted as he had bought another place for himself and his wife. We took a little time to arrange our home, taking great pride in spreading our meagre possessions as widely as we could.

In Julie's office a ceiling fan stirred the pages of the local English language newspaper. The dour expression of a local politician flipped over to reveal a smug tourist posing alongside an enormous blue marlin on the next page.

I wondered if Pat had tried this magnificent fish as an attention-grabber on the market.

As Joy and I sat and waited for Julie, I thought about what would be going on at the market at this time. It would be the final few minutes of trading time and for those shoppers in the know, the time when all the bargains could be had.

In a desperate attempt to eke out a few more sales, Pat would take to the front of the stall himself, bellowing his final offers. 'Five trays for a fiver. That's a freezer-full of Fleetwood's finest for just a tenner. Try saying that when you've had a shandy, love,' he'd wink.

Even with such discounts, the wily shoppers who hung back until the last moment knew that for the stallholders it was a time when any sale was better than none.

One habitual bargain hunter never failed to show up at the eleventh hour. He was a wiry man who always wore the same clothes; brown scuffed shoes stamped down at the back, fawn trousers with an increasing variety of stains each day, a dirty dark brown raincoat with matted black woollen collar and lapel and a trilby cocked over a few strands of dull grey hair.

He would stand in front of the stall sucking his teeth, waiting until Pat shouted for us to start packing away. Then gingerly, he'd shuffle forwards and go through the routine of prodding various pieces of fish, asking how much for each and shaking his head at the response.

'Three-fifty? Noooo, I haven't got three-fifty. I'm a pensioner you know. I can hardly afford to eat nowadays. I'll give you two pounds.'

'I'm a fishmonger not Father Christmas,' Pat would reply. 'Gerroff with you,' he'd say, waving him away. 'You're on more money than me, you jeffin' robber.'

The man knew the score and would shrink a little further into his coat looking hurt before turning slowly around as if to leave.

'Here, Grandad. Give me three quid and I'll throw in the plastic tray. You can put some soil in it and grow yourself some new hair.' Pat would have already wrapped the fish aware that a deal had been reached.

Back in Julie's office it was now approaching 5 p.m. and she still hadn't seen us. This was normal for our *g storia* appointments but nevertheless irritating.

Another British couple had joined us in the waiting lounge. Both faces were caked in white sun cream and they wore matching safari hats. They smiled nervously and hesitantly sat down in the threadbare sofa opposite.

'Hot today,' the man offered meekly.

'Scorcher,' I replied. 'Been on the island long?'

'No, just arrived yesterday. We've bought a bar, The Rum Jug, just down the road. Julie's sorting our paperwork out for us,' said the man. Like many other British bar owners, the previous owners of The Rum Jug were regulars for our Sunday roasts. Theirs was one of the first English bars in the south. They'd seen many comings and goings from other sunshine landlords and landladies. 'If you can get through the first six months and you've not got divorced, gone mad or killed each other, you might just make it in the bar world. In Tenerife it's called the six-month itch. 90% fail in that first half year,' they warned.

'I hope you're not in a rush then,' Joy was becoming agitated in the stifling heat of Julie's poky waiting room. She started to fan herself with a copy of *Island Connections*, the local newspaper.

This was by no means our first foray into Julie's world of ceiling-high paperwork, half-empty coffee cups and interminable waits. Time was of no importance. Specific appointments were merely general indicators of the day you were requested to camp in her office. A quick drop-in to pick up a piece of paper could take three hours – one hour waiting for her to show up, another hour before she managed to disconnect herself from the telephone and another hour whilst she complained about how busy she was and what new problems this latest addition to our library of forms would ensue.

When we were eventually seen, at 5.30 p.m., Julie went through the lengthy process of repeating how we were running a high risk of Joy getting deported and that we should legally employ her and pay her a wage. However, if we contracted her as a part-time worker this would save on the tax bill and mean we only had to fork out a small amount on social security payments.

This simple solution hadn't been mentioned before but Julie offered it as though it was old news.

'Why didn't you suggest that before?' asked Joy.

'They've only just changed the rules,' replied Julie. 'It's hard to keep up. Until recently all businesses had to offer any jobs to locals before employing a foreigner.' Joy was to be contracted as working 10 hours per week. There was still a slight risk as the hours she was supposed to be at work had to be specified on the form but at least if she was found out now it would only lead to a fine, not deportation.

It was true that the rules were changing on an almost daily basis. Since the foreign invasion, bureaucracy had replaced bananas as the number one preoccupation for the Canarian workforce. As the influx of foreigners was more sudden than anticipated, the authorities had to quickly develop a system of registration formalities and administrative procedures. This they did with great aplomb but nobody told them when to stop. Sheaves of forms were produced in varying colours, all demanding the submission of supporting coloured copies that could only be procured by the presentation of certain other legal documents.

Every form had to be presented in quadruplicate, accompanied by three other supporting documents, two brown envelopes plus a note from your mother explaining why you were late returning it. Invariably this was because the letter urging you to do so arrived five days after the demand date thanks to another of the Canary Islands' inadequate institutions, the postal service.

Our legal adviser had also informed us that it had been decreed that all catering establishments were required to obtain a health and hygiene certificate before an opening licence would be issued.

In theory we weren't supposed to open the bar without this but as it was two years since Mario served the first customer, we regarded this lack of paperwork as a triviality. However, a routine inspection by two uniformed officers from the local police further enforced our intention to do things by the book.

To gain the health and hygiene certificate the kitchen department, namely David and me, had to attend a two-day course on correct practice in the workplace and apply for medical certificates validating that we were free from contagious disease and any hindering impediments. This certification proved easier to obtain than we feared. An appointment was made with a local doctor who seated us at his desk, smiled and asked us if we were feeling OK. On hearing a positive response he stamped two proclamations of good health in exchange for the equivalent of 20 quid and wished us a good day. We were now medically entitled to carry out culinary operations. We just needed to go on the course to prove we were of sound enough mind not to poison too many people.

Inevitably, Joy's form-filling involved yet another one-hour drive north to Santa Cruz, the island's capital. We had already been this way before to register our residency at the consulate and also to apply for work permits for David and me. It was not a trip we enjoyed. The bureaucracy required both David and me, as official partners, to go and sign everything. This meant at least two of us were out of action for most of the day, putting extra strain on the girls.

On this particular occasion, Joy, as the intended employee, also had to present herself, which meant we had to shut the bar for most of the daytime and lose money. But the most aggravating thing about our paperwork quests up north was that more often than not they were unsuccessful.

We knew that as soon as we entered the police station or foreign office or department of health and social security, a frumpish bulldog would be assigned with the sole intention of barking a curt 'No!' even before we'd had the chance to explain our *raison d' être*.

And this was no normal 'no', delivered with a hint of pity and suggestions of alternative routes. The rejections that we were served with were full-blooded, self-satisfying absolute refusals served with a strong side order of condescension. Apparently we either produced the wrong documentation, or presented it in an unsatisfactory manner, at the wrong time, wearing the wrong clothes and with just the wrong inflection in our voices. The official 'No-ers' would not be moved, no matter that we had a business to run and couldn't afford to return the following day and thereby lose a consecutive day's profits. No matter that we had risen at 6.30 a.m., driven all the way from the south and spent an hour trying to find a parking space in a city that had none, and negotiated an interminably stupid one-way system that flung you back south if you accidentally missed the unsigned turnoff.

It might have made an inkling of difference if the capital was a pretty city. But in 1991 it wasn't, by any stretch of the imagination. The first monument that greeted travellers from the south was a shoreline oil refinery whose odour was twice as unpleasant as its intestinal architecture. Once in the centre, a hotchpotch of architectural styles dotted the ubiquitous *Plaza d' Espaã*, a place where gypsies would swarm at you waving linen tablecloths and frilly pillowcases like a fright of ghosts. And that was your reward for enduring a white-knuckle ride along the TF-1, a testing ground for kamikaze taxi drivers and 16-year-old rally wannabees.

We entered the police station with a large sigh, a foreboding sense of doom and a bulging folder containing every piece of paper we'd collected since history was invented.

Inside, all seemed calm. The only noises were the low hum of fluorescent lighting and a periodic 'clack' as a large bespectacled man in the background cautiously poked at his computer keyboard. Every tap was followed by an uncertain glance up, checking that every letter typed was in fact making its way from fingertip to screen. Satisfied that it was, he would then gaze around looking for someone with whom to share his accomplishment.

'Take a number' the sign said. I looked up at the electronic counter – it read 13. Our ticket said 112. We sat down and flicked disinterestedly through a couple of faded *Hola!* magazines that had been thoughtfully provided in 1987.

The minutes moved on but the numbers didn't. Whatever problem befell the elderly English couple at the desk; it was not being rectified despite their exasperated insistence in front of the shoulder-shrugging assistant. They had given up struggling with the local tongue and were now remonstrating in strong Geordie accents. The girl behind the counter had suddenly acquired an inability to speak English and was having none of it. She shooed them off with a wave of her hand and summoned the next in line. The Geordies sauntered off, red-faced, clutching the wad of seemingly ineffectual forms. They had my sympathy. Several times we had failed to impress a paper-shuffler, only to return the following day with a different clerk on duty who would then process our paperwork with not the slightest of fuss.

Eventually, with a colossal leap from 18 to 112, the counter indicated that it was our turn. I passed over the bundle of papers.

'Do you have the 123 and the 234?'

I lifted the top copy and there they were. The girl scanned every detail trying desperately to find a reason why they shouldn't be accepted.

'*Resid ncia,*' she demanded, annoyance now creeping into her voice.

This we produced, and frustrated again, she moved up a gear, converting back to Spanish to try and throw us.

'Did you submit your double 'O' seven, fill in a 36C and receive a signed copy of the B52s?'

'Yes'.

'Have you ever taken an A2B, forwarded a 4-4-2 and been given a T4-2 or a 2-4T?'

'Yes.'

'When?'

'Last month.'

Her face lit up as if she'd tripped over a bucketful of gold.

'Then it's expired.'.

She sat back in the chair contented. Her smug expression and folded arms evidently insinuated that she was done with me and victory was hers, but we were not giving in this time. We'd faced worse than her. We'd been to the foreign office and fought with the best, where, after half a dozen trips north trying to secure my work permit, I was only narrowly defeated by a classic jobsworth. She feigned everything from selective deafness to complete ignorance (although looking back I don't think there was much feigning about that) and beat me on a technicality – an eleventh hour change of rules.

From our folder I slowly produced another form. Our eyes locked in a Mexican standoff. As she saw the form, her mouth dropped and we both knew I had won. We had the notorious re-submitted, double stamped, top yellow copy of form 666. A valid extension from hell. The lights flickered, horrified heads turned to stare and the girl behind the counter shielded her eyes.

'Sign it,' she screamed, tossing a chewed biro onto the desk. The clock chimed 12 as we flung open the doors. The daylight streamed in causing the clerks to wince and groan. We had won. Joy was at last going to be legal, well, almost.

There were around 20 of us huddled in a small lecture room at the town hall, ready to be hygienically educated. The Canarians were seated at the front, notebooks, pens and pencils at the ready. The other half were foreigners like myself who had not been advised as to what may be necessary and were trying to borrow pens from each other.

From what we could gather, day one would involve learning about what we could and couldn't do in catering via a slide show, lectures and reading material. Day two would be concerned with seeing how much of it we had absorbed by means of a multiple-choice questionnaire.

The lights dimmed and the slide show commenced. Pictures of pans, chopping boards, cats struck with large red crosses and various examples of fire extinguishers slid before our eyes as the young man in charge explained the relevance of each and answered questions from the Canarian contingent.

It became quickly apparent that no English was going to be spoken that day and the Brits looked at each other as we realised the maximum we could contribute was our attendance.

After a short break for lunch, the course resumed. Within minutes a pack of cards was produced and whist broke out at the back. For three more hours, occasional glances were thrown at pictures of cattle and cauliflowers projected onto the front wall.

The test paper consisted of 35 questions of which you were expected to get at least 30 correct to qualify for a certificate. There didn't seem to be too much fuss made when consultations were made over some of the more obscure questions. Others, like, 'Are cows allowed in the kitchen?' needed little help to choose the right box to tick from 'Yes', 'No' or 'Sometimes'. All the foreigners passed with exactly the same score – 34 out of 35. The question that baffled us all was so obscure as to defy all logic and neither of the multiple choice options provided a satisfactory response. But we had passed and been certified and could now add this qualification to the bundle of papers that were required by law before you could boil an egg for payment.

Equal informality was apparent on our health and hygiene inspection that surprised us one particularly frantic morning. We had both woken up late after a frustrating night struggling to separate a table of six French timeshare salesmen from two glasses of beer that they had been nursing for over an hour. It was 2 a.m. and everyone else had left. We had washed up, swept and mopped around the remaining table. We cashed up in the kitchen and finally turned the lights off but still they remained resolute. Finally they left when we took the half-full glasses and told them we were going.

In the morning we had less than an hour to get to the cash and carry *and* prepare the restaurant for opening. A queue of people clutching newspapers had formed outside the bar as I pushed past with the last of the boxes of supplies. With no time to put them away I dropped the boxes wherever there was a space and lit the oven in readiness for the orders. A tray of chicken fillets lay half-tenderised to one side and several oranges rolled off a box of Iceberg lettuce that was balanced precariously on 24 double-ply toilet rolls.

'Four full breakfasts and a scrambled egg on toast. Then two full and two bacon sandwiches,' Joy looked around at the mess but could see my eyebrows were raised and said no more.

The eggs were spitting viciously at me when Joy returned. 'Joe, the health inspectors are here.'

I turned around and over Joy's shoulder could see two teenage girls holding a clipboard. I wondered for a second if it was a wind-up.

'Them?' I asked, waving a spatula at the two girls who had now started giggling.

They strode over the packets of serviettes that were littering the floor and asked in broken English if they could look around.

'*Si, si.* Be my guest. We're in a bit of a mess this morning though,' I started to explain but they were too busy trying to find out how to open one of the fridge doors.

'Handle came off yesterday.' I smiled and kicked the bottom rim with my foot. It sprung open. The girls looked at each other. The one with the clipboard wrote something down. The other seemed quite impressed with my Tupperware collection. '*Bien,*' she said. They seemed to be playing 'good cop, bad cop'.

'*Tienes un uniforme?*' asked the clipboard.

I motioned towards the aprons that were hanging from the First Aid cabinet. She asked me to put it on. After checking the interior temperature of the freezers, looking into the extractor hood and standing on one of the stray oranges, they signed a form, asked for my autograph and disappeared giggling again.

I didn't know if we were to be congratulated or condemned. A week later a letter arrived telling us that we were officially regarded as healthy and hygienic and the confirming certificate could now be proudly displayed on the wall. 'Possibly in the kitchen,' I thought, over the hole through which cockroaches made a hasty retreat from our napalm bug spraying.

CHAPTER 9

Having been informed about the latest rule change that abolished the need to employ Spaniards before foreigners meant that we could now think about taking on some extra help over summer. Faith was becoming increasingly discontent, adding to the strain.

Her latest outburst involved a kilo of sugar and a box of Golden Delicious. Apparently she had now developed a fear of baking and couldn't sleep because of crust-topped nightmares. In order to save her last remaining shreds of sanity, Faith was relieved of pie-making duties.

Fortunately one of the very few culinary skills that we had imported between us was Joy's knack of baking apple pies. The Smugglers had recently gained a reputation for its exceedingly good cakes, apple in particular. Holidaymakers with all the time in the world to chat (but a disproportionate lack of subjects about which to chat) would bask around the pool and make plans for their next meal, which invariably would include the famous Smugglers Tavern apple pie.

Sunlounger marketing was so efficient that by mid-morning we would receive a procession of people popping their heads into the kitchen to save a slab of Joy's speciality. No matter how many we made, the majority of slices had already been claimed by the time the evening meals started.

The same was true of our weekly fish and chip special. David had developed his own batter, trying out various secret ingredients before choosing half a pint of Dorada as the winning addition. The crispy cod was another sure-fire winner, especially with the older set who 'knew what they were getting with a nice piece of fish'. For some stalwarts even our Hawaiian burgers, simply chicken breast crowned with a pineapple ring, would prove too exotic for simple palates: 'Hawaiian burger? Oooh nooooo. Foreign food doesn't agree with me. Have you not got anything like curry or bolognaise?'

Although the menu could hardly be called inventive, aside from the odd, extravagant excursion offered by David, it consisted of meals that we knew would sell, principally steak, chicken, pork chops, mixed grills, burgers, salads and omelettes.

By now our meal count averaged around 40–50 breakfasts and lunches combined, and 70–90 evening meals. Naturally we had had to increase our efficiency to turn around more tables but it was no mean feat in the searing temperatures. All the more draining as we now also provided entertainment in the evening. We needed help.

We knew it was going to be almost impossible to find anybody that could cook and that would endure the heat and pace of the kitchen for the paltry wages we were offering. The biggest help that we could hope for would be a couple that could come in after all the food had been served and clean up and run the bar until closing time. This would at least put an end to some of the 3 a.m. and 4 a.m. bedtimes that we were suffering now it was summer.

The most annoying nights were when only one or two tables remained at a relatively decent hour. Thoughts of an early night would prevail especially if all remaining tables ordered the bill before midnight. It was hard to resist breathing a sigh of relief and start visualising fluffy pillows. But, as Murphy would have it, the plot would always change. Just as the last people were bidding their goodnights, after the floor had been mopped and all the tables cleaned, a taxi full of young revellers who had been turned out of a club in Las Americas would shatter the pre-sleep calm and crash into the bar like a herd of rabid cattle.

Having slowed to almost a standstill, trying to shift from first to fifth gear in one go required a major effort, both mentally and physically. We'd smile, we'd serve, and we'd even laugh at their drunken banter. Tonight's idiots could be tomorrow's breakfast crowd and having been rebuked by the nightlife downtown, there was also the possibility that they would choose to dump their entire binge budget in our till if we pushed the right buttons.

This involved much more than jolly smiles and chirpy banter however. Picking diced carrot out of the washbasin plugholes was a real delight, especially after we'd already cleaned the bathrooms ready for the morning. Oh how we would chuckle at that little jape coming as it did at the end of a 13-hour shift!

We also had to persuade latecomers that high decibel renditions of 'I'm Too Sexy' were not a particularly good idea at 1 a.m., especially as they'd normally be followed by a visit from the local constabulary with threats of arrest and deportation for them and early closure succeeded by a stern warning from the community president for us.

But to be truthful, most of our efforts were focused on getting them out, our persuasion based on the theory that if they didn't let us close we wouldn't be able to open again for breakfast.

If you've ever tried to have a serious discussion with a group of radically inebriated youngsters whereby the main aim is to convince them to give up their drinks, you'll understand that it's something of a an uphill battle.

'Come on now, last orders has long since gone. We're closing up now. We'll see you in the morning.'

'Oh you can't close yet, it's still early. Look, it's only...' Several attempts at focusing on a watch face would prove futile. 'It's... it's still early. Here, here's some potatoes. Buy yourself one. Sit down with us. Chill. How long have you been here? Do you like it? Don't you miss home? Will you ever go back? I'd love to live here. Have you got any jobs going?'

This was part of the same interrogation that we faced dozens of time each day. We toyed with the idea of putting a notice up behind the bar answering all the enquiries including, 'We're not going to tell you,' in answer to question number seven – 'How much did you pay for the bar?'

There was certainly an element of envy in the tone of the questioning. There aren't many people who have been on holiday and not at least momentarily flirted with the idea of making their stay longer than intended. To come in contact with someone that had more or less done that seemed to elicit a certain amount of awe. Some had to justify why they hadn't taken that step, 'I thought about moving out here, but my girlfriend/boyfriend/wife/husband didn't fancy it.' You could tell some were always going to be "just about to" move over. And then there were those that after seeing it *was* possible, became fully committed to changing their lives. Wayne Greaves was one.

Wayne was on holiday with his girlfriend, Becky, a pretty but painfully thin slip of a girl who wouldn't have suffered adversely from a couple of weeks of force-feeding. Wayne was an ex-gas fitter who we coerced into fixing our oven when the four rings suddenly developed delusions of grandeur, throwing circles of flames high into the air like four Rolls Royce jet engines.

We had attempted to persuade a gas engineer to pay us a visit after Frank had removed the safety catch from the propane bottles, but our hopes were not high in securing a return visit in time to stop the kitchen ceiling being cooked. Wayne and Becky were sitting at the bar early one evening when David came out from the kitchen with distinguishably less eyebrow hair than he had gone in with.

'I think we've got a problem with the gas,' he said and steadied himself with a shot of brandy.

'What's up with it?' asked Joy.

'I can't turn the rings down.'

'Us'll have a look for you. Us used to be a gas fitter,' said Wayne, making his way towards the glowing kitchen. Memories of Frank's near-deadly meddling caused frowns all round. As it was, Wayne discovered the problem and without need for any spare parts had the flames tamed within a matter of minutes.

He emerged covered in black grease but with a big toothy smile. Becky welcomed him like a hero, like the rest of us, except thankfully she was the only one he pawed with greasy hands.

The young couple spoke in singsong Wolverhampton tones, an accent that I'm ashamed to say I find hard to take seriously. It was as such when Wayne announced on his last day that he'd be back in a few weeks. 'Sure he would,' I thought. However, one morning after a frenzied breakfast rush, Joy and myself sat flicking baby cockroaches across the bar top when suddenly Wayne appeared in the doorway. 'Alright?' he waved. 'Us told you I'd be back didn't I?' He was alone. Becky had not been as convinced as him about stepping out of the dole queue in Wolverhampton to make a new life for herself overseas. 'Us dumped her, us did. She wasn't for moving, boring cow.'

Wayne was one of the many wannabees who we had automatically strung along with half-hearted suggestions of employment if he ever returned, which naturally we thought he wouldn't. 'If you come back, look us up. We might have work for you,' we said. It's surprising what benevolence four large beers can evoke.

Fortunately for Wayne, he arrived at a time when we were wondering who we could find that would work for low wages in appalling conditions and be trusted to put more pesetas in the till than they would take out. We had all liked Wayne. He was cheeky but sincere. He had no reservations about telling us of his dodgy past and short spells spent at Her Majesty's pleasure but he was also evidently honest and eager to please.

We decided that we would give him a few DIY jobs coupled with a few hours collecting glasses during the busy times. In return, we could pay him just enough money to afford rental on a studio apartment and would also provide him with a meal whilst he was working.

Wayne fancied himself as a builder, though his actual skills had been greatly exaggerated. However, what he lacked in construction know-how he made up for in determined aggression and he usually coerced a project to be more or less accomplished by using brute strength and loud obscenities. Building a stage was one such example.

The French timeshare line in the office above us had renewed their efforts at attracting fly-buys to the Altamira and the hotel was swarmed with more bewildered Gallics than they knew what to do with. To take advantage of this new trade we enlisted the help of Romaine, one of the timeshare reps, to find us some entertainment that would appeal both to his nationality and also to the Brits. Romaine recommended Mystique.

Some people take light entertainment very seriously. Their act is their life and more often than not their life becomes an act. 'I... am Gaston. She... is Monique,' said Gaston as he swept an open hand in the direction of a timid blonde teenager lurking several feet away. Romaine had sent them to introduce themselves and for us to see if they'd be right for the bar. The elevated nose and pigeon-chested stance of Gaston suggested that *he* was seeing if *we* were right for him.

They were a magic act, or '*illusionistas*' as Gaston preferred to be known. 'I am a member of the Magic Circle,' he offered, pausing for a suitably admiring response. None was forthcoming so he continued anyway. 'Our act is a mixture of *son et lumiere* and tricks of the mind. We can only perform if the conditions are absolutely perfect. The slightest noise will disturb my concentration and there will be a disaster. Your customers will love us. They will want more. We will leave them pleading. You will pay 30,000 pesetas.' This was roughly £150 at the time, twice the going rate.

'How long is your act?' I asked.

'It depends how good your people are,' replied Gaston loftily. 'You have a stage of course?'

'Of course,' I lied. I had taken an instant dislike to Monsieur Mystique but Romaine had convinced us that the French would love him and enthused that we should book him for at least seven nights a week.

We agreed to try out the act the following week and if it was success-ful we would give the couple a regular once-a-week spot. Wayne was set the task of building an outside stage and a backdrop using four sheets of hardboard, a dozen plastic beer crates, a double bed sheet and a can of black spray paint.

The next two afternoons rang with the sounds of a hammer knocking, a stapler thudding and a Wayne cursing. The excessive din drew the atten-tion of some of the older residents in the Altamira. 'What the hell is all that noise? It's siesta time, stop that infernal racket.' Phil was one of our older regulars. An old sea dog from Dorset, he would often come into the bar wearing a nautical-themed hat and sit with his long-suffering wife Yvonne, who would do nothing but wince at his eternal moaning.

Unfortunately, amiable though Wayne was, public relations were not his forte; 'Fuck off, you old git, before us wrap this hammer round your wrin-kled face.' Phil was battle-savvy enough to know when to retreat and saved his admonishing for a more congenial occasion.

We had commandeered the patio space immediately to our right, in front of the round empty locale next to us. Although we knew it had been sold, it remained unfurnished and didn't look as though it would be put into use for some time. Above this space was a second short walkway connecting the commercial units upstairs. From this we draped the bed sheet down behind the stage. A backdrop was born. We also positioned a couple of stage lights that we had borrowed from another bar. The result was impressive, though immoveable. With four nights to go before the French debut we were stuck with what looked like a huge washing line airing erotic black bed linen.

Fortunately, the laundry show only proved to add to the mystery of the forthcoming performance and on show night an eager crowd filled the entire area outside the commercial units. In between washing up, garnishing orders and helping to deliver and collect plates, I was also dashing upstairs to 'borrow' more plastic chairs and tables from Bar Arancha which had fortunately closed for the night.

Unsurprisingly, a large contingent of the audience was French. Romaine had done a good job of 'selling' the night and was wandering amongst his clients, spilling sangria over them from two earthenware jugs that he was waving about in a welcoming fashion.

By the time the show started the terrace was packed to capacity. Joy was having trouble delivering drinks to the distant tables and was reduced to asking people to pass them along. The British cooperated gladly but the French weren't impressed at having to work as waiters. More curious onlookers lined the railings above us, all poised to enjoy the free entertainment but reluctant to buy even one drink.

Joy made it a personal mission to extract some money from them. She took a tray up and started to take drinks orders. The majority were brazen enough to admit they weren't staying: 'No thanks, love, we're just watching,' they smiled. Joy was in no mood for reciprocating the friendliness. This act had cost a lot of money, not forgetting the extra strain on the four of us. Her subtle looks of annoyance were wasted on the majority who hadn't fathomed that somebody – namely us – had to pay for this spectacle.

Wayne was doing his best to gather empty glasses but he quickly became marooned in a corner, trapped by a group of expectant French, so happily resigned himself to admiring his beautiful stage.

The show was due to start at 10 p.m. but the flood of people had caused a deluge of food orders and we were all too busy to even think about the entertainment. By 10.45 p.m. our artistes were growing tetchy. Gaston grabbed Joy's arm as she was scurrying back to the kitchen with a stack of dirty plates. 'We need an introduction. At once.' It was something we had overlooked. Although we had no compère, we couldn't expect Mystique to suddenly start their act without so much as a '*Monsieurs et Madm es*'.

'Wayne, can you introduce them?' shouted Joy across the terrace.

'I'm not introducing that poof. You can bog off,' replied Wayne at the top of his voice. Joy had no option but to dump the plates on the nearest table and jump onstage. Faith flicked the stage lights on and stopped Van Morrison's *Brown-eyed Girl* in her tracks, swapping the cassette for one provided by Gaston.

'Ladies and gentlemen... is this working?' She patted the microphone as is traditional for low-grade compères. 'Welcome to the Smugglers Tavern. Sorry for the late start but I'm sure you'll find they're well worth waiting for. Put your hands together for Mystique!'

There was a slight delay before the electronic fanfare of Jean Michel Jarre rolled from the speakers. Gaston swished in from stage left, one hand pointing skywards. His black cape followed his expansive gestures like a faithful dog. Monique swished from behind the other side of the bed sheet with slightly less enthusiasm. Her red and black basque, fishnet stockings and high heels had already stolen the focus. Gaston grabbed her arm and spun her into his body, rolling her away again with equal gusto. David and I had abandoned the washing up and were stood watching in the doorway with Frank. Wayne was still at the front of the crowd, sitting on the floor nursing a pint of beer and openly rolling a spliff.

Even from where I was standing I could hear the crack. Wayne looked up, his tongue still sticking out from licking a Rizla. He leaned forward to bring his eyes level with the stage and raised his eyebrows then looked over at us with a pained expression.

'What was that?' I mouthed but he shook his head dismissively and continued rolling.

Feathers were procured from the most unexpected angles; gold rings were balanced precariously; jewellery was begged, lost and then miraculously found in unlikely places. The audience were enjoying the show, with the French contingent particularly vocal in their praise. Frank had trudged back to his bar stool, unimpressed, and was slumped over a Dorada, idly picking pieces of gold label off the bottle. He had no time for such flamboyance.

'Can't be doing,' he murmured to nobody but himself and the bottle.

As the music changed from triumphant to ambient, the *pièce d résis-*

tance began. A black rectangular box was wheeled from behind the backdrop. After much posturing, Monique climbed inside and waved *au revoir*. Only her head and feet remained visible.

Gaston pushed the box from one side of the stage to the other to show that both Monique's feet and head were moving. As he did, I thought I heard another loud crack. Wayne was beyond caring at this stage having smoked himself into oblivion. He was sitting cross-legged on the floor, his eyes half-closed and a grin plastered across his face.

Gaston began to saw the box in half, pausing occasionally to check if she was alright. As the blade was nearly halfway through the box I noticed the right hand side of the stage had begun to part company with the left. Unfortunately, Monique was positioned over each half of the separating sections. Gaston began pumping frantically with the saw to keep up with the rapidly widening gap.

The saw broke free at the bottom of the box and Monique, who was oblivious of the external problems, cried out theatrically as if in pain. Gaston stepped back, raising his saw in mock horror and stamping a foot behind him for effect. This was as much as the right hand side of the stage could take and the outer supports collapsed. The two pieces were now only held together by a handful of assorted screws that Wayne had used to unite them. The discrepancy in levels was enough to start Monique's feet on a slow roll to the right. Gaston stretched out his left leg, jamming a foot under the castors to foil the escape whilst trying to maintain a smile. The sudden shift in weight caused the screws to release their grip and the left side of the stage kicked free. Monique's feet trundled right, her upper half began to roll left. Trapped inside her wooden coffin, she could do no more than strain her eyes to see where she was heading. Gaston threw down the saw and made a brave effort to jam his other leg under this half of his assistant but having adopted the 'splits' position he discovered he was in no shape to sustain it. He toppled backwards with a fit of Gallic expletives, watching Monique's boxed head gain speed as she edged closer towards the left hand lip of the stage. Fortunately – although Monique may not have viewed it that way – rather than rolling straight off and toppling over, the first set of castors dropped over the edge, tilting the box just enough to thud Monique's head firmly against a store cupboard door, wedging her at an unlikely angle but saving her from any further injury.

The audience was in hysterics. Wayne had contracted an almost suffocating bout of giggles. He was now lying on the floor gasping for breath underneath the neatly boxed Monique, whose pleas for help were drowned out by the laughing. Friedhelm sat on his barrel table, tears streaming down his cheeks. His shoulders convulsed up and down with every rasping chuckle.

Needless to say, after releasing his assistant, Gaston was rather less amused. *Merd* was about the only word I could comprehend and there were plenty of those being thrown about.

'I have never been so embarrassed. What business do you think you run here?' he ranted, but I was far too amused to pay much heed.

'I can only apologise for the stage,' I said, trying to keep a straight face. 'I'll look into it. Can you come back next week?' Gaston snatched his money from my hand and waltzed out, hurling more French profanities over his shoulder. We took that as a *non*.

A post-mortem was held the following morning, the general conclusion being that the night was a complete success financially and the collapsing stage routine was a fitting tribute to a stuck-up Frenchman. Wayne was most apologetic and in true British spirit blamed his poor workmanship on inferior quality materials. We awarded him a sideways promotion into painting duties and for the next few days he was a permanent fixture, applying dabs of paint where unruly children had left their mark.

Our thoughts turned to staff again. On the nights when we clocked off at 10.30 p.m. both Joy and I had taken to going for a nightcap and a bite to eat at the local 24-hour service station. Not the most romantic of settings it has to be agreed, but it was one of the few bars within short driving distance where we could get something decent to eat in peace. The favourite was a plate of rice, bananas and fried eggs, which, if you haven't tried it, is as good as any doner kebab at plugging the phantom hunger that follows late night beers.

The service station bar was beginning to fill up with the usual assortment of moonlight crazies, reminding me of the scene in *Star Wars* where Harrison Ford is in the intergalactic bar with all manner of ill-featured life forms. The atmosphere wasn't exactly threatening but as a 24/7 hangout for alcoholics and drug-induced insomniacs, it did provide an element of uncertainty.

Two stools away, a gaunt youth with ill-fitting clothes and teeth was concentrating on making a sugar pyramid on the stainless steel bar top. He had opened and scattered at least 20 sachets before the barman whisked away the margarine tub in which they were piled. The youth looked over at us and mumbled something in Spanish. His eyes were glazed and his focus appeared to be a couple of inches to our left. I just nodded obligingly and picked at a plate of *pimientos d pad on*, hot roasted peppers in sea salt, that I had chosen as a starter.

Despite there only being one person working, the actual service was unbelievably fast. We enjoyed just sitting around the bar marvelling at the haste and efficiency of the barman taking orders. He could heat up tapas, keep tabs on everybody's bills and simultaneously pour drinks with frightening efficiency.

He was the perfect barman. His white shirt and black trousers might be soaked in sweat, yet he managed to maintain an air of collectiveness. He was never shaken in the face of adversity, such as a drunken local trying to get away with not paying, or spilling his beer all over the floor.

He moved from task to task seamlessly; pouring two beers, cutting a slab of tortilla, collecting payments and wiping the bar top like it had been perfectly choreographed. He moved with the agility that only someone fuelled by Latino blood could manage, flexing his physical and mental presence like a world-class salsa dancer.

It may be that the UK remains one of the few nations in the developed world where waiting staff are looked down upon as though they aren't capable of securing a more worthwhile profession. Perhaps it's our history of the upstairs, downstairs world of servant and master that still lingers in the British psyche.

Our only help behind the bar to date, apart from the junior crew, was from a 50-something retired flight attendant who had offered to work for free just for something to do. Unfortunately he turned out to be more of a hindrance than a help. His peripheral vision was non-existent which, combined with an acute deafness, meant that anybody waiting to be served and not standing directly in front of him would be thirsty to the point of dehydration by the time Barry would notice.

If there was one good point about him though, it was his glass washing. He would become totally engrossed, spending so much time with his head down, hands in the sink making sure that every glass was as shiny as the day it was blown, that he quite forgot that the principal responsibility of his position – to keep the customers watered. On the sporadic occasions when he would be satisfied with the lustrous sheen on a wine glass, he would raise it to the light like a winner's trophy where he would be genuinely surprised to see a gang of thirsty holidaymakers glaring through its shiny curve.

In spite of this, our regular customers loved him. He was a kind man who spent much of his spare time – of which he had plenty – ferrying people about on errands or playing golf with the less industrious. Every now and then we would call him in but more as an act of friendship than for the actual benefit we gained from his presence.

We still needed someone who could maximise the profit potential behind the bar. In summer, over 90% of our customers were British holidaymakers whose holiday enjoyment is directly proportional to the amount of alcohol consumed. Every empty glass on a table is a missed opportunity at making the till ring. We needed someone who would not only draw customers to the bar and keep them all night, but also who would make sure that the length of time between one drink finished and another started was kept to the bare minimum. If Barry was the antithesis of what we needed, the service station attendant was our apotheosis.

We had become friendly with Gary, a satellite system installer who had also risen to saintly status having blessed the Smugglers with the gift of live English football – an amenity that was as vital as draught beer in the British holiday pub world. We mentioned that we were looking for part-time staff and it so happened that he and his stunningly beautiful girlfriend Michelle were looking for extra work and volunteered to take on a couple of shifts.

Michelle had worked behind a bar before and her visual appeal, though some might consider it a sexist notion, provide a definite draw for custom. Her green eyes, blonde hair, tanned size eight physique and flirtatious manner were the perfect bargirl CV. To even the score, Gary had equally piercing eyes and the body of an athlete. There were no doubts from all four partners that they would be the ideal stand-ins.

We had reached the level of friendship where they were naturally included in any social plans we had on our separate nights off. Joy and I seized the opportunity to catch a real band whenever the shifts allowed, real being any act that included a live drummer and not two balding folk guitarists relying on a digital orchestra and a Bontempi drum machine. Gary and Michelle would often come along with us and what was intended to be a quick drink would always extend into a hazy session of inharmonious singing and over-exuberant dancing.

We were all more than happy to leave them in charge of running the bar from 10.30 p.m. until 2 a.m. or 3 a.m. and trusted them in all aspects, from cleaning to cashing up. For several nights they provided the pressure release of a little time off.

CHAPTER 10

Gary and Michelle had relocated to Tenerife after her aunt opened a hairdressing salon in the south, initially employing Michelle as a stylist. Michelle, like many, had decided that a new life abroad should also entail a move away from the job she had stuck at since leaving school at 16 and accepted her aunt's offer on the understanding that it was temporary.

Bar work wasn't exactly what she had in mind for a breakaway career but the couple had their eye on buying their own restaurant and knew that having temporary responsibility of stock control, cashing up and customer diplomacy at the Smugglers would serve as valuable experience eventually.

'No problems last night. Usual dickheads and drunks but no spew. Love Shell and Gaz, XX'. Their customary report was stuck to the till with Blu-Tack.

'Bar looks good again,' said Joy, noting the cleanliness. The chairs had all been up-ended onto the tables meaning last night's sweep and mop was not the usual poke between wooden legs that our end of night routine had degenerated into. All the cutlery had been rolled in paper serviettes, the bar top was free from patches of beer and all the bins had been emptied and cleaned.

As usual, Joy checked the till roll to see how busy they had been and what time the last bill was tilled in.

'Blimey, the bar must have emptied after we left last night. There's only a handful of entries. They only took 8,000 pesetas after meals but they didn't close till 1.30 a.m.,' said Joy.

'Well, you know what it's like. A lot of regulars only want the four of us there. Having other people on won't make them stay. It can't be helped,' I replied.

Joy wasn't convinced. 'Even so, 8,000 is crap, especially in summer. We need to take more than that.'

She was right. Summer was our time for raking it in before the lull in

October and November. We needed to put some money aside to cover the mortgage, loan and other payments for those months.

'We can't have it both ways. We need time off,' I argued. 'Either we lose a bit of money or we lose our sanity.'

We had all been feeling the strain, all showing signs of wear and tear in different ways. Cutting back on our hours was imperative for us and our relationships.

Spending every waking minute with each other is not conducive to sustaining a happy relationship. If all that we did all day and night was work, and at the same place, there was little to talk about out of hours. Added to that, the exhaustion of being on your feet for so long in such hot conditions, putting on the friendly front for long periods of time and working under the pressure of being understaffed was sure to take its toll.

On the nights when we clocked off at 10.30 p.m., Joy and I decided that bar talk was banned. Unfortunately that left a gaping hole in our conversation and we often sat drinking in silence like the married couples that had outgrown their interest in each other that we observed in the bar.

But the silence was sometimes preferable to the alternative – sniping. The tension was palpable. Our eyes were red, sunken above stormy shadows, shoulders hunched and knotted. The strain had to be released somewhere and firing pot shots at each other was one of the more effective ways.

'You're drinking too much.'

'I'm thirsty, I'm off duty. What's the problem?'

Or, 'Have you phoned your mum recently?'

'No, what's the point. I've nothing to tell her. All we do is work, sleep, work, sleep. I'll only cry if I speak to her.'

'You should still phone.'

'Don't tell me when I should speak to my own mum.'

The same was true for David and Faith. When not working in our bar, they could usually be found in someone else's, usually comparing notes and complaining about the same things – drunken customers, the latest licence requirements, the interminable questions.

We had begun to notice that Faith had stopped talking about anything recently. She was becoming more withdrawn and isolated. Any decisions that we had to make about the bar as partners inevitably saw Faith casting herself in the role of outsider, the underdog, seemingly choosing the contrary line of thinking – whatever the debate. It was as though she was revelling in the minority role almost to the point of self-pity.

'You don't consider me as one of the partners do you?' she would argue with the rest of us. 'Whatever I say, you always do what you three want anyway.'

'It's called democracy,' said David, calmly.

'We have to make the decisions by majority vote. How else can we do it?' I added.

'Well it always seems like you've already decided what we're going to do whatever I say,' Faith would counter. 'You two are brothers and Joy just follows what Joe says anyway. I might as well not be here.'

'If I follow what Joe says it's only because I agree,' said Joy, 'not because I'm some obedient lap dog. I do have my own mind you know.'

'I'm not an equal partner though, am I?' replied Faith, 'I mean, come on, at the end of the day we're never going to do what I want, are we?'

'If we agree on it, yes we'll do what you want. But the majority have to agree on it,' said David trying to appease her.

With Faith's argument running out of steam, this usually brought on another apron-de-robing, door-slamming episode.

When Faith had gone, David, as usual, apologised in her absence; 'She's missing her mum at the moment and she thinks we're all ganging up on her. We need to just tread lightly, give her a bit of slack. I think she's on the verge of a breakdown.'

Faith's tantrums became more frequent the deeper we sank into summer. A few customers had started to complain to Joy, citing her snappiness and the fact she looked miserable behind the bar. The truth was, she wasn't fitting in. She wore her heart on her sleeve but when behind the bar it has to be kept under wraps. Also, due to her paranoia, the slightest inference of hostility from anybody would cause her to bare her claws like a cornered animal.

The first day of reckoning came on a particularly sweltering Saturday in early September. The mercury was loitering around 100, the humidity energy sapping. Joy and I had survived one of the busiest afternoons so far. She had to sprint between bar, kitchen and tables non-stop from 1 p.m. to 4 p.m. and I had been battling with the seemingly insurmountable list of orders, trying to ignore the teetering mountain of washing up. By the time David and Faith clocked on at 6.30 p.m. we had just managed to piece together the bar in time for the evening rush.

Usually, the afternoon shift would complete a few menial tasks like cleaning the bathrooms or emptying out the bar fridges to scrub away the mould. This day we had barely managed to wash all the glasses and polish the glass tabletops.

Kevin and Brian, the two representatives for the British timeshare line, had approached us about hosting their welcome party at the Smugglers instead of the Altamira lounge. Some of the more affected residents of the hotel associated timeshare with con-artists and had made a point of hissing their opinions whilst walking past on the way to the pool; 'Don't do it,' 'It's a scam,' 'Just say no.' Naturally this made the two reps' tasks of extracting large deposits all the harder.

Another reason why they thought it better to use our bar was that it meant free drinks for themselves – the single most important reason for doing anything amongst the British expat community. In return for us providing free jugs of sangria and a smattering of peanuts, Kevin and Brian would extol the virtues of the Smugglers Tavern to weekly groups of around 20–30 new arrivals. More often than not, several of the timeshare fly-buys would stay after the welcome meeting and order food enabling us to recoup the cost of our meagre giveaways and showcase our hospitality talents at the same time. However this extra crowd of customers was in addition to our regular breakfast trade and once or twice whoever happened to be on shift that morning would be faced with 30 full English breakfasts and 30 coffee orders all at the same time. Understandably the bar was not looking at its best when David and Faith walked in.

'There's no fizzy water or bottled beer in the fridge,' said Faith during her habitual inspection.

'Don't start, Faith,' warned Joy. 'We've done 65 meals this afternoon as well as hosting the timeshare meeting. I've not got round to stocking the bar yet.'

But Faith was clearly in offensive mode.

'It's not good enough. Now the bottles won't be cold enough for tonight.'

'We can put them in the freezer like last time.'

'Yeah, and they'll all burst like last time. It's not a lot to ask...'

Fortunately a family of four walked in, forcing a cessation of hostilities, but the tension still simmered.

The evening turned out to be even busier than the afternoon. By 9 p.m. we were running out of food. 'No half-chickens, no pork chops, no gammon,' shouted David as Joy brought in the 80th order.

'Why didn't you tell me that before?' snapped Joy. 'I've got four pork chop orders here.' She raced out of the kitchen huffing, her pink T-shirt claret with perspiration. As she left, Faith rushed in with another order.

'Two pork chops...'

'No pork,' I shouted, manically ripping apart a lettuce to make some more garnishes. Faith huffed.

'For fuck's sake... well, two half-chickens, one...'

'No half-chickens either,' I interrupted.

'This is ridiculous. I haven't got time to go back and explain, I've...'

'I haven't got time to stand here arguing, Faith,' I interrupted again. 'Just go and tell them, no half-chickens, no gammon and no pork chops.'

'Who do you think you are? You're not my boss. See? You're at it again. You don't see me as a partner do you?'

'Faith,' intervened David, '*Now* is not a good time.'

Faith's paranoia was rising again. 'This is what I mean. You three all stick together. I'm nothing here. I'm sick of it.' Faith threw her pen and pad at the wall, stomped back through the bar and out of the front door.

'Jesus,' muttered David and carried on cooking. Anybody, even Jesus, would have been a welcome pair of hands at that stage. We were eight orders behind, all four rings and the hot plate were full and still customers were craning their necks at the door looking for a vacant table.

'Do you want to go after her?' I asked.

'No, I'll let her cool down first,' said David.

Joy panted into the kitchen. 'Where's Faith? The bar's three deep.'

'Done a runner,' I said, 'Buggered off in a huff.'

'Oh that's great. Well, one of you two are going to have to help me out here.'

I threw more garnishes on the plates, left them wobbling three-high on the table in the middle of the kitchen and raced out to face a bar full of impatient faces. We had been completely cleared of bottled beers, including those stacked in the freezer. We were also on our last barrel of draught. If that ran out there'd be a riot.

I spent the remaining hour dashing from bar to kitchen. We were all trying to fill the gap left by Faith and by 11 p.m., with the last order out, I was pleased to get back to the barrage of washing up that had commandeered every flat surface in the kitchen.

David was supposed to clock off at 10.30 p.m. but stayed an hour to help with the clearing. 'So what's up with Faith, then?' I asked.

'She just needs a break. She not good with stress.'

'It's not great for any of us,' I said. 'Especially when she just dumps her workload onto us. We're going to have to sort it out. We can't have her throwing in the towel every other night.'

'I'll talk to her,' said David. 'I think she needs to go home for a while.'

He was right. Faith was threatening to leave Tenerife for good.

After she had regained a little composure, she apologised to the rest of us and admitted she needed a break. Although it wasn't the most convenient time to jump ship, coming in the middle of the summer season, Faith had decided that she was going back to the UK the following night. She'd spend a fortnight with her mum and then return for the end of the busy period.

That left the problem of who would partner David on his shifts. We needed someone who could work 80 hours during the week, someone who could walk straight into the role without training. Michelle was the obvious choice but she wasn't available for all those hours. Barry was available but wasn't anywhere near capable. We had less than 24 hours to find someone. If we didn't, the alternative was to close during the day and the three of us just manage the evening shift. That meant a substantial drop in income at a time when we had to make sure we banked all that we could. If not, when the season slackened we might not have enough to pay the mortgage, Jack's loan or one of the dozens of other outgoings for which we'd assigned envelopes.

It was a basic system but one that we all could manage. From just a handful of different envelopes, our financial distribution now had to be apportioned to almost 20 needs that we had to save for, including Holidays, Emergencies and Christmas Bonus. Faith's disappearance was considered an emergency and as such it was this envelope that was raided.

The Rum Jug couple were sat at the bar. It was evident from their tired faces that all was not well. The enthusiasm and excitement that they had portrayed in Julie's office was no longer evident.

'I didn't think it would be so hard,' said the man.

'We don't seem to have any time for each other now,' added his wife. 'We decided to close for the afternoon. We had to get away. I wish we'd never bought the bar now.'

'So are you thinking of selling already?' I asked. At that moment Justin bounded into the bar wearing his T-shirt like a Saharan head-dress.

'D'you want me to do anything,' he asked. 'Everybody's gone for a sleep. I'm bored.'

'It's a bit quiet at the moment,' said Joy. 'If you really want to do something you can check if the toilets need more loo rolls and soap.'

'OK,' he chirped, happy to be of use.

The man continued. 'We'll stick it out for the summer but I reckon we'll put it up for sale after that. I came out here for an easy life, not to work my arse off. I'll try and get my old job back at Marconi.'

'Trouble is, we sold everything in Britain to buy the bar. We've no house, no car. We'll have to start all over again.' The woman was watching the bubbles rise in her half-empty glass, sad that hers had burst already.

The man could see she was on the point of tears. 'It'll be alright,' he said, putting an arm round her shoulders.

'You said that about coming over,' she snapped, pushing his arm away. 'I should never have listened to you.'

I began to pull them another two halves but was distracted by a knocking. 'What's that banging?'

'Sounds like it's coming from the toilets,' said Joy.

In the men's room I found Justin hammering frantically on the outside of the cubicle. 'Justin? What's the matter, mate?'

'I've locked myself out of the toilet.'

I tried the door and sure enough it wouldn't open. It was a door that could only be locked from the inside.

'Are you sure there's nobody in there?' I knocked just to be sure.

'Yes, I was in there. But I locked myself out.'

'Well why are you knocking?'

'Cos I'm locked out,' he said impatiently.

I gave up on this line of reasoning. 'How did you manage to lock yourself out?'

'I was checking on the toilet rolls and the door closed.'

'With you on the outside?'

'Yes.'

'And the door locked from the inside?'

'That's right. How am I going to get back in?'

'What do you want to get back in for?'

'I've got a toilet roll.' He lifted his arm. He was wearing a toilet roll on his puny wrist like a bracelet.

'Uh... don't worry about that, I'll put it in later. Go and get yourself a drink.'

He skipped out of the toilet leaving me to fathom how he'd managed this mysterious Houdini act.

'Justin!' I shouted after him.

'Yes?'

'You're still wearing the toilet roll.' He slipped it off his wrist and disappeared. It took the best part of the next hour and a 12-inch monkey wrench to unlock the cubicle door from the outside.

The couple from The Rum Jug had since made their exit. I felt a pang of guilt and was just glad that we had happened upon a location that was away from the centre where so many bars were having to undercut each other to stay in business.

To own your own pub is a pipedream for many British men. To have that pub in a sunny climate just adds to the attraction. But the majority who fulfil that dream in a resort destination like Tenerife return home to the UK with their vision in tatters having acquired a lighter pocket, an alcohol addiction and a severely strained relationship.

There are just too many bars in the resort areas to provide a profit for them all. In Las Americas, whole streets are dedicated to George and Dragons, Red Lions, White Horses and other British-themed pubs and they all compete for the same custom. Few have anything new to offer, all relying on the lure of David Jason, John Cleese, Jeremy Beadle or pints of beer five pesetas less than the bar next door.

Although competition helps shave the price of beer down to the bare minimum, it also means that corners are cut to make up for the narrower profit margins. Soft drinks would be of the lowest quality, the calibre of food served somewhere between barely fit for consumption and adequate pet food.

More often than not, the focus would be switched from efforts to attract the clientele to plans to stay one step ahead of the bar next door. This invariably resulted in not only a cut in income for the neighbour but also a drop in profit for the instigating bar.

Sooner or later the books would show that the business was going nowhere fast, except towards bankruptcy. Eventually the baffled owners would be forced to sell up for far less than they paid.

Even for the experienced landlords and landladies who had swapped snug rooms in the UK for sun terraces abroad, the competition usually proved too much. Despite this, there was one advantage in having customers who were on holiday as opposed to the drinkers back in the UK. Those propping up a bar in a resort destination had cash that was destined to be spent before the holiday was over rather than loose change that was diverted to alcohol and crisps rather than the next utility bill. The battle was getting them to spend it in our bar but we were lucky, we had a monopoly. Even so, some of our takings were now going to have to be spent on the unforeseen need for extra staff.

We managed to persuade one of Patricia's daughters to take over the shifts that Michelle couldn't manage. We were a little hesitant to take her on, mainly due to the fact that she was only 14 years old but she had the confidence and looks of a thirty-something.

Robin was far from immature when it also came to negotiating a wage. On top of the basic hourly rate she demanded a half-share of the tips, plus meals and drinks on the days she worked. The latter proved to be the most costly addendum.

We soon found out that Robin had the drinking capacity of a rugby team captain and on the first night her flirting ability was turbo-charged with half a dozen tequila shots.

'Four pints of lager, and one for yourself, love.' The man at the bar winked as he handed over a 1,000-peseta note intending Robin to keep the 200 pesetas change.

'Ta. I'll have a vodka orange. That'll be one thousand two hundred please.' Robin held out her hand.

'Blimey. You're an expensive girl to keep aren't you?' The man gave her two more coins.

'Thanks,' said Robin. 'You get what you pay for in this world.'

'I bet you're worth a fortune then, princess.'

'Too much for you.'

'I'm not short of a bob or two,' said the man. He took a sip out of one of the pints, peering at Robin over the ridge of his glass. 'I could give you a good time.'

Another customer was waiting to be served. 'I bet you could,' laughed Robin over her shoulder.

On average Robin was propositioned three times a night behind the bar. She felt safe with two feet of wooden bar top between her and her admirers but I wondered how long it would be before she took the flirting too far. Getting off with the bargirl was considered quite a trophy for the many beer-brave groups of lads who would egg each other on.

Joy also had her fair share of propositions. It was something I didn't particularly like at first but I soon realised it went with the territory. The male customers expect a certain amount of flirting, and if it brought them in night after night with the heady notion that they were in with a chance, so be it.

Despite her flirting – or perhaps because of it – Robin was fitting in well. Whether drunk or not, she was coping admirably with the drinks orders that Joy was firing in her direction. She would also take the initiative to wait on tables if she could see that a group had been sitting for too long before Joy could get round to them. Despite the fact that she was regularly consuming more alcohol than the majority of our customers, we were happy to employ her.

But Robin is perhaps living proof of the existence of a 'resort child'. In Tenerife, for non-Spanish speaking youngsters, night-time diversions revolve around a British bar or at beach barbecues, both of which involve copious drinking no matter what the age. Friends come and go in fortnightly rotation and because of Robin's mature looks and demeanour, these friends were often several years her senior. To her temporary friends this world might seem sunshine yellow but the simmering discontent and boredom was making the danger signs grow ever more red.

It doesn't take a sociologist to see that this is a breeding ground for juvenile alcoholics. We all took Robin to one side at one time or another during her fortnight with us and warned her that her life was centred around drinking, but we couldn't argue against her defence that she was performing well regardless. We just had to hope that for her sake one day she would be taken away from this environment.

Michelle was also maintaining an efficient – although sober – partnership with David.

For Joy and me, the difference in atmosphere when working with David and Robin or David and Michelle rather than with Faith was blinding. There were no long faces, no moodiness and for a while at least, there was no tip-toeing from one eggshell to another.

CHAPTER 11

'I think we've struck it lucky this time.' I sat in the living room of our new home surveying the space. Joy was stretched out on the sofa watching a midday movie full of righteous morals and wholesome families. We'd hardly seen Ron or Micky since we moved in but that wasn't to say the house was quiet. There had been a steady succession of mean and moodies knocking on their door at all times of the day and night.

The first time I met Adam was at 2.30 in the morning. 'Go and see who it is,' urged Joy quietly. The banging persisted for several minutes and any hopes of the knocker buggering off had faded. I opened the door a few inches and scowled in the most menacing way that anybody wrapped in a Sylvester the Cat beach towel could. The man scowled back. He had me beaten. He was dressed in a black leather trench coat and towered a good foot higher. His neck gave the impression of being wider than his head, a head furrowed with a much more convincing scowl than my own.

He held the scowl for a second, waiting for the wheels of recognition to whir into place but they buckled under the pressure and the scowl fell apart. 'Who are *you*?' he grunted.

'Joe. Who are you?'

'Adam.' I wrongly anticipated further explanation.

'What do you want?'

'My money.'

I gave a quizzical expression.

'What money?' I asked, after the quizzical expression failed to make him elaborate.

'Who *are* you?' he repeated.

'Joe.' I said it slower this time.

'Where's Micky?'

'Ah... Micky.' I opened the door and padded out to point to his door two apartments down.

'When did he move?' asked Adam.

'He never lived here...' I started to explain, but Adam was already bounding towards Micky's door, knuckles skimming the floor.

Joy's film had come to an end. Although our shift was due to start in a couple of hours, my eyelids were beginning to droop.

'Joe! Look,' whispered Joy. I looked at my watch. Half an hour had passed since we dropped off. I followed her gaze to the garden.

Our next-door neighbours had been sweeping and tidying their garden ever since we had sat down. Now, they were both leaning over the thigh-high wall trying to peer into our living room. The sun had started its decline, throwing a bright reflection on the patio door window panes and making it impossible to see in from the outside.

The woman began to brush our lawn, eyeing the patio doors for signs of life. Satisfied that there was none, she climbed over the wall and continued to sweep the grass.

'What's she doing?' sniggered Joy.

'Brushing our lawn, I think.'

The woman bobbed her head from side to side trying to catch sight of what lay inside. She manoeuvred a little closer to the glass doors, still sweeping back and forth. Her husband remained on the other side of the wall, encouraging her to go closer.

As she reached the short width of patio tiles directly outside the doors, she flicked the brush to and fro once more before pushing her nose against the window, shielding her eyes from the reflection to get a better look.

Her gaze moved methodically from right to left; from the white sideboard, to the black armchair, the arched reading light, the magazine rack at the edge of the sofa, and then... her eyebrows shot skywards taking cover behind a fringe of tight ginger curls. Joy and I smiled and waved from the sofa. She jumped back and began sweeping in double time back to the wall. Her husband must have heard her hisses of 'They're in, they're in!' and had ducked behind an expertly manicured bougainvillea before scuttling towards his own patio doors, head down as if dodging sniper fire.

The next morning, obviously embarrassed by their failed undercover operation, the snoopers came a-knocking. Maureen and Pete were in their late 50s. She was a highly-strung redhead with a screeching Midlands accent. He stood at least a foot shorter and had disproportionately small eyes, like a premature piglet. His black hair was combed in defiance of a balding crown, a flop of unchecked fringe sprawled across a barren expanse.

It was Maureen who tried to make light of the previous night's mission. 'I hope you didn't mind me sweeping your patio,' she squealed. 'Only I know how busy you must be. Obviously you never have time to do any cleaning.' She was looking over my shoulder, scanning the hallway for dust.

'It's nice to see some young ones doing something for themselves,' said Pete. 'Keeps you from mugging old ladies doesn't it, son?' We barely knew them but already they had spied on us once and insulted us twice. It was not the standard cup-of-sugar introduction that many neighbours opted for.

'Would you like to come round to our house for a drink?' asked Maureen. Caught off guard we could think of no excuse, apart from the fact that we already loathed them.

'Yes, that'd be nice,' lied Joy.

Maureen and Pete's apartment was astounding. Not for any design innovation or eye-catching ornaments but for the fact that it was immaculate to the point of sterility. The floor shone like a mirror, replicating the room perfectly in a translucent pool of pale grey marble. The cream leather three-piece suite was arranged around a smoked glass coffee table edged in sparkling gold plate. Three Lladro figurines stood on circles of trimmed lace positioned at precise intervals along the length of glass. More Lladro statuettes posed inside an upright glass display cabinet. Despite so much glass there wasn't so much as a speck of dust or a fingerprint, even on the patio windows, where thick gold drapes had been harnessed in perfect symmetry. Equal precision had been employed in positioning five gold and black tasselled cushions along the back of the sofa.

'It's beautiful,' said Joy dutifully.

'You can see we like to keep things neat and tidy,' said Maureen. 'Please, sit.' Joy hovered over the sofa, uncomfortable about causing ripples in the perfectly plumped cushions. I lowered myself into one of the armchairs but Pete made a dash for my elbow halting me before I made contact. 'Not there, son, that's my chair. Call me queer... not that I am, mind,' he gave a little laugh, 'but I'm the only one who sits there. Isn't that right, Maureen?'

'He's a funny one about that chair, he is,' smiled Maureen proudly. 'Here, sit there next to your wife. That's it... no... a bit closer... closer...' She motioned with her hands for us to move in as if composing a wedding photograph. I hutched a few inches closer to Joy so that we were both exactly the same distance from each arm. Maureen was scrutinising our positions. 'That's it. Perfect. Now, what would you like? Coffee? Good.'

Four dainty cups were brought in on a silver tray, each presented with a foil-wrapped biscuit on the saucer. Maureen unfolded cream linen napkins onto our laps. 'There's no need to make crumbs if we can avoid it now, is there?'

'So,' said Pete in between slurps of coffee, 'it must have cost you a pretty packet to buy the Smugglers. Did you borrow it?'

'Uh... we borrowed some and took out a mortgage for the rest,' I said, taken aback by the directness of questioning.

'You can't have had much to put down as a deposit, I guess. Were you working in England or on the dole, bleeding the country dry like all the other youngsters too lazy to get off their backsides?'

'We both worked in retail,' said Joy.

'In what capacity?' continued Pete.

'Sales,' I replied.

'Selling what?

'Food.'

'What kind of food?'

'Seafood,' said Joy.

'And game,' I added for effect.

'Ah! You were poachers?' Maureen had risen to her feet and was hovering, waiting for me to put my cup down. The moment I obliged she whisked all the crockery into the kitchen. I could hear her humming as she filled the kitchen sink with water.

'You been here long, Pete?' I asked, attempting to deflect the interrogation.

'Long enough. I've seen a lot of people coming and going. People like yourself. Youngsters who start a business and then realise it's not all fun and games.'

I looked to see if he was intending to insult us for a third time but his smile suggested it wasn't intended as a personal judgement.

'Take Forgreen next door.' He thumbed towards Micky's apartment. 'Started off selling apartments here, all nice and bonny. We bought ours from him. All kosher, no problems. Mind you, he knew not to mess with me. Then he got greedy, like all you youngsters do. Started doing deals on the side, taking all the commission instead of splitting it with his two partners. Anyway, like most people on this island, he couldn't keep that closed.' He put a finger to his lips. 'His partners wondered why he was driving about in a flash open-top while they were in battered ex-rentals. So he got found out. Trouble was, one of his partners was married to the sister of a wrong 'un who didn't take kindly to her being taken for a ride. Forgreen had to do a runner. They caught up with him in London and tied him to a radiator for a week until he agreed to sign over all his ill-gotten gains in Tenerife. Like his house. Now he's gone and spoiled it for all of us...' Maureen had returned and was still humming, busying herself around Pete's feet with a portable vacuum cleaner. Pete turned up the volume to compensate for the electronic sucking. 'NOW WE'VE GOT THE SODDIN' MAFIA LIVING NEXT DOOR.' The timing was immaculate. Maureen turned off the vacuum just as Pete delivered his condemnation. They both looked at each other, silent, eyes stricken with alarm.

Maureen held the vacuum nozzle aloft in pink washing-up gloves; 'Are they in?' she whispered.

'What time is it?' Pete whispered back.

Maureen looked at her watch. '11.45.'

'No. Tennis lesson.' Pete's shoulders dropped in relief.

Maureen tightened her lips in a reprimanding look. 'One of these days…'

'Well… it's been entertaining,' I said, nodding at Joy to stand up. Maureen reached between us to straighten the cushions. 'But we've got to get ready for work.'

'No rest for the wicked I guess,' said Pete. 'Don't go mugging anybody on your way up.' As the front door closed behind us I could hear the vacuum rev up again.

We had all been taking advantage of the fact that someone else was available to work the most loathed shift of the day. Loathed because it was a time when the majority of customers were getting steadily drunk and expected us to join them in their frivolity no matter how tired we all were or how early we had to get up the next morning.

For my brother and me, four and a half hours cooking for over a hundred people in 100-plus degree heat and then having to deal with the subsequent washing up was not the best way to raise party spirits. Just when the physical work was over, it was necessary for whoever was rostered for the late shift to switch hats and play the jovial host for the next three to four hours.

Running a bar is certainly not the 24/7 party whilst propping up the proverbial that casual observers may think. You have to be nice to people who you would much rather slap, pluck regurgitated vegetables out of urinals if you're a true follower of the hands-on approach to management and watch everybody stagger to bed whilst you fill the mop bucket.

Every day brings a new drama, a new dilemma and more often than not a new drunk. But there are worse jobs, like folding knickers on a conveyor belt for eight hours a day or jabbing at rock hundreds of metres below the earth's surface. This needs to be remembered occasionally, when drudgery and heat gets the better of you and you just wish all the happy smiling faces would sod off so you can scrape the vomit off the upholstery in peace.

Everybody gets sick of their job every now and then, but bar work is a 'party' business, especially in a holiday resort and being a miserable git just isn't an option. A drink or two to lift the mood becomes unavoidable especially if you want your customers to continue depositing their cash behind your bar.

It can't be denied that a mighty thirst was worked up in our sweatbox of a kitchen. The first ice-cold beer that dampened the parched lips and bone-dry throat of the kitchen crew after a lengthy shift was pure *manna*. The problem – though understandably many wouldn't see it as such – was that if you stood at the bar for more than a minute another drink would miraculously appear courtesy of a customer. 'Looks like you needed that,' they'd say slapping you on the back. 'Faith! Get him another, put it on my bill.'

'No' was not an option. It wasn't worth the argument. It's an unwritten law that to refuse a beer from a holidaymaker causes great offence – like turning your nose up at sheep's testicles during a Bedouin feast. Well, almost.

Unless you are a paid-up member of Alcoholics Anonymous it's surely reasonable to not want to drink every single night. And although the calories flooded off in the kitchen, accepting beery gifts seven nights a week was a sure way to acquire the familiar expat gut.

'The gut' is just one of the attributes of the expat crowd. In a holiday resort they always have a certain demeanour that makes them stand out from the holidaymaker. It's not just the difference in confidence from knowing 'the street'. More often than not there is also a physical variant. Usually this is manifested in a tasteless surfeit of gold jewellery in an attempt to distract the focus from sun-shovelled wrinkles on leathery skin. The male of this species often looks like he's just swallowed a deflating Space Hopper. Such customary swelling is due to a combination of too much time on his hands and a sub-culture where the sun sets over the yardarm as soon as the Rice Krispies have stopped crackling.

Within this sub-culture exists a micro-culture. The BBC, or Boring Bullshit Crowd. The BBC are not only afflicted with the physical traits mentioned above, from the moment they wake to the moment they start dribbling on the pillow (and beyond, for the worst cases), they have a compulsive obsession to bore the arse off those unfortunate enough to wander into conversational proximity with tales of their business acumen.

'Oh yes, you should come down to my boat for a glass of champers.

She's a twenty-eight footer you know,' blabbed a member of the BBC whom I encountered in the bar one night. He patted his rotund affliction in a gesture of smug satisfaction, sublimely managing to slip this information into a casual comment about the price of Dorada.

The topic then ricocheted from how much money he had, to how he was a self-made man, followed by a detailed analysis of where his wealth had been recklessly distributed.

Fantasy Island is one of the pet names for Tenerife, for the very reason that people arrive here, choose a personality, and spend their time convincing themselves and other unfortunate listeners that they *are* that character.

'Oh aye,' the globe continued, 'I might get meself another, you know, something a bit bigger for the weekends, when all me mates come over. Mind you I'm not here much anymore. I like to go to me villa in Florida every now and then. It's got an infirmity pool, you know.'

His bulk blocked the only escape route and my hands were beginning to tremble with the weight of two pints in each.

'Well, it was nice talking...' but he was off again.

'Do you know how much money I made last year? You couldn't possibly guess.' I had no real desire to, but in the hope that I might just flatten his ego I estimated that it was thousands.

'Millions, son. Now, if you want a tip from me, start early. Invest all your money in a few houses, sell them and then buy bigger ones, then bigger ones, then bigger ones still.' He had spread his arms as wide as his chubby body would allow in a demonstration of enlarging wealth in case I hadn't grasped his amazing formula for success.

As he bent towards the bar top to take a slurp from the fruit and vegetable-laden cocktail, I spotted daylight and made my exit. It was an untimely move; a piece of pineapple perched dangerously on the rim of the glass stabbed him on the nose and his whole body jolted back. Four pints of chilled Dorada slopped onto my new trainers and down the back of an old fellow who was slowly gnawing his way through half a chicken. He stiffened sharply as cold beer raced down the back of his Y-fronts.

'Watch what you're doing with those drinks, son,' said BBC. 'These are

Gucci shoes. Had 'em made 'specially, when I was in Italy. Now there's a place with style...'

One thing you notice is that despite the abundant wealth, the BBC always drink alone. Money may be able to buy you Gucci, but it can't buy you buddies and without friends, with whom are these people going to share their success? Well, with me it would seem, though previous experience has taught me that this is no time for British politeness and feigning interest. You move away from the BBC like he's a nuclear reactor on fire.

This wasn't our first encounter with a resort fantasy character. Two years earlier Joy and I had wangled an idle six weeks at a family friend's apartment in Majorca whiling away a summer in between jobs.

Actually, 'in between' is a bit of a misnomer as there were no jobs to be in between. Joy had just finished drama college and was inactively pursuing her first big break. I had just returned from a stint of drumming in the USA with a band teetering on the verge of mediocrity but dismantled in an untimely manner by the United States Department of Immigration. They had decided that our guitarist, a Sid Vicious look-alike, did not fit their profile of 'desired persons'. My last communication with him was a phone call informing us that he might be a tad late for our showcase gig in Boston, as he had been deported and was currently thumbing his way from Heathrow airport in a desperate attempt to get his Gibson Emperor guitar, himself and a K-Mart carrier bag of possessions back to Manchester.

Needless to say, our spectrum of sound, somewhat limited as a 3-piece, was hindered irreparably as a duo and like most wannabee pop groups, dreams of stateside stardom were unceremoniously dunked in the Atlantic. British fame and fortune had proved equally elusive, unless you count having a photocopied flyer of your band on every fifth lamppost in Marple Bridge as a publicity coup.

And so it was, with an air of resignation and a nagging demand from parents to settle down, that Joy and I fled with all the money we could muster. The idea was to see how long we could survive on £200, blagging the odd day's work whenever the cupboards looked bleak.

In times of trouble, faced with the prospect of having to go and find work, it's amazing just how far you can stretch a measly subsidy. Mealtimes forced a creative compromise between economy and edibility. One-pan cooking was the trend, and the limit of our culinary repertoire, the ingredients being relatively inconsequential. Tuna, sausages, cheese, potatoes, eggs, rice, tomatoes, peppers, vinegar and oil were united in what we called 'stir-fry surprise' and what usually proved to be only palatable if preceded by copious quantities of carton wine. The ingredients were donations from kind holidaymakers whom we befriended by the resort pool. 'Meet us on the hotel steps on Friday and we'll give you whatever food we've got left over,' they would say. Fridays were like Christmas, racing home to see what presents had been left in Santa's supermarket bags.

In the evenings Travel Scrabble saw a lot of action and when word blindness set in we would master an ability of seeing how many coins we could simultaneously spin on the apartment's marble floor. Occasionally we would baby-sit for holidaymakers, introducing their toddlers to the wonders of Monopoly or impressing them with our coin-spinning prowess.

During our stint, Joy did manage the odd shift in the local supermarket and I was promised a job with one of the island's pioneers in bullshit.

We were savouring the sterility of the hotel bar in celebration of a new world record in gyrating 25-peseta coins - 11, if you're interested. All the furnishings were from the 'sit on the fence' school of design, created neither to offend nor favour any particular taste. The chairs were busily patterned with green and white leaf motifs, the tables faux bamboo. As much thought had been given to mood lighting as to the gallery of pictures hung on the wall. Spanish tourism posters showing impossible-to-find coves were clipped behind smudged Perspex.

We made two pints of beer last as long as possible so that our petri dish of complimentary peanuts was kept replenished. A conversation in the adjacent quartet of armchairs had caught our attention. An orange-tanned man in his mid-forties was trying to play it cool with a young, suited Spaniard. No easy feat when you're wearing Elton John sunglasses

'You tell me,' said Elton. He raked his fingers through his thinning hair. 'I've shot films with three cameras, four cameras, a dozen cameras. It all depends on the budget, baby.' The Spaniard was clearly unsure what to make of this extraordinary Englishman.

'Well... I thought... err... we'd need at least three crews. We need to put on a big show for the ministers.'

'Three?' Elton extended an upturned palm at the man and turned his head towards a lady slumped in the next chair. She was either his secretary or his long-suffering wife. Perhaps both. He threw her a 'see what I'm dealing with' look, which was reciprocated with 'I really don't care'.

'Sure, I can put out three crews but between you and me you'll still get a better effect with just the one. Besides, all the other cameramen are tied up with my other movies.' Elton leaned into the man revealing a lopsided stump of a ponytail that protruded beneath a bald patch like a capital Q. 'There's a lot of exciting stuff in the pipeline,' he whispered.

'OK, I'll have to get back to you when I've spoken to my boss,' said the Spaniard hurriedly. He stood up and shook hands.

'These people,' sighed Elton. He shook his head as the man made a sharp exit.

'Can we go now, Norman?' whined the lady, 'I'm starvin'.'

Elton snapped his fingers in an attempt to attract the waiter. 'Fuck. Where am I going to get a crew from?'

Joy and I stopped crunching.

'I hope you don't mind us eavesdropping,' said Joy, 'but I heard you were looking for a crew?'

The man switched back into Hollywood mode. 'Yes, all my regulars are finishing off my latest film. I'm Billy Rhodes, Billy Rhodes Productions. This is my wife Margaret.'

'Hi. Pleased to meet you.' Margaret slowly lifted a hand without disturbing her slump.

'We're looking for work over here. Joe's worked in video production before if you need any extra crew,' said Joy.

It was true. Whilst in America I had managed to get part-time work with a video production company in Boston. I'd been given the opportunity to help in various departments including camera, lighting and sound but due to circumstances, namely my lack of ability in all three, my role generally fell under the title of gofer, fetching and carrying for whoever demanded on set.

The catalyst that finally convinced me the glamour of tinsel town wasn't coming my way came during a blizzard whilst shooting a car commercial. I was assigned the responsibility of persuading a dog to pee on cue at a pre-lit spot.

I soon realised that a friendly word in its ear was not going to work and was reduced to trailing after another dog that happily wandered the street where we were filming. With bucket and spade at the ready I kept my eyes firmly fixed on the mutt's butt waiting for signs of bladder action. Every three or four paces it would cease sniffing at the ground, stand still and look nervously over its shoulder at this strange, two-legged stalker. The idea was to scoop a bucketful of pee-coated snow and deposit it next to the parked Buick that we were filming. When the cameras rolled, I'd then release our actor-dog who, if he ever wanted to work in TV again, would toddle straight over to the alien scent and cock a leg up to regain his territory.

I had become so engrossed in tailing the rogue up a nearby driveway in pursuit of its urine that I didn't notice the door of the house open or the family of four who peered anxiously from behind it.

'Aha,' I muttered to myself as the dog delivered the liquid prop, 'Good boy. Now if I can just have that...'

'Can I ask what in Christ's name you're doing?' said the head of the household, arms firmly folded.

'Ah... I'm... err... collecting dog pee to film... for...' I backed off waving my plastic spade apologetically as the winter storm carried the words 'crazy fucking limey' into my hood.

'I might just be able to help you out then,' said Norman, Billy or whatever his name was. 'I run a production company here in Spain. My last film was a big hit, shot entirely on location in Majorca. I was just negotiating a deal for another one but to be honest I've got that much work I'm only going for the big bucks. What have you worked on? Anything I'd know?'

'Well, probably not. I'm just a production assistant really but...'

'Great, I need a cameraman for a film I'm making next week.'

'I have to admit I've not really had much experience as a cameraman...'

'That's OK, I'll book you in anyway. Probably three days' shooting. How are you at editing?'

'I've done a few rough cuts but...'

'Fantastic. I'll put you down for a week in the studio as well. How about you, babe? What do you do?'

'Uh, I'm an actress,' tried Joy.

'Hmm, talent eh? Done any presenting?'

'No, not really.'

'Never mind, you'll be fine. It's all simple straight to camera stuff. How about you both come round to the house tomorrow and we'll sort out the details?' He wrote his address on the back of a flimsy business card and strode off, leaving his wife to pay the bill.

The following day we decided that to save costs we'd walk to the village where the film mogul had told us he lived. Even in a straight line it took us the best part of three hours to reach the old part of this hillside town. It was mid-afternoon and the place was deserted. Doors were closed and shutters were down. The only sign of life was a lone buzzard that circled overhead like an aerial undertaker in search of clients. Dehydrated and glowing red from the sun, I tapped on the door of Norman's house. There was no answer. I rapped harder. Still nothing. Joy and I looked at each other in despair, still panting.

'Try one more time,' urged Joy.

A voice answered from within. 'Just a minute.' It was Margaret.

We heard a shuffle of commotion and Norman hissing at her, *'You* get it'.

'Sorry about that. God, you look hot. Come in, I'll get you a drink.' Margaret led us past a stairway into the cool dark interior. The furnishings were surprising. As with many Spanish houses, the exterior promises little. Unlike the British, the Spanish aren't obsessed with what the neighbours think. They don't care if the place looks like the remains of a Baghdad barracks from the outside, all the love and attention is lavished within. Comfort is the key, not vanity.

Norman and Margaret's house was not exactly Malibu beachfront but the black leather furniture and dark wood furnishings were obviously not inferior products. The kitchen was open-plan revealing a large American-style fridge and a plethora of modern appliances.

'Beer, Coke, water, wine?' asked Margaret. We both gratefully accepted ice-cold beers. 'Billy's on the roof, he's on the phone.' She rolled her eyes then motioned towards the staircase. 'He said to go up.'

With beers in hand we emerged onto a large rooftop terrace. Norman was reclining on a sunlounger in the centre of a barren rooftop. A can of beer rested on his purple Hawaiian shorts, a thick gold chain looped across his chest. 'Hi guys,' he shouted. He covered the mouthpiece of his mobile phone, 'Just on the phone to the States, I'll be right with you.'

On one side of the roof, T-shirts, tea towels and oversized underwear hung motionless on a washing line strung across his neighbour's roof. They obliterated the best view, which was back down towards the ocean. On the opposite side, the village climbed further up the hill to the point where a dark green mountain soared skywards, culminating in a jagged double point.

Behind where we had emerged, only a low wall divided our concrete plateau from a plunging ravine. A long, deep swathe had been scythed out of the dark rock, the far side striped with various hues of ochre. Huge boulders littered the ravine like giant marbles. Such dramatic scenery can't help but slam your own miniscule presence firmly into place. Or at least that was the case with most people. Those with grossly inflated egos like Norman needed a little more prodding to pop their self-importance.

'Yeah, no problem. You just get them to sign and I'll take care of the details. I've worked with his type before... yep, sure, George Clooney was also a pain in the ass but we worked it out... yep, yep... exactly the same with Meg Ryan, yep. She came round to my way of thinking eventually. Now Meg and me, we're best of pals.' Norman had acquired a mid-Atlantic accent and was eyeing our reaction to his name-dropping. He saw he had our attention and upped the ante. 'Well you can tell Mr De Niro he's not worth it.' Holding the phone at arm's length he gesticulated 'wanker'. 'OK, OK, I've told you what I want. Now it's up to you to get that spoilt bunch of Hollywood starlets back on line and tell them Billy Rhodes only asks the once.' He covered the mouthpiece: 'They're all the same these Hollywood stars, stuck so far up their own...' Suddenly the phone he was talking into started to ring. He pulled it to his chest trying to mute the sound then turned away to hide his embarrassment. He put it to his ear again. 'What? I'm in a meeting with Joey and Joyce,' he hissed. 'Yes, yes, I'll do it later... no, *later*! I haven't been yet. Yes I know they close at one... yes, I know... rubber gloves and a new toilet seat. Right. Yes. Thank you. Bye. Bye.' He turned back to us. 'Damn mobiles... they never work properly up here. Now where were we?'

We went downstairs for another beer and to watch Norman's latest film. It was a 10-minute video selling the sights and sounds of Majorca. The voiceover had a strangely familiar mid-Atlantic accent: 'Soft, silky sand and soothing surf abound on many superb beaches.' Margaret suddenly appeared strolling along a beach and tugging at an uncooperative dog. 'Peace, tranquillity, the space to do whatever you want,' the sickly voice continued. Not for the dog though, I thought. Then the theme changed. The sound track hit overdrive as the camera zoomed in on an ample backside that wiggled from side to side, framed for what seemed an unnecessary long time. 'Club land,' boomed Norman's voice, 'where you can dance the night away or just sit back and experience the sights and sounds of party time in the Balearics.'

It was nothing more than an elaborate home video that had been commissioned by a local timeshare company for use in their sales presentation.

Joy and I spent the next four hours experiencing the sights and sounds – mainly sounds – of Norman's rise to fame as the island's top 'cinematographer'. We listened politely in case just one fraction of the truth could lead to paid employment but it quickly became evident that this would require a great deal of special effects, so we made our excuses and left. We had more worthwhile endeavours to attend to, including a world record to beat. Little did we know that two years later we would be trapped in a similar world of make believe artists.

Holiday resorts are infested with all manner of bullshitters, con artists and parasites, keen to sink their teeth into your wallet. However, once they've been on the streets for a few weeks they evolve a fairly accurate radar for distinguishing the expat from the visitor.

For the expat, there comes a stage whereby you suddenly realise you're no longer being approached by the likes of timeshare reps. A line has been crossed and you have subconsciously acquired the persona of 'a resident'. Maybe it's because you've learnt that to make eye contact is an invitation for him or her to sell you something.

'English and friendly? Here mate, take one of these.' The pimple-chinned teenager would push a scratch card into my hands.

Dutifully I would fill my nails with silver coating to reveal that I'd incredibly won the star prize – a two-week holiday.

'You've won! I don't believe it!' He would start jumping up and down as if he were a contestant on *The Price is Right* .

'That's the first time I've seen anybody win the top prize. Well done, mate.' After several slaps between the shoulder blades he'd continue the charade.

'All you've got to do is go up to El Scabby Goat Resort in Torviscas, have a look round, tell them what you think, and the holiday's yours. I'll even pay for your taxi. Shall we go?'

After attempting to herd Joy and me towards a conveniently waiting taxi, I would bring the game to a halt.

'It's timeshare, isn't it?'

'Nooooo, mate. Absolutely not. Nothing to do with timeshare at all. It's a co-ownership holiday scheme that means you actually own your very own piece of paradise.'

'So how's it different to timeshare then?'

'Well, it... it's... it just is. You actually own the property.'

'What, all of it?'

'Well, no. Not all of it. You own a share of it and you can use it when you want.'

'So I could use it all year if I wanted?'

'Uh... no, you just use the weeks that you buy.'

'So you buy a share in an apartment and have a set time in it. Kind of like sharing it over a period of time.'

'Well, yeah, but...'

'So it's timeshare, no matter what you want to call it.'

The timeshare PRs were the worst of a bad bunch of street mitherers. Young, cocky kids trying to entice you to take a timeshare tour by all means, fair or foul. However, like me they had probably escaped the drudgery of Britain's treadmill or dole queues and figured that standing in the sunshine all day being annoying was preferable to standing in the rain all day getting annoyed. And who could blame them?

CHAPTER 12

On her first day back, Faith was completely different. The break had proven effective. She was smiling, joking and altogether calmer. Even Frank's antagonising couldn't draw a snide response. The real test would come in the evening though, when the pressure of a full bar would stretch the nerves.

Much to our surprise, despite the additional trial of two temporary power cuts, Faith managed to sustain her congeniality and refused to be fazed. It was as if she was on tranquillisers, laughing off any impatient complaints and over-demanding customers.

The relief all round was palpable. David had been on tenterhooks, expecting another blowout and his mood was lifted by the 'new' Faith.

The effect of Faith's break wasn't all positive however; in Joy's mind it had caused resentment as she too was feeling pangs of homesickness and longed to see her family back in Bolton. She had kept quiet though, knowing that it was totally unfair to take time off before the end of the busy season. Faith's excursion had sown the seeds of a deep-rooted resentment and even though Faith may have chilled out, Joy's patience with her had now expired.

Michelle and Gary resumed their two afternoon and two graveyard shifts but Joy was finding fault with everything. Unable to express her anger at Faith in case she reverted back to the ways of old, she vented her frustration at anybody who made the slightest error. The early September nights had become as hot as the days and sleep was hard to catch, adding to her short temper.

School term was about to start in the UK, which meant our first summer was nearing an end. It had been a hard slog for all of us and it was starting to show on Joy. Nearly four months of smiling and being nice to people you'd rather slap was beginning to take its toll. It was like being on stage all day every day. She had always wanted to be an actress but even the busiest stars weren't expected to keep in character day in, day out for such a lengthy period of time.

'There's something wrong with the figures again,' she snapped one morning. Michelle and Gary had been working the previous night and Joy had totalled up all the bills that were outstanding. We had left the bar at 10.30 p.m. with four tables still eating and a further two still to settle up. Added to that there was a good crowd of drinkers in full flow. 'The till's down,' she announced.

'Are you sure? Have you double checked it?' I said innocently.

'Do you think I can't count?' she shouted. 'It's down! I've been through it twice and it's definitely down. Even if everybody paid the bills I left and the bar emptied straight away, there should be more money in the till.'

'There's probably a reason,' I said. 'Ask Gary and Michelle when they come in.'

Michelle and Gary were taking the afternoon shift today and when they arrived at 2 p.m., Joy confronted them. 'Can I have a word, Michelle?' said Joy. She took her into the kitchen whilst Gary went to outside to bring a spare beer barrel in. I stood in the doorway keeping an eye out for customers. 'I couldn't figure out the money this morning,' said Joy. 'I left six bills unpaid and there were about five tables of drinkers but the money doesn't add up. I reckon it's about 30,000 pesetas down. Can you shed any light?'

Michelle smiled, 'Oh, dozy cow. You know what I'm like,' then realised the implications of Joy's questioning. Her smile dropped and her face flushed pink. 'Joy? Why are you asking me this? It's me, Michelle. I hope you're not saying what I think you're saying.'

'I'm not saying anything, Michelle. I'm just telling you that the till reading doesn't stack up with the amount of people that were in last night and the number of bills that were still behind the bar.'

Michelle's eyes had begun to fill up. She shouted for Gary who sauntered into the kitchen.

'What's up?'

'I'm trying to find out what went wrong with the money last night. It's about 30,000 down.'

Whilst Michelle seemed genuinely upset at the insinuation, Gary remained unperturbed. 'I don't know,' he said calmly. 'Everybody paid, though it did go quiet just after you'd gone. I can't see how it's down though. Must be something wrong with the till, I guess.' He shook his head. 'Oh, here we go.' A customer had come to the bar and Gary went to serve him. Michelle had true shock on her face. She continued pleading her innocence and voicing disbelief that she was being accused.

'Joy, we're friends,' she continued. 'I can't believe you're saying this.' But Joy was resolute. She was tired, angry and beyond compassion and Michelle and Gary, whom we classed as our only friends, were bearing the brunt.

We left them to run the shift and returned at 6.30 p.m. to take over with David and Faith. They had arrived before us and Michelle had already told them about the run-in. Michelle was trying to catch Joy's eye but Joy was ignoring her and went straight into the kitchen. Michelle followed.

'Do you still think we stole some money?' she asked. Her mood had now changed from one of shock to one of anger.

'I never said that, Michelle,' answered Joy. 'I just want you to know that money went missing while you were working here last night. Look at it from my point of view. You'd be suspicious, wouldn't you?'

Michelle had obviously been preparing her speech. 'Well, I'm sorry you think that. I can assure you that I have never taken anything from here. I feel guilty even pouring myself a beer. But if you think I'm a thief then there's no point in carrying on working here. Or in being friends.' She walked out, apologising to David and Faith on the way.

'They've just quit,' said Faith as Joy came out of the kitchen.

'I know,' said Joy. 'They've been taking money.'

'How do you know?' asked Faith.

'The till's been out a few times after they've been on,' said Joy.

'You can't prove anything though, can you,' said Faith. 'You don't know for sure. It could have been a mistake.'

'It wasn't a mistake. It happened too often. They've been taking money... or at least one of them has. I don't think Michelle had a clue. But I could tell Gary was lying. I think he's not been tilling in some of the bills and then pocketing the money.'

'Well that's great,' sighed Faith. 'You've just lost us the only relief staff we had...'

'Hang on a minute. I haven't lost them. They walked out...'

'But you accused them of stealing,' interrupted Faith. 'You should have consulted me and David first before wading in. It's not up to you who we fire. You can fill in all the shifts they've left. I'm...' But her protests were left mid-flow. Joy had stormed out.

Faith and Joy were no longer speaking. Joy's policy of light-footing around Faith had been superseded by a general disregard. On evening shifts, the only communication was to ask for drinks or to take bills. The antipathy was noticeable and although they continued to put on a fake smile and chirpiness for the customers, those who knew them better could tell there was friction.

In a show of spite and to reassert her own authority on the business, Faith had banned children from coming behind the bar, Danny included, and Frank was not pleased. 'Given our Danny the sack, have you?' he asked Faith.

'Danny's just 13 years old, Frank. If the work inspectors came in they'd close us down.'

'Didn't bother you last week though, did it? What's he going to do now? I'll tell you what he's gonna do, he's gonna mither me all bleedin' day, that's what.' Danny was sitting between his dad and Sam, looking forlorn.

'We're not a crèche,' said Faith. 'He shouldn't have been working here in the first place. He should be at school.'

'Oh, telling me how to look after my kids now, are we?' He gulped down the last dregs of the half he was drinking and got off the bar stool, nodding at Danny and Sam to follow. 'If I want parental guidance I'll soddin' well ask for it. OK? C'mon you two.' Frank slouched off into the sunlight, tailed by Danny. Sam shrugged her shoulders at Faith and smiled but she was busying herself in the bar fridge trying to hide her damp eyes.

We had now lost Michelle, Gary and Danny all in the same week. We still had at least 10 days of the busy period left and desperately needed help. None of us could face going back to running all the shifts and besides, it was so busy that even with the four partners overlapping between 6.30 p.m. and 10.30 p.m., we still needed more help.

We now had entertainment on Saturday, Sunday, Monday, Wednesday and Thursday night. Friday and Tuesday, the changeover days, remained act-free, as depending on what time the departing flights left and what time the new arrivals landed, the night could be completely dead or packed with a crossover of white faces and those waiting to go home.

Karaoke had proved such a hit both in drawing the customers and making the till ring that we had begrudgingly booked Maxi Belle for Saturday and Wednesday evening. Sunday was reserved for a Neil Diamond soundalike who also happened to be from Bolton and had offered us a cheap rate because of the connection. From behind a walrus-like moustache, Tony Delrosso would belt out such hits as 'I Am… I Said', 'Song Sung Blue' and the sing-along 'Sweet Caroline' to an assorted collection of British, French and German holidaymakers impressed by his effort, if not his melodic precision.

Monday night was David's quiz night when those who wanted to check if their cerebral matter was still working could test their general knowledge in teams of four. David was quite happy to spend a couple of his rare spare hours compiling 25 questions with a difficulty level varying from 'What's the nearest mainland country to Tenerife?' (most people would answer Spain, 10 times further away than Morocco) to 'Name the 10 commandments'. Considering the prize was a bottle of the cheapest sparkling wine we could find, the competition was taken extremely seriously, with more than one competitor walking out, adamant that they were right and the quizmaster was wrong.

It was Motown Madness on Thursday night. Maxi Belle had recommended a soul act who apparently used to be in The Drifters. It was not an uncommon boast, half of the black singers who threw the obligatory 'Under the Boardwalk' into their set also made the same claim. If you believed all the claimants, The Drifters would have had more members than the London Symphony Orchestra and that was just in Tenerife.

Having seen his act, whether he was ex-anything or not, we couldn't deny that he was good. Gene Alexander had an ultra-smooth voice, dazzling footwork and was one of the most professional acts that we had seen on the island. However, he didn't come cheap, especially when he found out that he'd have to travel out of town to accommodate the Smugglers into his schedule.

Gene didn't disappoint. He was a huge hit with the holidaymakers and many residents from far afield who would make their only appearance at our bar on the Thursdays when Gene was performing. Joy's theatrical aspirations were briefly fulfilled as she joined Gene in a dance routine that they had worked on for 'Up on the Roof'.

It was only after a few weeks of Gene's gigs that we found out he was capable of getting much higher than just on the roof. One Thursday he had arrived over half an hour late and the audience were growing impatient. The two Johns were having a particularly annoying day. 'I think your ex-Drifter's an *ex*-Smugglers now,' said John One.

'Aye, *d ifted* off, I reckon,' added his sidekick.

'You want to sack him if he comes in now,' said John One trying to stir things.

'You can't put up with it,' agreed John Two. 'Tell you what, we'll sing a few songs for you. How about that? What do you reckon, John? Reckon we could put on a better show than monkey man?'

'Easy, John. I'll go and get me accordion, you tell the crowd he's been sacked, Joy.'

'I'd rather chew my own arm off than listen to you two,' said Joy. 'Bugger off if you don't like him. It's no loss to us.'

When Gene did arrive, he ambled down the steps with his black jacket over his shoulder and a bow tie dangling down his white shirt.

'Where've you been, Gene?' I asked, taking the cassette from him. He always gave it to me without rewinding it from the last show. I discovered this on his first night when his show opened with two minutes of static hiss before I realised what was going on.

'Hey Joe, how's it going? No problem, man. I'm ready.' He jigged from side to side to demonstrate the fact but there was definitely a problem. His eyes were completely glazed, his eyelids heavy and most noticeably, one of his nostrils was powdered white.

'You okay, Gene? You look a bit fried,' I asked.

'I'm ready, man, I'm raring to go. Get me on.' Joy took the microphone and introduced Mr Gene Alexander to the audience outside. The music started but Gene missed his cue and came in late. Not only that, he seemed to be struggling to remember the words and ended up singing the same line over and over again, 'It's just too good to be true, too good to be true...'

I looked at Joy. 'What's he doing?'

'Too good to be true...'

Joy shook her head, her smile was still fixed but her eyes were looking aghast.

'...trood to be goo, doobie doobie-doobie doo...'

'He's off his head,' I said. Even when the song burst into the chorus Gene couldn't veer off that one line, though it didn't seem to bother him in the slightest. He continued moving his tiny, shiny shoes in time with the music and swaying his body to the rhythm regardless.

'...to be true... oh yeah... true... oh yeah... too... good... too... goo... ooh...' Obviously Gene had an entirely different tune coursing through his head and when the song finally came to an end the crowd applauded graciously, if not a little baffled. All of his El Beril and Altamira fan club were there – grumpy old Phil and his wife Yvonne, who clapped along oblivious to the deranged state of the performer; Betty and Eric, the Blackpool landlord and landlady who were so intoxicated themselves they wouldn't have known the difference; Friedhelm, who sat sobbing at his barrel near the door, dabbing at his sagging eyes with a handkerchief; and the whole of supermarket Patricia's family, who were taking great delight in this variation on Gene's act.

I threw Gene a confused look before the next song started but like Gene himself it was wasted. 'Mr Bojangles' burst from the speakers and this time Gene didn't even bother with any vocal accompaniment. He attempted to throw his feet around in time with the music but they were having none of it and he resorted to static swaying whilst waving his hands above his head like a drama class tree impression. It was becoming clear why, if Gene Alexander was ever a member of the famous Motown five-piece, he was now an ex-member.

I let him continue with his own private party for another three songs whilst he improvised and blurted out nonsensical lyrics at random points before telling Joy to get him off. Even Phil and Yvonne were having trouble keeping in time with their clapping as Gene's drug-induced spouting was competing with a different rhythm.

'Ladies and gentlemen. Sorry to cut it short but we've had a complaint from the Altamira so unfortunately we'll have to end it there. Give Gene Alexander one more round of applause.'

'That set just zoomed by, man,' said Gene as he glided to the bar.

'That was crap,' I said. 'You're completely wrecked. If you turn up at our bar off your face again, you won't be singing here – ever!' Gene looked genuinely hurt, as though he was expecting his usual praise and backslapping. Thankfully it was the last time he turned up wrecked. Gene knew he was on good money, plus I assumed it wasn't the first time he'd nearly lost work through his illegal recreation.

CHAPTER 13

'Excuse me, you don't know anything about TVs do you?' A chestnut-tanned woman was leaning on the low wall dividing our two gardens. Long brown hair framed a model's face, high cheekbones etched below sparkling emerald eyes. She was dressed in a microscopic yellow bikini, the perfect showcase for a taught stomach and brimming cleavage.

Joy and I were dozing on recliner chairs in the shade of the overhanging balcony. We had woken in the middle of the night to a commotion from next door. The apartment had remained unoccupied since we arrived but the banging and clomping of high heels on marble signalled we had a new neighbour.

'A little. Depends what you need to know,' I said, rising to shake our neighbour's hand. 'I'm Joe... and this is Joy.'

'Hi, I'm Charley. I got here last night. I hope I didn't disturb you.'

'No, no, we never heard you come in,' I lied. 'You here by yourself?'

'At the moment. My sister's coming out next week.' Charley beckoned us both into the house. 'Would you like a drink? Beer? Wine? Juice?' She held the fridge door open, waiting for an answer. Every shelf was full, mainly with booze. The foil of champagne bottles protruded past cans of imported beer. I could also see an unopened punnet of strawberries and another of cherries. Either Charley had brought a Samsonite full of Sainsburys with her or someone had provided quite a welcome pack.

'Now *that's* a fridge,' I said, and nodded as she pointed to a can of Red Stripe. 'You didn't bring all that with you, did you?' It was not as dumb a question as it may have seemed. Many holidaymakers used more of their luggage allowance on catering packs of bacon, frozen sausages, boxes of PG Tips and tins of baked beans than on summer clothes and sun tan lotion. It's amazing how many British people spend months looking forward to escaping from their everyday surroundings only to spend a great deal of time and money recreating that same environment once they reach their destination.

'No,' laughed Charley, 'I'm not that sad. My boyfriend had somebody stock up the fridge and cupboards for me. Fancy some champagne?' I glanced at my watch. It was only 11 in the morning. 'Why not? Joy?' I finished what was left in my can whilst Charley poured three glasses.

'How long are you here for?' asked Joy.

'I'm not sure yet. Two, maybe three weeks. I'll see how it goes,' Charley answered vaguely.

'Does your boyfriend live here, then?' continued Joy.

'On and off.'

Now it can't be denied that in general women are more adept at picking up on small details than men. The fact that she was being cagey about her boyfriend had made a pleasant whooshing sound as it flew above my head. Joy had locked in on this strange vagueness. Whilst I was happy with the simple sum of one free beer plus one free glass of champagne equals nice person, Joy was already trying to piece together a more intricate equation. She wanted to know the who, why and wherefores of Charley, not content until she had built up an assailable profile of her new neighbour.

At the risk of sounding like David Attenborough, I presume it's to do with selectivity. Women need to have a secure foothold before they'll throw out a line of friendship. Men are more happy to immediately play tug-of-war with the same line, throwing in nuggets of self-achievement and material possession in a head-to-head for higher status. Most women are subtle at extracting this information. Joy isn't one of them.

'What does he do?'

'He's a successful businessman.'

'What's he into?'

'Sales mainly.'

'Selling property?'

'Partly.'

'What else?'

'Other things.'

'Like?'

'Bars.'

'What's his name?'

'John... well, I don't like to be rude but I've got to go out. I'm going to have to get ready. It's been nice meeting you. Come round for a drink again.' Charley was ushering us out, taking the half-finished glasses out of our hands.

'What about your TV? Do you want me to take a look at it?' I asked as I was shepherded onto the patio.

'Oh it's not important. It can wait. Bye, now. See you later.' Charley shut the patio doors before we had time to climb over the wall into our own garden.

'Seems like a nice lady,' I said, the early morning alcohol switching on my 'everything's alright with the world' frame of mind.

'She's hiding something,' said Joy.

The bar was surprisingly quiet when we arrived to take over from David and Faith at 2 p.m. Frank and Al sat at one end of the bar. Frank looked concerned. Al was visibly shaking. His eyes and skin were a sickly yellow and he was sweating profusely.

'You don't look so clever,' I said.

'Aye, I found the daft fucker sparked out on his bedroom floor. He's been on the pop for four days and nights,' said Frank.

'Well there's shite all else to do round here, is there?' croaked Al.

'I told you. Go home, then,' shouted Frank. 'If you want to fucking kill yourself, don't fucking do it in my house. Get yourself on a plane and go and top yourself in Liverpool.' David and Faith were standing by the till. David was sucking deeply on a Marlboro Lite, something he always did in situations where he didn't know how to react. Faith was standing slightly behind him, gripping a bottle of water ready to refill Al's glass.

'Go on, get that down you,' barked Frank, holding the glass of water in front of Al's face.

Whilst Al sipped on the water, creasing his face as if it was medicine, David filled me in on the morning's activities. They'd had a busy breakfast time and then it had gone dead. The brilliant sunshine and temperatures in the 90s had presumably sent everybody scuttling for the beach. Well, at least the British. Other nationalities had probably headed for the wisdom of shade or an early siesta. It was Wednesday, the day after changeover Tuesday so we were bound to see the usual assortment of flaming red hues in the bar tonight.

The Brits tend to parade sunburn like trophies. The more defined the lines between pre- and post-sun the better. Behind the bar we were often treated to the sight of pallid groins neatly crowned by fire-red bellies as pants were tugged down and tan lines were compared. Blisters on the males were even better, like battle scars. 'Nope, can't feel a thing,' they'd say, oblivious to the fact this was only because they'd just ingested four pints of the local anaesthetic.

However, the real test was in the morning, when they woke up and wondered why someone had swapped their soft cotton bedclothes for sheets of sandpaper and why acid was coming out of the shower rather than water. No amount of fabric softener would reduce the abrasiveness of barbed wire T-shirts nicking away at raw shoulders and the flimsiest of flip-flops would feel like bear traps clamping down on swollen red feet. But after they'd contemplated their pain, where would they head? Straight to the beach again of course, to make doubly sure that on their return to the UK nobody could be in any doubt that they had been abroad. Sunburn is the wearable banal postcard – 'Weather hot, don't you wish *you'd* been there?'

Outside the bar, the two Johns were teaching pool to a couple of teenage girls trying to get them to lean further over the table as they practised cueing up. 'Smooth action. That's it. Let it slip through your hands slowly, then bring it back,' said John Two. 'Slowly. Smooth. Imagine you're making love to your boyfriend.'

'Aye, like you're giving him a hand job,' added John One. The girls giggled. 'Got a right pair 'ere, John. Think they know what a hand job is?'

'Doesn't look like it John. They're a right pair.'

A French couple were silently sharing a bowl of tuna salad whilst reading their respective paperbacks. Behind the gas cupboard protruding from the bar sat Micky and Ron. They seemed to be having a heated debate over some matter, or rather Ron was getting heated and Micky was trying to cool him down. I went to fetch the tea towels that were hanging from a clothes maiden several yards behind them, lingering long enough to get snatches of Micky's hissed placating, '...because I say so. It's my outfit now and what I say goes. Alright?'

Ron was still arguing. 'But if we don't, somebody else will. You know JP's lot will be here sooner or later.'

'Let them 'ave it. It's no skin off our nose,' whispered Micky.

'You're going soft, son,' countered Ron.

'Listen, it was you who told me you don't shit on your own doorstep. Remember? Isn't that right, Joe?' Micky knew I was listening in. 'Never shit on your own doorstep, right?' he shouted.

'Right,' I agreed, though I wasn't entirely sure what I agreed with. I carried the pile of faded tea towels past their table.

'You're a lucky bastard,' sneered Ron through gritted teeth.

Micky immediately intervened, 'Leave it, Dad,' he said sternly. Since finding out about their radiator treatment of Richard Forgreen I had naturally grown more nervous of the father-son partnership, especially when they were around the bar. However, enough time had passed since their first insinuated threats to make me believe that we were not about to become one of their 'clients'.

Micky left, leaving his father drinking rum and Coke. It was clear that he wasn't in the best of moods. One of the girls playing pool over-hit the white ball. It jumped off the table and rolled past Ron's foot coming to rest under the chair now vacated by Micky. ''Ere mate, can I have me ball back,' laughed John Two. The girls giggled again but Ron didn't flinch. John Two tried again, still laughing. 'Hey, me ball's dropped.' The girls nudged each other smirking but still Ron continued sitting with his back to them, rum and Coke held to his lips.

'I think he's deaf,' said John One loudly, more for the girls' sake than Ron's. He put two fingers to his mouth and let out a shrill whistle. 'Hey, ball boy! Hablez-vous Inglés?' he shouted. Ron remained still.

'It's a bit rude that, isn't it John?'

'That's definitely considered rude where I come from,' said the other. The girls had stopped laughing, having perceived more than the two Johns. Namely that Ron could definitely hear them and that his mouth had now curled into a menacing sneer.

'I'll get it,' said the taller of the two.

'No you won't,' said John Two. 'Mister ignorant over there is going to pass us the ball, aren't you, Mister ignorant?'

Unbeknownst to the Johns, Ron's dark eyes had widened at the goading. His scarred jawbone had tensed, the grip on his glass tightened. He slowly turned around, smiling. The two Johns lost their smirks. The girls smiled back awkwardly. Ron leant back in his chair to reach the ball then rose to his feet clutching the ball in front of him. Keeping his stare fixed firmly on John Two, the smaller of the pair, he strode towards him, stopping with his face inches from John's. I was watching from behind the bar and could sense trouble.

'What did you facking call me?' he asked quietly.

'Nothing, mate. I didn't call you nothing,' said John Two quickly.

Ron's shoulders were rising and falling with every raging breath. 'Ball boy was it?'

'That wasn't me,' replied John, his eyes gesturing towards his accomplice.

'Think I'm deaf, do ya?'

John shook his head silently. 'Not me again, mate.' Once again he signalled with his eyes that it was John One.

'Ignorant? Is that what you called me?' Ron's voice was getting louder. John Two laughed nervously.

I could see that Ron's hand had formed a fist over the white ball and was about to be launched at John. Despite my dislike of the two troublemakers, as one of the landlords I felt obliged to intervene. 'Hey, Ron. Micky's looking for you.'

'Huh?' Ron turned to look at me. As he did, the two Johns made a dash up the stairs, falling over each other as they fled. Ron turned back, his senses impaired by the afternoon alcohol. 'Get your facking northern arses back here,' he shouted, but John One and John Two were pushing each other towards the safety of their apartment. Ron muttered to himself. The two girls were now clinging to each other for comfort, their eyes wide in panic. 'Here you are, girls,' said Ron passing the ball to them and setting off to look for his son. 'You tell those two wankers they're dead,' he barked from halfway up the steps.

The rest of the afternoon passed uneventfully; the usual straggle of dads escaping from the beach for a quick pint under the premise of fetching ice creams; three generations of a French family sitting down to a late lunch that took one third of the afternoon to order, another third to eat and the final third spent trying to split the bill.

Unfortunately, as the time came for David and Faith to clock back on, Ron returned – having failed to find his son. He had obviously continued drinking heavily and sat at the bar barely coherent but still trying to pick a fight with somebody. Any shape, size or nationality had become a target. 'You're a fat cunt, aren't you,' he offered to Des, an ex-bouncer on holiday from Bolton, with whom we had become friends. Frank also knew Des and had warned us that he was 'as tough as fuck' and was not to be messed with. Unfortunately he hadn't shared the same information with Ron. Not that it would have made much difference to Ron's pickled sense of logic.

'And you're an ugly twat,' replied Des calmly, accepting his change from Joy.

Ron stood up and tried to raise himself to his full stature but his neck had lost its grip on his head, which lolled loosely at Des's right shoulder. 'Whadya say, fat boy?' slurred Ron.

Des turned to Ron, smiling. He'd seen it all before. He leant into his face, 'I said you're an ugly twat... but I'm sure your mother still loves you.' He picked up his two drinks, kissed Ron on his forehead and walked outside before he had time to react. Ron touched his forehead and with a puzzled look sat back down.

Suicide Sid was next in the firing line. 'Joooooyyyy! One big beer,' he rasped, plonking himself at his usual barrel. Ron's head shot round, dropped to his chest and bounced back up again. 'Aha! Is that a facking Kraut I hear? Oy, Kraut. Fack off back to your own country.' Suicide was a little taken aback and looked pleasantly surprised that somebody had started a conversation with him even though he had no idea what was being said. 'Please?' he enquired, leaning forward.

'Yeah, you're not so facking 'ard now, are you? You Nazi wanker.'

'Please?'

'Think you're 'ard with your facking goosestep army but get you on your own and you're facking shitting it, aren't you?'

'Faith? Please?' Suicide was asking Faith to translate.

'OK Ron, leave him alone or we're going to have to stop serving you,' said Faith.

'So you're on their side now, are you? That's facking gratitude for you. I fight the fackers off and you join sides with 'em. Well *you* can fack off 'n' all.' The early eaters, namely young families, had started to arrive in the bar. Joy, David and I were now stood around Ron.

'Come on, Ron. Go and sleep it off. There's kids here now,' said Joy.

'Fack 'em.'

'We're not serving you any more today, Ron. You've had enough,' I said.

'Get me another drink.'

'No, no more,' said David.

'I want a facking drink.'

'No more. I'll go and get Micky,' I warned.

'Don't bring Micky into this, you cants. The only reason you're still in business is because that soft fack doesn't believe in shitting on his own doorstep. If it was up to me you'd all be facking payin' your way.' With that, he slid off the barstool onto his feet, faced the open door and after a moment's pause to line up a route, made unsteady progress out the bar, stopping momentarily to raise a finger at Suicide before deciding that he couldn't think of anything else to say. He staggered into the early evening light still holding his finger aloft.

'Shit,' I said. 'So we *were* on the hit list.'

'It's a good job they moved into Forgreen's house,' agreed Joy.

'But who's JP? I heard them talking about JP's lot coming in?'

'No idea,' said David.

Faith had become visibly anxious with the confrontation. Her hands were shaking as she tried to light a cigarette.

'Here, let me, love.' A customer had come to the bar to order drinks and was in the process of lighting one himself. He took out a box of matches from his shirt pocket and pushed open the little door.

'Aaaghh!' shouted Faith. 'Put them away.'

'They're just matches, look.' The man held the box closer to Faith.

'Get away, get away!'

David snatched the box out of the man's hand. 'Here, have a lighter. She's got a thing about matches.' Faith had run into the ladies toilets, locking herself in.

'Her nerves are shattered,' David explained to Joy and me. 'She's not slept for two nights, says it's too hot. Just give her a few minutes to calm down.'

Eventually Faith returned to the bar. It was a slow start to the evening. A worrying sign as it meant that we would have a late rush. The heat was making people eat later, once the sun had gone down. I stayed behind the bar to help Faith whilst David dealt with the few food orders we had.

She had just regained her composure, managing to force a smile here and there when she suddenly leapt back from the till with a muffled shriek. As Faith pressed the 'enter' button on the till, a mouse leapt from one of the coin compartments and landed on the glass shelf just below bar level in front of her. It rattled the glasses as it scuttled the length of the shelf then dropped to the floor and disappeared behind the bar fridge. Faith in the meantime had fled to the toilets again, this time in tears.

I swapped roles with David, cooking the food whilst he attended to Faith. Minutes later he was back in the kitchen. 'She's not coming out 'til we've got rid of the mouse,' he sighed. The bar had now begun to fill up and the last thing we wanted to do was disturb the mouse, sending it scuttling out into the open.

'There's nothing we can do now,' I said.

'I know, I know. I told her that,' said David. I agreed to swap places with Faith again so she could work in the rodent-free kitchen but things turned from bad to worse. Faith joined David just as the orders came flooding in.

'Two chicken in wine, chips and salad. One pork chops, one mixed grill, two cheeseburgers, all chips, no salad. Steak rare, steak medium and two Hawaiian burgers no mayo. All chips and salad. One pork chops with Canarian potatoes, one half-chicken, chips and salad. Two egg and chips. Two tuna salads, one no cucumber, extra tomato and one portion of chips.' Joy was writing the orders on the wipe board stuck to the fridge door as she spoke. 'Oh, and can I have two portions of chips ASAP.'

Faith had her mind elsewhere and was falling behind with the garnishes, chips and washing up. David was starting to snap at her and the tension was rising.

'I can't keep up. I'm tired,' complained Faith as David attempted to fulfil both roles.

'Here, you take over with the cooking, I'll do the prep,' he said handing her the spatula. 'Two chicken and wines on, first pork chops on. You need to make up the mixed grill and bash the steaks.'

'Say it again,' she said shaking her head. David started to repeat it, impatience in his voice, but Joy was back interrupting with new orders.

'Two mixed grills, one Canarians, one chips, salad on both and four steaks, three medium, one medium rare, all chips and salad. Then...'

'Joy!' shouted Faith. 'I can't concentrate. No more orders for a few minutes OK?'

'I can't stop people ordering,' complained Joy. 'There's four tables with menus at the moment. Come on, step it up.'

The sweat was pouring off both David and Faith as I brought them two pints of shandy. 'Courtesy of table seven,' I said. David was dashing from the microwave to the sink, arranging salads on the way. Faith was standing with her back to me, idly flipping one pork chop and one burger. I could see that there were at least 20 more meals to cook but Faith was in a daze.

'You OK, Faith?' I asked. David looked at me, then at Faith.

'Faith! What are you doing? You've got a pile of orders stacking up and you're playing with a chop and a burger.' Faith turned round. Her eyes stared straight at David, then at me. There was no flicker of emotion, stress or otherwise. She had shut down mentally.

Joy appeared in the doorway. 'Table two wants to know how long for... why is there nothing cooking?' Faith was already untying her apron.

The following morning when Joy and I came to open up the bar we found the security bars had already been removed, yet the doors were still locked. My immediate thought was that we'd been burgled.

'There's someone in there,' whispered Joy, cupping her hand over her eyes. In the dark interior I could see toes sticking up from a bench behind table one in the far corner near the kitchen doorway. We tried unlocking the main door but the key wouldn't turn. I could see that there was another key already in the lock on the inside. The Paddington Bear key ring was Faith's.

We banged on the window and Faith padded to the door, her short black hair wildly askew on one side only. 'What's going on?' I asked.

'Sorry, I must have slept through the alarm. What time is it?'

'Five past nine,' answered Joy. 'What are you doing sleeping here? Have you had a row?'

'No... it's just cooler in here with the fans on. I can't sleep in the apartment. I'll see you later.' She grabbed her shoes and strode out of the bar in her bare feet, still clutching the peach tablecloth she had used for a blanket.

'She's been sleeping there for the past week,' said David, drawing deeply on a cigarette. His face had lost any trace of colour and his eyes bore witness to his own troubled nights. Arguments had become commonplace, subjects ranging from Faith's role in the Smugglers to whether they should buy filter or non-filter cigarettes. Having agreed to move to Tenerife, albeit reluctantly at first, the root of the problem seemed to be about bullying. Faith was now saying she was bullied into coming and once here was being bullied by the rest of us.

We'd had this discussion with David before and several times had agreed to tread lightly when voicing our opinions, or rather, disagreeing with Faith's. The truth of the matter was that my sister-in-law no longer wanted to be here but David was financially tied to the business. The decision had to be made whether she was prepared to leave David as well.

David and Faith grew increasingly exhausted over the next 48 hours. Their eyes bore the red marks of too little sleep, too many tears. Faith had decided to leave, despite David's pleas for her not to go. She argued that she didn't want to move to Tenerife in the first place nor get married in circumstances that she felt had been forced on her. Now she found herself in a business partnership where she not only disliked the nature of the business but also where she wasn't treated as an equal partner. She was leaving Tenerife and David for good. The marriage was over.

On the morning of her departure we didn't open the bar until 6 p.m., allowing David time to help Faith pack and take her to the airport. Joy and I didn't see her before she went. Instead she wrote us a letter explaining her reasons for leaving and apologising if the decision left us in the lurch. It did, but the inconvenience was secondary to the rage I felt at her abandoning my brother.

He came in to the bar at 7.30 p.m. and worked silently in the kitchen until the last order had been sent out. He left the bar with two bottles of red wine, returning to an empty apartment, and his marriage in tatters. David's bid for a golden opportunity had already cost him dearly. I wondered whether he had contemplated following Faith back to save his marriage or if he felt more compelled to stay with the business. Time would tell.

CHAPTER 14

'Surprise!'

J oy was in the kitchen, scrawling down a breakfast order. She stopped writing on the fridge. I turned my back on the spitting eggs. The cavalry had arrived. In the doorway stood Carole and Faye, our mothers. Both had broad beams and outstretched arms as though welcoming back a long-lost relative.

'Mum!' Joy couldn't hold back the tears, which instantly released a tide of emotion in Faye. My mum, never one to miss out on a good cry, dabbed tears from her eyes. I wiped away some sweat that had begun to trickle down the bags under my eyes. To a passer-by it may have given the impression that I was also crying.

'What are you doing here?' I asked, having removed the perspiration. When David had phoned to say that Faith had left, my mum telephoned Faye and they decided to fly over to lend a hand and give David some support for the last week of summer, adamant that they wanted to start straight away. Or at least after a gin and tonic. They sat down on table one beneath the only fan that still had the energy to respond to a 'high' setting.

After wrapping paper napkins around 65 knives and forks, it was time for another gin and tonic. The bar had become progressively busier and three people were waiting at the bar whilst Joy was delivering lunches and clearing tables. Encouraged by the midday aperitifs, Carole felt compelled to go behind the bar to try and alleviate the wait. Whilst a noble gesture in theory, in practice she had overlooked the fact that she neither knew where all the requested drinks were located nor what to charge for the drinks once she'd hunted them down.

'Two Cokes, a white coffee and a pint of lager please, love,' said the first man.

'Uh... OK. Jooooy?'

Carole tried to flag Joy down as she dashed back and forth from the kitchen to the terrace. 'Just a minute.'

Faye could see that Carole was getting distressed and decided to try and help.

'How do you work this machine?' she whispered to Faye.

'No idea,' said Faye.

'Coffee won't be a minute. What else did you ask for?' said Carole brightly. 'I guess this is the beer,' she said, pointing at the beer pump.

'Dunno. Try it,' said Faye.

Carole held a pint pot under the spout and pulled at the handle. The liquid hit the bottom of the glass filling the interior with white foam.

'Hmm, beer's lively today,' she said knowingly. She'd heard that uttered on *Coronation Street* once. Carole passed the man an inch of pale yellow topped with five inches of froth. He held it up to his eyes, mouth ajar but before he could say anything, Carole had turned her back in pursuit of the Coke. Both she and Faye searched in the beer fridges, on the shelves, under the sink but neither could locate it.

'Jooooy?'

Joy flashed past again. 'Just a minute.'

'*Tae pins ena fissy pope.*' Faye had moved on to the next person waiting. The man stood at the bar shirtless, his bony body almost luminous in its whiteness. Faye was staring at him blankly. An uncomfortable silence developed before he repeated his order.

'*Assad tae pins ena fissy pope. Whirrsat ootie front.*'

'Can you speak Spanish, Carole?' asked Faye looking over her shoulder. Carole had been a patron of Linguaphone for several years but was disappointed to find her tutorials to be of no use on this occasion.

'Right, who's first?' Joy joined the parents behind the bar.

'This Spanish gentleman,' said Faye nodding at the exasperated man.

'Hi Campbell, the usual? Two pints and a fizzy pop? You sitting outside? I'll bring it to you.' Joy smiled. 'They thought you were Spanish.'

'Aye, a-spose a heave got that Latern look,' said Campbell, stiffening proudly.

Joy dealt with the three at the bar and then rushed back to the kitchen to answer the bell. Faye and Carole continued chatting until another customer interrupted.

'Can I pay?' asked the man.

'Err... sure.' Carole turned the piece of paper around in her hands but couldn't make any sense out of it.

'Jooooy?'

'Just a minute,' came a muffled response from the kitchen.

She passed it to Faye. 'Where's me glasses. I can't see a thing without them.'

'They're on your head,' said Carole.

'Nope, still can't make any sense out of it. Jooooy?'

'Coming.'

Both mothers graciously attempting to help without the slightest knowledge of what they were doing was causing Joy more work than it was saving. She suggested they go for a siesta and return for the evening rush. They eagerly obliged. A surfeit of midday gin and tonics had merely added to the spiralling confusion.

David arrived with the two mothers at 7 p.m. to clock on for the evening shift. Thankfully the night started off quietly enough for us all to have time to show Carole and Faye various trivialities of the job such as how to pull a pint, how to work the till and how to succinctly write down an order in the kitchen without including too much detail on the diners' backgrounds and interpersonal relationships.

There were few problems with the British diners but Faye in particular appeared somewhat alarmed to discover that there were entire tables of foreigners lying in wait.

'Hello, what would you like, love?'

'*Pardne z-moi.P arlez-vous Francais?*'

Faye stepped back in horror as though she'd just confronted a man wielding a machete.

'Who?' she barked, then scuttled off in search of reinforcements.

At 9.30 p.m. we made them sit down and take a break. Neatly coiffured hair had matted with perspiration and dissolving mascara was making a steady descent south. They looked like a couple of Alice Cooper fans.

Opting to escape from the heavy heat, the two women flopped down at a table on the terrace. The two unoccupied white plastic chairs facing them flagged their 'single' status. I spied the two Johns coming down the stairs. Carole and Faye were sitting ducks.

John One and John Two were both dressed in black. They were obviously on a mission. Like sharks to blood, they immediately honed in on the two women.

'Evening, ladies,' said John One, his eyes lingering as he made his way inside to the bar.

'Evening,' repeated John Two, as usual he was two paces behind.

'My usual,' shouted John One as he approached the bar.

'Aye, my usual too,' echoed his namesake.

Joy handed them two halves with lime.

'You're putting a bit of weight on, lass,' remarked John Two. He straddled a barstool. 'It's not a bad thing, mind. Men like a bit of something to get hold of. You could do with a bit more up top though, don't you think, John?'

'You're right, John. You can never have too much up top. Bigger the better I say, eh? The bigger and bouncier, the better.' They both began to chortle like year three schoolboys.

So late into the season, Joy hadn't the energy to reply. Before taking over the bar she would have counter-punched with some biting banter, a skill perfected on Bolton market. However, five months of facing the firing line behind the bar had taught her that in this job reacting to all the petty goading took too much time and effort and she had already bored of the same old jokes and comments. A humouring smile was the most accommodating response for all parties.

To a holidaymaker, the life of a sunshine landlord may seem like heaven in a glass but in reality it was as much work, if not more, as running a pub in the UK. The most successful landlords/landladies quickly had to adopt chameleon-like qualities, changing personality to suit whoever they were playing host to. In a resort bar, although there were a few regulars, the patronage changed on a wholesale basis every Tuesday and Friday.

Letting the jibes fly over your head was just one example of the changes in behaviour that we all had to take on board. On the market, cheeky banter was encouraged. The customers who shopped at Pat's stall expected it and would have been deeply suspicious of straight-laced courtesy. But in the Smugglers, with its varied social stratum, the style of interaction had to adapt to whoever was commanding your attention at the time. We were sales people just like any other agent or vendor. Only we weren't just selling food and drink, we had to sell the atmosphere, a party, and a personality.

Sometimes even the odd whiff of a certain perfume would trigger a metamorphosis. From bawdy backchat with Frank and the other barflies, we would have to climb a few rungs of the deportment ladder to ensure that a 'swallow' or stole-wearing expat would contemplate returning.

The downside of being a chameleon is that it soon becomes hard to remember your original colour. Personalities get lost, engulfed in a wave of adopted guises worn to please other people. From minute to minute we were both business people and cleaners, bar top counsellors and entertainers, drinking buddies and bouncers, party hosts and diplomats. In a twist on Pat's favourite saying back on the market, 'We were losing a lot of ourselves, but making a lot of friends'.

The two Johns sauntered outside.

'Mind if we join you?' said John One, sitting at one of the vacant seats opposite Faye.

'Looks like you ladies could do with some company,' chirped in the other John.

Carole and Faye looked at each other

'No, we're fine,' said Carole.

John One chose to ignore the rebuttal. 'You two escaped from your husbands for a week of sun, sand and sex?'

Faye laughed. 'Not at our age, love. Sun, sand and sleep maybe.'

'A holiday's not a holiday if you don't sleep in someone else's bed,' continued John One.

'Aye, and we've got very big beds, eh John?' laughed John Two.

Carole and Faye continued to eat, ignoring the advances but John Two persisted.

'What's your names then?' he asked.

'I'm Faye, this is Carole.'

John Two extended a hand. 'Pleased to meet you. I'm John.' He shook Faye's hand.

John One took Faye's hand. 'They call me John Juan,' he said smirking and put her hand to his lips. Joy had been watching them from the bar and had seen enough.

'Alright, you two. Go and mither someone else,' she said, striding towards the table.

'We're not doing anything wrong. We're just keeping these two lovely ladies company,' said John Two, trying to look innocent.

'Well, go and keep someone else company. *My* mum and Carole, who happens to be Joe and David's mum, can do without your slavering. Bugger off.'

'But...' protested John Two.

'But nothing, bugger off,' repeated Joy.

'She said sling your hook.' Wayne had been sitting at a nearby table. He got up and stood at Joy's shoulder like a protective dog. 'Do you want me to throw them out?'

'No, it's alright, Wayne. Thanks, but I think they've got the message. Haven't you?' She glared at the two and they slunk off like scolded puppies. 'Watch those two,' Joy said to her mum, 'They're a pain in the arse.'

'Looks like you've got them under control,' said Carole.

'They're not my favourites,' said Joy. 'Just watch out, that's all.'

Unruly people weren't usually a problem at the Smugglers. The rare few that did get too boisterous were politely asked to calm down or leave. They realised that we were the only British bar within a two-mile radius so were careful not to fall out with us.

The only time when things threatened to get out of control was when Tommy Cooper threw a skull at one of our customers. Perhaps that needs explaining a bit more.

One night we had tried out a Tommy Cooper show. The comedy act included many props, one of which was a small plastic skull.

'Alas, poor Yorick! I knew him well,' cried Tommy, 'but not that well!' He tossed the skull to a member of the audience. Unfortunately, his throw went astray and instead of the skull landing in the man's lap, it bowled over a full pint of lager.

The man shot up, drenched. The audience assumed this was part of the gag and continued to laugh but the victim couldn't see the funny side.

'You stupid git, you've soaked me!' he shouted. His three companions slid lower in their seats as if they knew what was coming.

'Ever so sorry,' continued Tommy keeping in character. 'Get that man a nappy.'

Joy was taking drinks to another table at the time and could see what had happened. She whipped two bar towels off the bar top and went to wipe up the mess.

'Joe, can you get this man another pint,' she shouted from amidst the melee, but the soggy customer wasn't satisfied.

'That stupid sod spilled my mate's drink as well. I want another one for him.'

Joy could see that the other pint was still full but she shouted for two pints. Still the man refused to be appeased.

'In fact, I want a whole round. Get us another round.'

Joy stopped wiping the table and straightened up. 'Listen, it was an accident. I apologise that you got wet but I'm bringing a pint for you and a pint for your friend, even though he's still got a full one in front of him. There's nothing more I can do so I suggest you sit down and watch the end of the show.'

'That's not good enough. I'm wet through. I want a full round,' continued the man.

'Well I think you're taking the rip. You're not getting a full round.' Joy came to the bar to collect the two pints. I was just pouring the second when the man walked into the bar and stood behind Joy.

'If I have to be wet, so do you,' he said and tipped his friend's pint over Joy's head.

Tommy's voice came through the speakers, 'I bet that was cold.'

I hurled the beer I was in the middle of pouring. The man leapt back, wiping his face as I scrambled to get round to the other side of the bar. The man couldn't have picked a worse night to pick a fight as the majority at the bar were residents. Des, the bouncer from Bolton was one of them and I couldn't get round him. He'd already lifted the man off his feet. As he swung his arm back to launch a punch, his elbow caught me in the eye, sending me scuttling backwards.

'Ooh. That'll smart,' said Tommy dryly, continuing his running commentary.

Wayne had also fought his way through the crowd and was clamouring to grab hold of the man. Des was holding him aloft out of reach of the baying crowd. As he carried him through the crowd, each of the residents added to his sodden misery with the dregs of whatever they were drinking. Danny was following Des, jumping up to whip the man with a wet bar towel.

'Rawhide!' yelped Tommy.

'The man must have thought his time had come and was now squealing for his life. Wayne managed to wrest one shoe from the man in a tug of war with Des and was now using it to beat the man's bare foot.

'Get off, get off me! Put me down! Help! Help!' His cries could barely be heard above the rioting crowd.

I was back on my feet, nursing a swelling eye, dissatisfied with my part in the retribution and followed the throng outside to where Des had finally put the man down, drowned in beer, limping on one foot and striped with red welts on his arms.

'I think you'd better leave, son,' said Des menacingly. The man was close to tears.

'And don't ever come back, you're barred,' I shouted.

'Bard. D'ya get it. Bard,' said Tommy holding up his reclaimed Yorick.

As the man turned to climb the steps, a shoe sailed over the crowd and caught him on the back of the head, quickening his retreat.

'Juss like that,' barked Tommy through the microphone.

More time was spent herding animals away from the bar than placating the drunk and disorderly. Stray dogs and cats were a big problem in Tenerife. Packs would roam from community to community, seeking out the most rewarding territory and loitering for as long as possible before they were chased away with sticks and stones or fell victim to poison bait laid out by the *technicos*.

Some owners brought their pets with them to the bar. Most would lie patiently under tables waiting to go home again but there were one or two pampered pooches whose owners clearly had an unhealthy emotional attachment. I would be happy to bag up any leftovers for the masters to take away. I also had no problem in providing something for the pet to drink from whilst it waited to go home. What I did object to however was the dog sitting on a chair, being fed at the table. Even worse, I was asked to cook a chicken in wine and serve it on a plate for one particularly babied poodle whose owner ought to have been sectioned. The embarrassed pooch strutted around in a plaid vest. Pink ears poked through holes in a matching sunhat and its tail wagged a pink bow like a baby shaking a rattle. I refused to serve food on a plate to the dog and told the owner it had to be fed on the floor. She looked at me as if I'd just dug up her grandmother. Outraged, she whisked the blob of fluff off the chair and disappeared through the door, vowing that she and Mr Cuddles would never step foot in the Smugglers Tavern again.

Whether invited or not, animal incursions were part of day-to-day life at the Smugglers and except for mounting a permanent guard, there was not much we could do about it. Until Buster arrived.

Despite a sign requesting patrons not to feed the strays, most of our British customers actively encouraged cats and dogs to their tables. The unfortunate few who liked to eat their steaks without the front paws of a salivating Alsatian resting on their laps would glare at us with contempt for allowing such behaviour. But we were too busy to keep shooing animals away only for them to trot back down the steps again once our backs were turned. A recent invasion of mongrels and scrawny cats had forced us into finding a solution.

Thankfully the solution found us. I was crouched underneath one of the wooden tables located in the middle of the bar. One of the legs had fallen off, another victim of the curse of Justin. He had been sitting at the table with his parents the night before. His hands could be seen disconcertingly fiddling with something below waist level, a grin on his face suggesting he was gaining pleasure from the activity. It was only when I came to move it whilst mopping that the heavy wooden support clattered down onto my flip-flop and the focus of his errant hands was revealed.

As I strained the monkey wrench to force the nut tight enough to withstand any other playful fingering, a swathe of black fur raced past my left side. A split second later the black was followed by a blur of ginger. The scene was then repeated on my right side, accompanied by a pitiful yelping. The gap between black and ginger had narrowed. I backed out of the table on my knees just as the black and ginger blur – now merged into one – hurdled the back of my legs, skidded round table seven at the end of the room and shot out of the doors at the other end. A cheer rang out from the terrace.

A sturdy ginger cat swaggered back into the bar on paws the size of junior boxing gloves. For a second he stared at me through half-closed eyes, like a gunslinger expecting trouble. On realising there was none to be had, he jumped up onto the padded bench seats near the door and began to lick his paws. His face bore the scars of combat and when he yawned I could see that he had the teeth of a bout-weary boxer.

He stopped licking his outstretched leg for a while and looked at me as I pondered what to do. He was clearly at home on this bench although I'd never seen him before. Unlike the other emancipated and timid strays that followed their noses to our tables, he had the stature of Des the bouncer with a self-assurance to match.

'He's a tough nut,' said a voice from behind. It was Wayne. He'd been watching the antics from outside. 'He just chased a big bastard dog up the stairs. If he can see off a mutt, maybe he can get rid of the mouse.'

I'd forgotten about our other lodger. Since his acrobatics in front of Faith, he'd kept a low profile, only appearing when the bar was empty. He'd still managed to leave his mark on our stash of crisp boxes. Quavers were obviously his favourites judging by the number of packets he'd infiltrated, though smoky bacon also bore the hallmarks of a rodent fan.

We decided to call him Buster after Buster Gonad, the *Viz* comic book character. Unlike some cats, Buster's gender was never a matter of debate. Not only was he as burly as a builder, two little cannonballs swung under his tail with each John Wayne stride

He had turned up to offer a security service for which he expected to be fed fresh chicken and fillet steak as and when necessary and be given his own room (a sturdy cardboard box would suffice). The deal seemed fair to us but I doubt it was negotiable anyway, so we started him right away.

Over the next few days Buster lived in the bar 24/7, emerging only to charge at four-legged foes who dared to stray onto his new patch. One of his first official confrontations was with a lunging mongrel that had become a regular caller at the bar.

The dog had spotted Buster lying under one of the tables and, duty-bound, scampered towards him, barking and snarling. Buster was taking one of his many daily siestas and thus was officially off duty. He opened one eye and disdainfully sniffed at the dog's snout, now less than a few inches away. The dog, not used to this breakdown in social order – dog barks and runs at cat, cat scarpers, dog laughs and tells all his friends over a can of Chum and a bowl of water – was a little unsure as to how to react so he flopped onto his stomach to bark and snarl some more. Buster slowly stood up, arched his back in a slow stretch, and moved to within licking distance of the dog, staring him straight in the eye. The dog began to whimper in confusion.

As is the custom of all professional doormen, Buster had given the cus-tomary warning, allowing the offender the opportunity to back off. But the dog didn't. Without a trace of fear or trepidation Buster's paw scythed across the dog's nose, sending it scampering backwards. His legs skated on the terracotta tiles as if in a cartoon as he raced to escape this anarchic ginger demon. Buster leapt after him, chasing the howling wretch outside and up the stairs. Happy that the matter had been dealt with, he sauntered down to the applause of those seated outside. His tail went up to acknowledge the adulation, then he turned round and ran half-way back up the stairs for an encore. He had proved his worth. The job was his for keeps.

His notoriety as a dog in cat's clothing soon got round and he became as big a draw as some of the artistes that were performing. Nobody could fail to be impressed by his sheer fearlessness and determination. This determination also had its downside. For much of the afternoon Buster would lay comatose on his back, snoring at full stretch whilst brazenly displaying his cat-hood and occupying the whole bench seat at table five. No amount of cajoling could persuade him to vacate the bench or make room for customers. The price for waking him from one of his deep slumbers was paid in blood. The only way to make him move was to carefully unzip the padded cushion, carry him outside like a pampered emperor and unceremoniously dump him onto the warm tiles.

He was most insistent at mealtimes. When hunger struck, customers would watch aghast as he strolled straight into the kitchen, where he would make a nuisance of himself around my feet until he was served his ration of raw meat. We naturally tried to discourage his kitchen forays and bought a water pistol in order to teach him the boundaries. However, after one or two days of being squirted in the face and skulking off, shaking his head, he realised that being shot at was a small price to pay for eating well and the water pistol became ineffective. As soon as the gun was levelled at him he would stand his ground, screw up his eyes and wait for the deluge to finish before continuing his demands.

Whilst Buster carried on his one-man mafia operation, terrorising the local four-legged population, Micky and Ron were introducing more and more dubious associates to the bar, something we weren't overly keen on. We had become the meeting place for trench coats and facial scars. Frank knew one or two of the disfigured faces as island hit men. 'As thick as shit, which makes them even more dangerous,' he whispered at a safe distance.

We truly had become their 'doorstep' and although playing host to a gang of hardened criminals was never in the job description, I figured that as long as Micky remained in charge, we were free from being shat on.

Ron was clearly still aggrieved from 'losing a client' and wasted no effort on pleasantries. Micky, on the other hand, had become a model of courtesy, even correcting his hit men if they forgot to say please and thank you.

Serving an armed hit man is a stressful event. Although at the back of your mind you know he's not going to stand up and shoot you if you spill a drink down his leather coat, the pressure to stay on the right side of him is immense. On one hand, you want to appear friendly and accommodating but on the other, you don't want to fawn too much otherwise you appear weak. As in their line of work, I adopted the silent approach – getting in, doing the job and getting out as quickly as possible.

'Hey, Joe. You got a minute, mate?' Micky had called me over to his table where six sinister characters had their heads down in deep discussion.

'I've got something coming up. You might be able to help me out.'

'Err… sure, depends what it is.' I laughed nervously.

'What have you got on tomorrow afternoon?'

'I… err… might have to work here if it gets too busy,' I lied.

'It won't take long. I just want to borrow you for an hour or so. Can you spare a friend some time?' he grinned.

I was trapped. Refuse and I was refuting friendship, agree and I could be destined for a stretch of long lonely days in Santa Cruz prison.

'No problem. What do you want me to do?'

'Have you got a tennis racquet?'

'Yes.' He could see my confusion.

'Meet me at the Altamira court at two. I heard you used to play and I fancy a game. None of these monkeys know one end of a bat from another.' He nodded at the assembled primates.

Although the dilemma was a fraction as troublesome as it could have been, it was still a dilemma nonetheless. I was naturally competitive. What if I thrashed him? What if he was a bad loser? How bad would he be?

After a fitful night's sleep and a morning shift in the bar, I dusted off my tennis racquet and met Micky at the court. He was dressed in brand new gleaming whites. Everything was top of the range; even the racquet looked like a sophisticated weapon.

The warm-up started well. We both appeared to be of roughly the same ability. Micky's aggressive forehand was matched by my devious drop shots and we parried the ball back and forth for 20 sweaty minutes.

'Shall we start?' Micky had approached the net. His eyes were steeled with determination. Mine were focused on anxiety. The first few games were close. I wasn't yet playing to my full potential. 'You're playing against the mafia,' my conscience reminded me at frequent intervals.

However, the further we progressed into the match, the more my natural will-to-win kicked in. My serves got harder, my returns more aggressive and my runs to the net more frequent. Micky was getting agitated. He was cursing to himself, beating his thigh with his own racquet after every point lost.

By the last game the match was tied one set all. I was serving to win. My first serve fizzed over the net landing a good six inches inside the box.

'Out,' shouted Micky.

The second serve dropped just in front of him and he returned with a strong backhand. I parried the shot more in self-defence than anything and the ball bounced off my racquet, dropping just over the net. I ran in to follow it. Micky also sprinted to the net, straining to reach the ball as it dropped to the ground. He just managed to scoop the racquet underneath it at full stretch and flicked upwards but his momentum caused him to lose balance. He fell forward. The ball gained height then began its descent. I couldn't tell if it was going to land on my side of the net or not. Micky crashed to the tarmac at full stretch. His head came to a rest at the bottom of the net, inches from my feet, where he lay motionless for a moment, watching the ball bounce just next to him. A wave of panic surged from head to toe. Not only had I beaten Micky the Mafia but I'd also drawn blood.

Micky picked himself up. 'Fack,' he said, looking down at his knees. A trickle of blood streamed down his left shin. Both elbows were also grazed, scraped raw on the unforgiving surface. 'Fack,' he said again.

I offered my hand. 'Well-played.'

He looked up. 'Fack,' he said once more, reluctantly accepting a hand-shake. I helped him limp to the Smugglers where my mum was filling in for my absence. I poured him a beer and offered him a handful of Elastoplasts.

'What happened?' asked Joy.

'I won,' I answered sheepishly.

'Oh, nice move,' she said sarcastically. 'I thought we were supposed to be staying on the right side of him.'

Micky didn't take kindly to being beaten but fortunately he displayed his displeasure in a passive manner by staying away from the bar over the next few weeks. It was nice to be mafia-free, if only a temporary situation.

CHAPTER 15

At last it was the final night of summer. The number of breakfasts and lunches served daily had dropped into the 20s and we were all desperate for a break. The bar needed touching up after a hot and hectic season. Handprints marked the white walls like shadows from the ghosts of customers past; hundreds of green bottles on a high shelf lining the interior were caked in dust; the bar stools and wooden chairs needed repainting; and the outside tiles were ready for yet another industrial clean.

Perhaps worst of all, the bar needed fumigating and for this we needed to vacate the premises for at least 12 hours. It was Frank who brought the matter to our attention. He spent so much time hunched over the bar in moody contemplation that he knew every knot in the wood, every cigarette burn and every hairline crack where the roaches sought sanctuary. Despite unleashing dozens of cans of killer spray through the summer months, the romantic procreation of our resident bug population continued unabated.

'You're going to have to do something about these fucking roaches,' said Frank, slamming his hand down on a procession of babies. 'They're getting worse.'

He offered to fumigate the bar himself, claiming he knew what chemicals to mix and a man who could supply them, but I declined. I had visions of his lethal crop-dusting leaving a legacy of toxins circulating for weeks, our bar having to be decorated with red and white ribbon, deemed a no-go zone, whilst a team of boiler suits tried to find an antidote to the hazardous cocktail Frank had created.

Buster had become adept at leaping on the bigger ones but he made such a song and dance out of his assaults that he was bringing unwanted attention to the infestation. He would bat the bug from paw to paw until it toppled on to its back and started to spin, then end the show with an unappetising crunch in front of a horrified audience of diners.

There was a celebratory mood in the air. We had got through the first season of a new life without poisoning anybody, making too many enemies or being set on by the locals. It felt like a victory, albeit at the cost of David's marriage. He and Faith were now communicating again but hopes of reconciliation were slim. There was no way she would come back to Tenerife and David, like Joy and I, was chained to the bar with a huge mortgage and loan.

In spite of our burdens, this last night of all-day opening was one to celebrate. A never-ending succession of beers were delivered to the kitchen by Mum and Faye who themselves were making the most of their last night helping out with generous proportions of gin and less generous proportions of tonic.

By the time the final meals had been cleared and the kitchen tidied, we were all in party mood.

'Are you lot on drugs or something?' muttered Frank. As is the way with excess alcohol, everybody was our friend that night. Even an appearance by the two Johns couldn't dampen the spirits, despite their usual antagonising.

'Hey, Joe must have given you a good time last night,' said John One to Joy. 'Look at that smile.'

'That's the smile of a satisfied woman that is, eh John?' added John Two.

'No that's the smile of a woman who doesn't have to face your ugly mugs in the daytime any more,' replied Joy.

'What do you mean?' asked John Two.

Joy explained that we were closing during the days and just opening at night until the Christmas crowd arrived.

'But you can't do that,' moaned John Two. 'Where are we going to go for our fry-ups?'

'Not my problem,' smiled Joy.

'Tell you what. Maybe Joy wants to deliver it in bed. Now that'd be good service. What do you reckon, Joy?' said John One.

'I think I'm going to throw up at just the thought of it,' replied Joy.

'Is that right, then?' asked Frank. 'The bar's going to be closed during the day? You lazy fuckers. I worked seven days a week when I was your age. I had to get up at five in the freezing cold and walk a mile to me uncle's garage.'

'Yes, and look what a happy chap that's made you,' I said. 'You know what they say about all work and no play.'

'No danger of that here, is there?' he said with a sigh. 'Anyway, what about my office? Who's going to answer my phone?'

'And where am I going to leave the keys for my renters?' added John One.

Frank had taken to using the bar as his daytime office. Phoned requests for his DIY services were frequent, more frequent than our own callers at times. It had come to the point that incoming calls were immediately assumed to be for Frank and we would pass him the handset automatically, although he was always reluctant to take it unless we knew the caller. He was convinced that sooner or later one of the calls would be from Shark Bait.

The bar's status as community HQ also involved taking on several other responsibilities. As one of the very few things that was guaranteed to be around for at least a few more months (so long as Frank resisted the urge to mess with safety valves again), the Smugglers Tavern had become more than a place to grab a drink and a meal. In addition to its crèche status, the bar also became a drop-off and pick-up point for begged, borrowed and returned goods.

'When you've finished with the stepladders/surfboard/stuffed cat, if I'm not in, leave it at the Smugglers. I'll pick it up later,' was common. Our tiny outside storeroom began more to resemble a catalogue despatch centre than a booze cupboard. Behind the bar we would have all manner of notes, letters and keys to be passed on to third parties.

Keys in particular were a constant hazard. Apartment owners who rented out their properties had bestowed upon us the honour of being judged as custodians of spare keys. The title came with the burden of being listed in their 'apartment manual' as the ones to go to if there was a problem. We didn't mind doing this for those owners we had befriended and who showed their appreciation in kind or cash. However, some saw it as our community obligation and at such a relatively early stage of our business we rarely refused if asked.

This key-holding service slowly developed into bigger and better things, at least for the owners. From time to time holidaymakers would ask us if there were any private apartments for rent. To save the effort of having to scroll through her phonebook each time the question was asked, Joy had compiled a list of telephone numbers of the four or five owners who would let their accommodation. The enquirer would then phone the owner direct and the owner could make all the arrangements with them. That was the theory anyway. In reality, the person wanting accommodation would make an initial enquiry and the owner would call Joy asking if she thought they were OK and could she pass them the keys if they booked.

In the eyes of the renter this tended to wrongly paint Joy in the role of apartment manager and any subsequent problems were then directed her way. More than once a complete stranger would walk into the bar and demand that we fix his leaking tap or inform us haughtily that his buttocks had been nipped by a broken toilet seat and what were we going to do about it? 'Nothing,' was usually the answer.

We had a final drink with David, Mum and Faye after we had managed to herd the last of the customers out, then staggered down Cardiac Hill to our apartment. There was a salty sea breeze blowing up the hill, the first inkling of fresh air we had experienced on El Beril. Overhead the sky was full of pinprick clusters, the moon casting a silver glow over the ocean in front of us.

We strolled past the apartment on our left and continued down some steps at the far end of the turning circle at the bottom of the hill.

The steps led to a part-finished promenade that ran half-way in front of the Altamira to the right and to the back edge of the El Beril complex to our left.

At intervals along the promenade were gaps in the knee-high wall where broken steps led to the black pebble beach.

We sat on the top step gazing at our world. A gentle surf raked the smooth rocks, rasping slowly back and forth at our feet.

'It's not a bad place to live, is it?' I said.

'No. It's times like these that you appreciate it,' agreed Joy. 'Now we're closed in the daytime we should start making the most of it.'

'You're right. Let's spend the day on the beach.'

We watched a line of lights dipping and rising like a Mexican wave several miles offshore; night fishermen stretching their nets from boat to boat in search of tomorrow's fresh catch. Beyond them, the dark silhouette of La Gomera rose from the water like a giant whale, the faint lights of Hermigua and Vallehermosa blinking above the moonlit ocean.

I thought about the view from Joy's mother's house where we had been living before we moved to Tenerife. Joy's bedroom looked over Belmont Road, a busy byway linking Bolton with Blackburn West via the bracken and heather of Belmont Moors. Austin Allegros and Vauxhall Vectras would be parked outside the neat gardens of the facing bungalows.

Lace curtains would frequently twitch, those inside disappointed as fire engines raced past from the station half a mile up the road, reminding the neighbourhood that there was something exciting happening, but always somewhere else.

Over the bungalows, the terraced houses on High View Street would reflect the pale yellow streetlight off damp grey roof slates, casting a sickly pallor on the community like a fevered jaundice. The pallid, damp glow of the night felt as claustrophobic as the low-hanging clouds of daytime. I felt pride, and relief, in our escape.

We wandered back to the apartment along the promenade.

'Who's that man in the car?' asked Joy.

As we climbed the steps up to Cardiac Hill, she noticed a man sitting in darkness behind the wheel of an expensive-looking jeep. His seat was reclined back as if he was planning to sleep there but his eyes were open, tracking us as we walked in front of the bonnet and through the gate leading to the back of our apartment.

'Seems a bit strange,' I said, unlocking the door.

'Go and see if he's still watching,' said Joy.

A hedge at the end of our garden obstructed the view onto the road so I slowly pulled back the curtain in the spare bedroom upstairs. The man was staring straight back at me.

'Is he still there?' shouted Joy.

'Yes, and he's watching us.'

'Should we phone the police?' asked Joy.

'No, I'll go and let the Altamira security guard know. He can keep an eye on him.'

'Wait a minute, you're not leaving me here alone.' Joy was already shutting the door behind us.

I found the security guard asleep on a sunbed round the El Beril pool. One arm flopped towards the floor, the other was resting on his stomach, his thumb hooked through a pair of handcuffs. His mouth was wide open and he was rasping the deep sleep of someone who clearly wasn't at his most vigilant.

'Señor?' I hissed without success. I tapped him on his arm but still there was no waking him.

Joy grabbed his shoulder, shaking him violently. 'Hey, wake up.'

His eyes shot open. '*Que? Que pasa?*' He looked at us as if we were going to mug him and fumbled for his baton whilst wiping a dribble of saliva from the corner of his mouth with the other hand.

I raised my palms to calm him down then signalled for him to follow us. Peering from behind a stack of bin liners piled at the top of Cardiac Hill, I pointed to the solitary car parked at the bottom.

'A man... *hombre*... watching our apartment... *mi casa*.' I scowled to show this was not good and gestured that the security guard should go and take a look but he didn't seem keen. He gesticulated that he'd keep an eye on him from a safe distance, i.e. from where he was now.

As usual, the sun exploded round the blinds in the bedroom. Today felt different. Almost like the day we were leaving for Tenerife. I wasn't sure why but then remembered that we weren't going to open during the day for the next few months. I felt like we were on holiday.

I drew the blinds up, filling the bedroom with light.

'He's gone,' I said.

'Hmm?' mumbled Joy. Her eyes were still closed.

'That man in the jeep. He's gone.'

'Mmm.'

'Beach today?' I suggested. A smile slowly spread across Joy's face as she came to the same realisation as I had.

An hour later we were on the way back from the airport, having dropped off Faye and my mum. It was late morning and I could feel a progressive hangover starting to kick in. 'Nothing that a day snoozing on the beach couldn't cure,' I thought. Thin wisps of clouds threaded a near-perfect sky. A perfect day.

Just then my mobile rang. It was the fumigation company. They'd be at the bar at midday.

Normally you could rely on the Canarians to need several pokes with a sharp stick before they'd fulfil their obligations several days later than requested. This was the first time that one had been so speedy and efficient. It was very inconvenient.

The beach plans were put on hold. Hopefully they would turn up by 1 p.m. and be gone again by 2 p.m., which meant we could still get a couple of hours on the beach. The night before we had given Wayne a key so that when the fumigation had taken place he could let himself in and wash all the crockery and glasses. It was a job we were glad to delegate.

As promised, the fumigation man turned up at midday. Only his midday was more known as mid-afternoon in our world. After waiting from 12.30 p.m., pottering with small jobs that needed doing, like dusting the fan blades and polishing the beer pumps, our bug-buster sauntered in at 3 p.m. The beach would have to wait until tomorrow.

The exterminator was smoking a cigarette, a rucksack slung casually over his shoulder. He greeted us with a rasping '*hola*' and a subsequent coughing fit. It sounded like he'd been inhaling toxins too long. He emptied the contents of two plastic bottles into what looked like a weed killer bottle and pumped on the top handle until the nozzle he was holding in his other hand spat a small globule of insecticide onto the floor.

'*Dónd están?* (Where are they) he asked, gazing round the bar.

'Well, everywhere,' I gestured. 'Here, and here, and here.' I showed the man the small cracks in the wooden bar top, pointing with my finger. He gave each area a blast, barely giving me time to move my finger out of the way.

'Do we need to cover the glasses?' I asked.

He shrugged his shoulders and shook his head, unleashing a stream of poison along the back of the shelf.

The insecticide was acting fast. Seconds after spraying, dozens of roaches emerged from the cracks and gaps, dropping onto the tiled floor like lemmings. The dozens turned to scores, then hundreds. Piles of tiny bugs lay at the foot of the bar like wood shavings.

'*Dios mío!*' My God, he exclaimed. The fumigator looked at me and raised his eyebrows. I felt ashamed.

Just then a young couple walked into the bar ignoring the 'Open at 6' sign on the closed door.

'Are you open?' said the man. I rushed over to block them coming any further. 'No, sorry. Open at six,' I answered. He spotted the man with the container and tilted his head to see what he was doing. I tilted mine to block his view.

'So we'll see you at six, then,' I said, my head still at an angle.

'What's he doing?' asked the man.

'Varnishing.'

His eyes flashed from me to the pale brown piles on the floor.

'What are those?'

'Wood shavings,' I said. 'We've been sanding. That's why we're closed. See you at six, then?' I took hold of his shoulders and steered him and his wife back out.

I continued to lead the fumigator around the bar, pointing to all the nooks and crannies; behind the bar, behind the dart board, in the store cupboard, in the toilet door frames, in the washing machine cupboard, under the benches, in all the joints of the wooden tables. Communities of various sized roaches occupied every conceivable living space. On seeing the devastation, I was only surprised that we weren't awash with them during opening hours.

Buster lifted his head, opening one eye as a cloud of chemicals engulfed him. He sneezed once then tucked his head under his massive paw and went back to sleep on his padded bench.

The kitchen was to be the final battleground. The fumigator refilled his tank and stepped into the front line. Anywhere there was the slightest gap between shelf and wall was inhabited. He pushed the nozzle underneath the serving top and sure enough within seconds a mass exodus was in progress.

I asked again whether we should cover the stacks of plates that were exposed on an open shelf above the sink. He shrugged and dismissed the suggestion again.

There was one area that I dreaded showing him. It was only a few days before that I found a small roach scuttling up the stainless steel doors of our main fridge, next to the oven. Despite several attempts to flick it off with a tea towel, it eluded my aim and disappeared under the rubber door seal and into the fridge. I opened the door just in time to watch its bottom wriggling inside a crack on the plastic door interior. We had cockroaches living in the fridge!

After satisfying himself that the kitchen was done, the man made for the doorway.

'*Perdne* ,' I coughed, opening the fridge door and pointing to the crack. He looked at me doubtingly. I nodded. He fired one tiny jet into the crack and waited. One by one a line of small brown roaches scrambled out of the crack onto the floor, kicking and flailing. He forced the tip of the nozzle into the opening and sprayed some more. We both stood watching.

'Hello.'

I peered round the open door. Justin was standing on the other side of it.

'Are those cockroaches?'

'Err… yes, Justin. Those are cockroaches,' I replied, looking at the pile of dead insects at his feet.

'They're dropping out of the fridge,' he said without emotion.

'I know.'

'So will they have been crawling on the food, then?'

'Look, Justin. How about you get an ice cream out of the freezer and pretend you've never seen this? What do you say?'

'Sure.' He opened the upright display freezer, releasing a freezing mist. 'Should I just tell my dad?' he said. His glasses had frosted over.

'No, no-one.'

'OK.' He wiped his glasses with a knuckle and skipped out of the bar.

After the man had left, I swept all the roaches into one pile in the middle of the bar, just out of morbid curiosity. It was the size of a large molehill. Although satisfying to know that we would no longer need to do subtle Michael Flatley impressions behind the bar it was also disconcerting to know that we'd been sharing our workspace with literally thousands of cockroaches. And God knows where they'd been stomping their little buggy muck.

That night the jeep had returned. The mysterious man was watching our apartment for the second night. We woke the security guard again to inform him. He dutifully sprung into action, yawned, and then trudged to his stake-out behind the bin liners.

Again in the morning he had disappeared and again we looked forward to a day on the beach. Joy made *bc ail llos*, long rolls, from some leftover chicken we'd brought back from the Smugglers the previous night. I packed a cool-box with beers and a bottle of premixed *tinto verano* or summer red, a heady concoction of red wine and Sprite.

'I'm just nipping up to the bar for some olives!' I shouted to Joy.

David was in the bar when I arrived. He was pouring himself a Fernet Branca, a potent herbal drink and supposed digestive aid. The Germans would drink it for fun but it was always served to the Brits as a forfeit in any drinking game. Nobody I knew could drink it without severe facial contortions. It had the colour and fluidity of treacle but the taste of creosote seasoned with stinging nettles.

I waited till he'd stopped convulsing. He looked like he was going to be sick. 'Hangover?' I enquired.

'No, got a god-awful gut ache and sore throat. I was sick twice in the night,' he said.

'Maybe there's something going around. Frank didn't look great last night either.'

'Frank never looks great,' replied David.

'That's true.'

'Hang on a minute... gonna be sick.' David rushed off to the toilets where I could hear him gagging.

'You look terrible,' I said when he returned. 'Are you going to be OK with the shop and prep?' We were taking it in turns with the daytime chores but David looked in no fit state to do anything but hang by his chin from a toilet bowl.

'To be honest, no. Can we swap and I'll do the prep tomorrow?' he croaked.

'No problem, I'll just go and tell Joy.' The beach would have to wait again.

Joy brought the sandwiches up to the bar and we shared them on the way to the cash and carry.

I had become adept at making our money go a long way at the cash and carry. All those months ago, Mario had showed us how to stack the trolley most economically.

'They so flickin' lazy they no get off their ass to check. They only charge for what they see.' It was true. The more expensive items were placed at the far side of the trolley behind bundles of toilet rolls and catering cans of Heinz beans. We had saved a fortune over the months and justified the cover-up by the fact that many a time we had been overcharged for items due to careless mistakes on the till. We rarely checked the receipt but when we did there was more often than not a mistake in their favour, but it was in-evitably always too late to complain. This 'careful placement' policy helped to balance the books somewhat.

That night Joy and I ran the bar by ourselves. David was still suffering with the mystery bug. The bar was strangely quiet and it soon became apparent why.

'Two portions of chips to take out,' shouted Justin, startling me. He had magically appeared at my elbow just as I was carefully slicing through a tail of fillet steak.

'Your mum and dad not coming in tonight, Justin?' I asked, sucking the blood from my finger.

'No. They're not very well.'

'Why, what's the matter.'

'They're both being sick and my dad's lost his voice.'

The mystery bug was claiming a lot of people. Several of our regulars had called in for a drink, then left early complaining of the same ailments. Even Buster was more lethargic than usual and his meow had turned embarrassingly pitiful for such a macho cat.

Late that night Joy and I started to suffer the same symptoms. We were too busy staring at porcelain to notice the jeep pull up outside again. Even if we had, we would have been in no state to kick-start 'the sleeping policeman'. By the following morning we were bedridden. The beach was the last thing on my mind.

Wayne called round later that day to see how we – or more importantly to him – Joy was doing.

'What you been eating then, youse look like shit?' he asked.

'Nothing unusual. We've been eating from the bar,' strained Joy.

'Ah, well, that's it isn't it?' he joke., 'The shit they serve in there would kill anyone.'

'What you been up to, anyway?' I whispered.

'I've just been to see your David, tell him I'm back and see if he wants me to do anything.'

'You're back? Where've you been?' croaked Joy.

'I had a mate come over from Wolverhampton so I've been off me face with him. Can't remember anything from the last two days.'

'Sounds like fun,' I said, nodding.

'Hang on.' Joy rose from the settee wrapped in a quilt. 'If you've been away for the last two days, when did you go in and wash all the plates and glasses?'

'I haven't been in yet. I'm still waiting for the bug man to come.'

I looked at Joy. 'Oh, crap.'

Wayne could see the alarm in our faces. 'What?'

'He's been. He sprayed insecticide everywhere,' I said.

'Including the plates and the glasses,' added Joy.

'Well no fucker told *me*,' said Wayne, sensing that he was about to get the blame.

One of my worst fears had materialised. 'We've poisoned everybody,' I announced solemnly.

CHAPTER 16

I broke the news to David. Fortunately he had recovered enough to go back into work. It was vital that we kept the revelation to ourselves or our reputation would be ruined. On a small and isolated complex such as El Beril, it was potentially disastrous.

Both Wayne and David immediately set about cleaning the crockery, glasses and work surfaces whilst I made my way back to bed. All the food had to be thrown out and the fridge completely restocked. We'd managed to poison twelve people that we knew about, not including ourselves. It had been a costly mistake but the price could have been a lot higher.

Both Joy and I managed to make it to the bar that night and were relieved to see a lot of the old faces back.

'Did you get that bug as well, Frank?' asked Joy. His colour had returned but his zest for life remained unchanged.

He nodded. 'Couldn't stop crapping all night.'

'It did the rounds, didn't it?' said Joy continuing to plant the idea.

'I fucking hate this time of year,' he said. 'When summer finishes and winter kicks in everybody always gets ill. It's those fucking Moroccans sending their germs from Africa. Should all be shot.'

The change of seasons could hardly be called drastic. The mercury might have dropped a couple of millimetres but we weren't exactly clamouring for hats and mittens. However, the frequent *calimas* or sand storms from the Sahara that shrouded the islands in a dusty haze for days on end were known to trigger various ailments.

Fortunately it seemed that we had escaped any finger-pointing and our regular array of cheerful patrons, plus Frank, soon littered the bar once more. There was also one addition to the regular barflies who would prove to be more trouble than the rest of them put together.

A dark-haired, dark-eyed girl sat at the bar. She appeared nervous as she asked for her second beer. She kept looking down at the bar top in an almost subservient manner, as though she didn't think herself worthy enough to look anybody in the eyes. Joy took pity on her and tried to engage her in conversation.

'Where are you from?'

'Czechoslovakia.'

'Are you on holiday here?' she asked.

'No, I am work here.'

'Where do you work?'

'I work Hotel Conquistador. I clean room, make bed.'

John One had come in the bar and headed straight for the girl. 'You can make my bed any day, love,' he said, putting his arm round her shoulders. She pulled away from him, eyes wide in horror. Even John was surprised at the reaction and raised his palms to apologise.

'Did you come to Tenerife by yourself?' continued Joy.

'No. I come with boyfriend but now I have big trouble.' Her head lowered even more.

'Why, what's happened?' asked Joy.

'My boyfriend he leave. I nowhere stay,' answered the girl sadly. 'I need find apartment.'

Joy tutted sympathetically. The girl looked to be on the edge of tears, holding her head in her hands. John began to beam, a smile he considered his most beguiling. He looked like a dog baring his teeth. Joy sensed he was about to play the saviour and quickly butted in.

'I have a friend who has an apartment on El Beril. I think it's free at the end of the week. I could ask her if you like,' said Joy.

The girl looked up. 'Thank you,' she said softly. She asked Joy for her phone number and said she would call in the next couple of days.

Joy hadn't managed to get in touch with Siobhan, the owner, but she did know that it was going to be free for two weeks before Siobhan's next friend arrived.

The only casualty who did not seem to be making such a quick recovery from 'the bug' was Buster. His puny call had deteriorated to a silent mouthing whenever somebody ventured close and any inclination to travel beyond table five had completely vanished. When one of the Spaghetti Beach residents ambled into the bar with a Dalmatian, Buster lifted his head from the soft padding of the bench seat, looked at the spotted enemy and flopped down again. It was clearly time to seek professional help.

Over the weeks, Buster had gained an enormous amount of weight. From being barrel-shaped and burly he had become more like a furry beach ball. His personal hygiene had also fallen by the wayside. He now sported a permanent black stripe running the length of his spine, a legacy of his favourite stakeout place underneath a parked car. However, whereas before he had been able to remove the camouflage once his mission was over, the middle of his back now remained frustratingly just beyond the reach of his probing pink tongue. Sitting on his haunches, he would strain his neck in an attempt to lick clean the oil but more often than not he would lose his balance, roll over his own shoulder and let out an indignant sigh of defeat.

Buster's attraction to cars wasn't restricted to the underside even though he spent a lot of time sprawled under chassis now the bar was closed in the daytime. After sleeping, eating and chasing dogs, going for a ride in the car was Buster's favourite pastime.

On those mornings when time was short and we had an insurmountable list of tasks that needed to be accomplished before the bar opened, speed was of the essence. Without fail, these mornings coincided with Buster's innate urge to be a passenger. He would have no qualms about standing resolute in front of a revving car until a door would open and in he would leap.

If the chores of that morning involved meetings and appointments at which Buster's presence wasn't required, he would content himself with a quick circuit of the car park before being dropped back off at the bar.

It was thus no challenge to entice him into the car for a trip to the vet. He jumped in and assumed his usual position. Two front paws rested on the dark grey dashboard, purring and dribbling saliva onto Joy's lap as he watched the world go by on the way to Las Americas.

'He's been poisoned,' announced the German vet.

'Has he?' we both feigned surprise. She gave him an injection, which he accepted without a flicker of pain or protest.

'He needs to be neutered,' said the vet, noting Buster's two appendages. 'Bring him back when he's better. It's time he had the snip.' Buster looked up at us and opened his mouth, aghast, but nothing came out.

With Buster on the mend and our stomachs the right way round again, the day was ours. There was only one thing for it. The beach bag was packed once more.

El Beril's offering was no Copacabana but it still attracted a few hardy souls who must have treasured the chiropractic qualities of lying prostrate on a lumpy stone mattress. I assumed these were the same people who forced themselves into freezing water, happy in the deluded notion that doing awful things to your body was healthy for body and soul.

Joy and I had no such wholesome intentions and headed to the nearest swathe of soft golden sand with the aim of plonking ourselves down and doing bugger all for as many hours as the day would allow.

We found a spot on the newly created Las Americas beach. I say newly created as the coastline, although beautiful in a rugged sense, was merely a series of rocky crags interspersed with pockets of coarse black sand, remnants of Tenerife's volcanic birth.

As the tourism industry quickly took hold of the island, it wasn't long before the authorities recognised the fact that north Europeans weren't in the least bit attracted to bitumen-coloured beaches. Buckets and spades were sent to the Sahara Desert to dig up the preferred golden variety and transport it back across the water, where it was dumped at the feet of huge hotels in a bid to cover up unsightly black roots.

Naturally, environmentalists were none too pleased with this trans-continental transfer of earthly treasure. Consequently, many of the south's other beaches had to draw on sub-oceanic reserves, sucking golden sand (and startled marine life) off the seabed, blowing it along lengthy sections of tubing and spitting it back out onto dry land.

Joy and I pitched camp between two families. One was Spanish, several generations sheltering from the sun under a marquee of overlapping beach brollies. A wall of towels draped from the umbrellas provided security from the gusts of sea breeze, protecting the picnic they had laid out on one of the white plastic sunbeds. A carpet of remaining towels protected the delicate feet of the younger members of the family from the hot sand.

If it wasn't for the fact that they were all dressed in swimsuits, except the grandmother who was clad all in black save for a straw boater, you'd be forgiven for thinking that you were peering into someone's living room. Huge efforts had been made to repel the conditions that you'd normally seek on a beach, i.e. sand, sunshine and a sea view.

A red-top newspaper protruding from the top of a straw shopping bag gave an obvious clue as to the nationality of our other neighbours. The family of four couldn't have displayed a more contrasting outlook on beach excursions. They were here to revel in all three enemies of the Spanish clan.

Mr Brit was standing, one hand cupped over his eyes, surveying the scene for a glimpse of the topless, oak-tanned girls he'd heard about back home. His white legs gleamed in the midday sun like flagpoles on a tropical parade ground. His other hand rested on hips housed in purple knee-length swimming shorts. Above this, a pale blue short-sleeved shirt was unbuttoned, flapping in the slight breeze. It still had birthmarks, two lines running parallel from top to bottom and one across the chest from left to right, a neat tribute to the packers at M & S department store.

Mrs Brit sat upright reading Jackie Collins whilst slow cooking in coconut oil. The wide brim of a straw hat threw shade over the novel and her shoulders, where both straps of her black one-piece had been pushed daringly off their perch.

The junior Brits were both lying comatose. The boy of about 14 lay on his back atop a Sheffield United beach towel, a glorious antithesis if ever there was one. Pale skin and red hair hinted that this wasn't an environment particularly suited for him. Nevertheless he slept soundly, blissfully ignorant of the pink glow fanning out from his freckled shoulders.

His sister was possibly a year older. She was lying on her front, bikini top unfastened, arms and legs spread wide to minimise the catastrophe of acquiring white bits. A teen mag lay discarded in the sand at the side of her head, its pages blowing back and forth from one Hollywood hunk to another.

We spread out two towels and flopped down. Joy smothered herself in sun cream, took out a magazine and immediately fell asleep before she had time to learn why a C-list soap star had decorated her bathroom in zebra stripes.

We had been living within a hundred yards of the ocean for nearly 140 days. We had driven past the beach six days out of seven for those four and a half months. We had welcomed hundreds of customers in various states of undress who had obviously come straight from the beach, expressing envy at our lifestyle while asking the inevitable, 'Why are you so white if you live here?' But this was the first time we had been able to enjoy for ourselves what 99.9% of holidaymakers came for – to lie in the sun and do nothing.

Beach-goers can generally be divided into two schools; those that see the sand as a giant communal mattress and those who see it as an activity centre.

For every comatose sun worshipper there's another indulging in a beach activity – some more traditional than others.

Just beyond the Spanish encampment, a tanned Latin girl sat astride her boyfriend who lay on his front. Her face was contorted in fierce concentration as she nipped his flesh with two thumbs, minesweeping for spots along the length of his back then wiping the results on the back of his shorts. His eyes were open, watching two portly British lads trying to impress a group of girls with their keepy-uppy skills, competing with the wind for control of their 200-peseta plastic flyaway ball; 'One... two... thr... damn! Right, this time. One... two... sorry, love.'

A small boy stood watching, open-mouthed. In one hand he held a red plastic spade, in the other his willy. Behind him, his father was putting the final touches to an intricate sand village complete with irrigation system and walled surround. His tongue was between his teeth as he lay on his front etching mullion windows into the houses oblivious that his son had wandered off, bored with the complexities of making sandcastles with Dad.

'It's time for a change.' Joy had woken from her doze and finished all the articles in her glossy on '*How to g t thin eating nothing t choco-late*', the latest cellulite treatment involving hydrochloric acid, a stiff wire brush and several months in intensive care and yet another conclusive study revealing that all men are crap. She was now propping herself up on one elbow, staring at my manhood.

Insulted by this deflating remark I stopped my posturing. As gravity let go of my shoulders, chest and stomach they slumped down towards the focus of her gaze. My ego fought hard to convince me that it was the packaging and not the contents at which she was expressing displeasure.

'Nobody wears those nowadays,' she announced.

I had to admit that there weren't many other bodies sporting red Speedo trunks but not being a dedicated follower of fashion this was not a concern. I'd had this swimming costume for years and apart from a quick dash into (and a quicker dash out of) Blackpool's icy offering, they had enjoyed a very restful life.

It's only in places like Tenerife that you realise beachwear is such big business. It's the least amount of clothing you're likely to wear in public yet produces the most amount of concern in the run up to summer holidays.

It's also come a long way since the days when extraordinary efforts were required to ensure that nobody got a glimpse of exposed skin. In the 18th century, a bathing machine was invented to save the blushes of the psychotically modest beach-goer. This contraption was the brainstorm of Benjamin Beale, a Quaker who was apparently troubled by the sight of women emerging from the sea in sodden dresses.

Choosing not to look didn't appear to have been an option so he went to all the trouble of inventing what was basically a shed on wheels. This would be towed by horses far enough into the water to enable the occupant to change out of her thick layers of land clothing into her equally thick layers of water clothing and enjoy an unsociable day at the seaside beyond the prying eyes of voyeurs like Benjamin Beale himself.

Joy's revelation that I looked a prat did little for my confidence amidst such eye-popping beach-goers. I was going to go for a stroll but opted instead to have a doze. Several yards away, a group of local girls were doing the same. As I lay there, it dawned on me what a particularly odd place the beach was, especially for the Brits. As a socially inhibited bunch, the last place that you would think a typically shy Brit would come for some relaxation was a wide expanse where you were expected to undress in public and lie shoulder to shoulder amidst a crowd of complete strangers.

Bed to most Brits is a most sacred place. Strangers, even extended family, are rarely allowed a peek at the room where… dare I say it… sex is practised. Sleep is an equally private affair. What happens beneath the sheets, whether active or passive, is strictly taboo to all but the closest of friends. To go through the same act in public (the passive one rather than the active one) but without the security of a fleecy bed sheet, runs against the grain of the British psyche. But I guess beaches are like that, exclusive zones allowing exceptional conduct. I mean, how else could you explain the fact that a woman may feel perfectly comfortable exposing her breasts on the beach but wouldn't dream of doing the same in other surroundings, such as around the hotel swimming pool?

I have to admit that I made very little effort to avert my eyes from the tanned flesh parading up and down. Back in Bolton I was used to strolling amongst anoraks, parkas, trench coats and hats, even in summer. Those considering a move from a muffled-up country like England should be forewarned about the culture shock of suddenly finding yourself living amidst a never-ending parade of near-naked, golden bodies. It's not a bad thing, may I hasten to add, but those of a weaker disposition should realise that distractions come thick and fast.

I was pondering these and other facts, about to doze off, when I sensed a shadow slide across me.

'You've not got a bad life, have you?' I recognised the Tyneside accent. It was a middle-aged teacher who was here on holiday with his wife. They'd been in the bar every night since their arrival last week.

'It has its moments,' replied Joy. I contemplated acknowledging the couple but thought better of it and feigned sleep. Joy immediately kicked into hostess mood. 'Look at the colour of you two! You're getting a nice tan.'

'Aye, we're real sun lovers we are, aren't we, pet?'

The woman was acutely aware that we were enjoying time off and probably didn't want to be mithered by customers. 'Aye, we are,' she smiled as she tried to usher her husband away.

'So is this how you spend all your afternoons, then?' he continued.

'I wish,' replied Joy. 'Believe it or not, this is the first time we've been on the beach since we moved here.'

'Aye, away with you. I might look daft but there's more up here than you think,' said the man, tapping his thin grey hair.

'Not a lot, mind,' said his wife. 'Come on, John, these people see enough of us when they're at work. They dinnae want to be mithered by us on the beach an' all. Leave them be.'

But John was having none of it. Two lunchtime pints had set him in bar-room mode and he wanted some banter. 'Joy's alright, aren't you, pet? She doesn't mind. Look, her hubby's asleep. I bet she's glad of the company.'

He sat down next to Joy while his wife remained standing. 'So you're telling me you live by the sea and you've never been on the beach yet? You must be mad.'

Joy was inwardly kicking herself. She took great pride in the fact that many of the customers thought they were her favourite but although it kept them coming back spending money, she couldn't drop the pretence now, even in her time off.

'So how long have you been here, then?' the man continued.

My heart sank at the off-duty interrogation. I could feel the stress beginning to rise. *'Leave us alone for God's sake.'*

'So what made you come out here? Do you like it? Will you ever go back?' The questions were coming thick and fast. The wife had given up. I had to do something. I opened my eyes and yawned as if I'd been in a deep sleep.

'Oh, hello. I thought I heard voices. What time is it?'

'Ten past three,' answered the man.

'Eek! Come on, Joy, we've got to go and meet Mike.' I stood up and shook my towel.

Joy paused for a second before realising what I was doing. 'Oh, right. Yes, I forgot. Well, it's been nice seeing you.'

'Yes, sorry about John,' apologised the woman. 'Two pints and he thinks he's everybody's best friend. C'mon, you.' She pulled him away by the elbow.

As soon as they were out of sight we set the towels back down again.

'You encourage them,' I said to Joy, lying back down.

'I can't blank them, can I?' she replied. 'We can't all be unsociable.'

I let the dig pass. It was bad enough we'd been ambushed. Bickering would certainly put a dampener on our first day of relaxation. I just wanted to spend an afternoon in the sun enjoying a comfortable silence.

'PIÑACOCOPEPSIFANTALEEEEEEEMON!' A man in cut-off denims stood at my feet, shouting in a Jamaican accent. He was holding a large, white plastic bucket. Sweat rolled off his face. 'ANANAS-COCO-PEPSI-FANTA LEEEEEEMON! You want, mister? Here, *ananas*.' Before I had time to ask what ananas was, I found myself holding a wedge of pineapple. The cold juice ran down my still extended arm and plopped onto my stomach.

'*Cuatro cientos*,' demanded the man, holding up four fingers. He held out his hand.

'Err… no thanks, mate,' I said, wiping the sticky mess with a sandy hand. I tried to give him the wedge back but he withdrew his hand.

'400,' he repeated.

'I don't want it.'

His English suddenly took a dramatic turn for the better, the Caribbean lilt subsiding into Liverpudlian. 'You've had your hands all over it. I can't take it back now. Look, it's got sand on it.'

I couldn't be bothered arguing and accepted the dupe, handing him a 1,000 note. He started to walk off, 'PIÑA-COCO-PEPSI-FA… *Que*?' I had hold of his bucket.

'Change. You said 400.'

'Sorry, mate. I wasn't thinking,' he said, handing me the change.

Joy was smiling. 'Want some?' I asked.

'You're a salesman's dream,' she said, shaking her head.

The wind had picked up and I was trying to shelter my wedge from the blowing sand, dripping pineapple juice all over my legs and towel in the process. I gave up, crunching sand between my teeth before spitting it out.

'What else have we got to eat? I'm starving.'

Joy handed me a cheese and ham sandwich from the cool-box but as soon as I put it to my mouth, another gust of wind peppered the bread with sand.

'Don't look,' hissed Joy suddenly, though where I wasn't supposed to look wasn't made clear. I hid behind the sand-coated sandwich, following Joy's gaze out of the corner of her eyes. Another two of our customers had laid down their towels just a few yards beyond the Spanish family.

'It's alright, they've not seen us,' she said. 'Just don't attract their attention.'

In the meantime, a passing fly had zoned in on the sweet pineapple juice that had formed a sticky patch around my belly button.

'Get off, you...' I flailed my arms, trying to shoo the stubborn insect away but it just kept taking off and landing like a trainee helicopter pilot. Another fly joined in the manoeuvres. Then another. Fresh pineapple juice and salty sweat apparently had a formidable allure to beach-bum flies. Before long, it seemed like a squadron had formed with the sole intention of trampolining on my stomach.

'Joe, pack it in,' hissed Joy. 'They're going to see us.' But it was no good. Joy obviously wasn't aware of the assault that was taking place. I stood up and ran to the sea, arms thrashing wildly like windmill sails in a hurricane. After losing the flies in the cold ocean I returned the long way round, hoping we were still inconspicuous.

Joy had started to pack up when I returned. 'Come on, we'd better get back.' It was only four p.m. but several others were also on the move. Judging by their smart clothes, some had come to the beach during their afternoon break, preferring a siesta in the sun to one indoors.

Others were probably more victims of habit, like the old couple who were changing for the third time that I had noticed. They seemed to have swimwear for arriving, swimwear for swimming, another outfit for just lying down and yet more clothes for departing. Both were currently in-between costumes, white octogenarian buttocks wobbling as they gripped each other's arms in a shaky attempt to remain upright. There were more pleasant parting sights to leave the beach with but unfortunately this was the one that was lodged in my mind.

Charley was smoking a cigarette in her garden when we arrived back at the apartment.

'Hi, you two. Had a nice day?'

'We finally got to spend a day on the beach,' answered Joy. 'Well, half a day anyway. I thought you were leaving last night?'

'Yes, so did I, but I've got a job. I'm staying on.'

'That's great. Where are you working?' I asked, climbing over the wall into her garden.

'I'm in timeshare, not selling though,' she added quickly. 'I'll be working in the office, in admin. Fancy a quick drink to celebrate?'

We stepped through the patio doors and into the kitchen. As we did I heard the toilet flush upstairs.

'My boyfriend,' smiled Charley. She shouted up the stairs. 'John? Are you coming down? It's Joe and Joy from next door.'

'Be down in a minute,' came the reply.

Charley poured four glasses of champagne and we toasted her new job and extended holiday.

'Have you noticed the jeep that parks outside our house some nights?' I asked Charley.

I noticed Charley's cheeks flushing. 'No, I can't say I have,' she replied.

'There's a man that sits in it all night, watching. He makes us kind of edgy. I'm thinking about calling the police. What do you think?'

Charley began to choke on the champagne. 'No... I... you... he's probably just a night fisherman, or something,' she spluttered. 'I wouldn't call the police, you know what they're like.'

The fourth glass remained untouched, as we had to get ready for our shift before the mysterious boyfriend made an appearance.

CHAPTER 17

I could delay the inevitable no longer. Buster had taken to spraying any-thing and anybody that remained motionless for more than 30 seconds and the stench was becoming unbearable. It was time he met the manhood scissors.

'He'll take a while to come round from the operation so we'll call you when he's ready,' said the vet. She obviously didn't know Buster.

The snip was scheduled for 10.30 in the morning. Less than hour later I received a call from her assistant, declaring with some amazement that Buster was already wide awake and ready to be picked up. Sure enough, when I arrived, Buster, although scowling and none-too impressed with his loss, was sitting patiently in the surgery waiting for his ride. He dutifully followed me to the car and jumped in without any signs of discomfort.

While Buster's lustful advances may have been nipped in the bud, the two Johns were still in full flow. The winks and insinuations would have been funny were it not that John One seriously thought that Joy was inter-ested in furthering their relationship.

This was another of the undesirable side effects of Joy's congeniality. Whilst most men, especially those old enough to be her granddad, would enjoy the banter and innocent flirting, there were some who mistook it for genuine enticement. She brought a twinkle to the eye and a shine to the heart of many a greying holidaymaker. On several occasions, the partners of these old, new romantics were less than impressed with their spouse's infantile obsession with 'the girl behind the bar' and occasionally Joy's seemingly undivided attention would backfire, the husband banned from any further visits to 'his new girlfriend' – a heartfelt loss for them, a financial one for us.

If innocent flirtation sometimes lost us custom, there was one thing that was sure to gain more patrons – clickety-click, 66.

It was now late November and the sea of faces viewed from behind the bar had changed from the lively surf of suntanned exuberance to the flat, silver calm of a millpond.

There aren't really seasons as such in Tenerife, merely different times of the year for different types of people. Summer, Christmas and most school holidays were obviously the time for families and groups of young students. November to April was the time for the 'fish brigade' as we referred to them due to their partiality for 'a nice bit of fish'. Clickety-click was more or less the average age of our post-summer, pre-Christmas crowd. It was also their favourite pastime abroad.

The stalwarts would arrive twenty minutes before we were due to start, order a tonic water or half a shandy and sit down expectantly, pens poised at the ready until business commenced. If the first card didn't kick off exactly at the time stated on our 'tonight's entertainment' blackboard at the top of the stairs, the clucking began.

'It said ten p.m. It's ten past now.' Bloody revolutions had started on the murmurings of less discontent.

Six cards were the norm for the specialists and as Joy read out the numbers, the concentration was intense. Comments such as: 'Hang on, I've dropped me balls,' as number thirty-three bounced along the floor, were not appreciated.

We never knew who was going to win of course but I could always guarantee who wasn't. Anybody with cards bearing numbers 6 or 84 were in for a long wait. Those particular balls had long since gone into hiding after a mass breakout during an uncharacteristic show of playfulness by Buster amidst our bingo premiere.

We were only playing for a fiver but the solemnity was all-consuming. The urge to laugh was as compelling as a fit of giggles in morning Mass. For Joy, this wasn't helped by the fact that I'd feed her an endless succession of extra-strong Bacardi and Cokes to liven up the evening for both of us.

'One and six, sweet 16.' Silence.

'Kelly's eye, number one.'

'Six and nine, your place or mine, 69.' Disapproving tuts.

'Erm... two little ducks, 22.'

The professionals responded, 'Quack, quack.'

The Bacardi would have kicked in by the second game. Combined with the tense atmosphere, it would only take the slightest silly gesture or daft comment for Joy to lose her self-control.

'Come on!' complained a large woman wearing Day-Glo pink. She glared at Joy like a reprimanding schoolteacher. 'Next number.' But Joy's eyes were watering and her shoulders shaking up and down.

'Eee, jiddy,' said Joy regaining some composure. 'Six and eight, 68. Oh no, hang on. I've got it upside down. Eight and nine, the Brighton line, 89.'

'That's not the Brighton line,' shouted the same lady. 'That's five and nine, the Brighton line. Can we do it properly, please?'

'I'll do my best,' replied Joy, wiping the tears from her cheeks. 'Five oh, blind fifty.'

'Five oh, five oh, it's... off... to... work... we...' the lady stopped singing, aware that it was a solo effort.

'Quite,' said Joy. 'Major's den, the number 10.'

'House!' shouted a squeaky voice from outside. It was Justin.

'How can you have house, Justin? I've only called out thirteen numbers. You need fifteen for a house.

'Oh. Oh yes, I've got two more to get here.'

'Doctor's orders, number nine.'

'House!'

'Justin, you need one more.'

'Oh, right.'

'Top of the shop, blind 90.'

'HOUSE!' It was Justin again. 'Oh no. That's not mine. I need number 30. Sorry.'

Unfortunately the next number to roll out of the little plastic cage was in fact 30.

'Dirty Gertie, number 30.'

'HOUSE! That's me, I've won.' Justin was already racing towards Joy, kicking a couple of chairs in his haste.

'Hang on.' The big lady was on her feet. 'I'm not having that. It's a fix.'

'Sit down, y'old bag!' shouted Wayne, waving his bingo ticket at the big lady.

'I will not sit down. This is a fix. He shouts out the number he's waiting for and next road up it's pulled out. I'm not having that. I want to speak to the manager.'

The other players had started to join in. 'Boo, boo. Shame on you. Sit down. It's only a game.'

'I *am* the manager,' said Joy over the microphone.

'Well what are you trying to pull here?' the fat lady asked, pointing a finger first at Joy and then at a bemused Justin. 'He's a ringer, isn't he? You're trying to con us. She's trying to con us,' she repeated, addressing the crowd.

Frank was shaking his head. He put his pencil behind his ear and folded his arms. 'We're not playing for millions here, you know. It's only a fucking pound.'

The big lady pulled in her bosom. 'Don't you swear at me. Manager! Are you going to allow that kind of language in this bar?'

Joy could sense bingo anarchy was breaking out. 'Can we all just calm down and carry on please!' she shouted through the microphone but her plea was in vain. Insults were being hurled back and forth as the big lady defended herself against the rest of the bar. Wayne screwed up his bingo ticket and flung it at the lady in the middle of the terrace. It struck her on the back of her head.

She wheeled round. 'Who threw that? Come on. Who was it? Did you throw it?' she said pointing a menacing finger at Frank, who was now smirking. As she turned to face him, another ball of paper was thrown from the other end of the terrace. It was Justin's dad. Normally meek and mild, he was visibly shaking and vented his fury using all the might of a scrunched, six-game bingo card.

It wasn't long before the trend had been established and the big lady was pelted from all angles before skulking off amidst a hail of missiles like a defeated sumo wrestler.

The next day, the Czech girl phoned to check if the apartment was still available.

'How much?' she asked.

'25,000 pesetas [£100] per week, 50,000 in total,' said Joy.

'I give 25,000 first, 25,000 after? I don't have more money until end of month.'

Joy agreed and arranged to meet the girl the following day in the bar to take her round to the apartment and hand over the keys.

'Have you told Siobhan yet?' I asked.

'No, I can't get in touch with her. I'll just give her the money when she comes out at Christmas. It'll be a nice surprise for her.'

The couple that had been staying in the apartment had left it immaculate. Scatter cushions were neatly placed along the benches at an alcove dining table. Black and white portraits of classic comedy characters were reflected in the bright sheen of polished pine. In the four corners of the living room, potted cheese plants and cacti added personality to the simple square geometry of the room.

Despite the neat state in which it had been left, Joy still felt the urge to go over the marble floors once more and sprayed the bathroom suite with Windex. She'd also bought a small bouquet of flowers, which she arranged on the kitchen worktop.

At the bar that night, we received a phone call from Julie, the *g storia*.

'You'll be getting a letter from Adeje Town Hall any day. They've decided in all their wisdom that all bars and restaurants in their vicinity have to have a foot tap installed in the kitchen.'

'A foot tap? We've got to wash our feet in the kitchen?' I asked.

'No, you dope. You've got to have a tap that's operated with a foot lever. They're saying that it's unhygienic to use your hands to turn on the tap.'

'More likely a cousin of the mayor has a lorry load of foot taps that he doesn't know what to do with.'

'You're probably right, but just thought I'd let you know,' said Julie before hanging up.

Frank was sitting at the bar complaining how boring life was in Tenerife. 'It's enough to drive you to drink,' he said, adding, 'Another half here, Joy.'

'You bored, Frank?' I asked.

'Shitless,' he replied.

'How are you with plumbing? Reckon you could fit a foot-operated tap in the kitchen for us?'

'I suppose it's something to do for half an hour,' he sighed.

The following morning, he trudged into the bar bearing an assortment of borrowed spanners and wrenches and a foot tap he'd eventually managed to track down at a builder's merchants in Las Chafiras near the airport. The Czech girl arrived at the same time, looking sullen and still upset. She grunted a hello at Joy, ignoring Frank and me.

'What's up with her, miserable bitch? Got a face like a bag of spanners,' said Frank, as Joy took her to see Siobhan's apartment.

'Boyfriend trouble,' I said.

'Mark my words. It's more than that,' he said. 'She looks shifty to me.'

I left him to vent his frustrations with the world by battering the pipes under the kitchen sink with a monkey wrench.

At 5.30 we returned to the bar to get it ready for the usual six o'clock evening start. The preparation was kept to a minimum during this quiet time, a bit of salad to chop, Canarian potatoes to boil and a few chicken fillets to tenderise. I grabbed an iceberg lettuce from one of the Tupperwares in the fridge, twisted the stalk off and held it in the sink whilst I turned on the tap. Nothing happened. I remembered Frank's mission and reached further under the sink for the pedal with my foot. I probed from side to side but failed to locate the new installation. Even when I stepped back to peer underneath there still didn't seem to be a pedal.

I was just about to phone Frank to ask him what had gone wrong when I noticed the shiny edge of new stainless steel hidden behind the rubbish bin three feet to the right. Now on all fours, I pressed it with my hand and sure enough a whoosh of water could be heard overhead in the sink. However, when I tried to turn it on standing in front of the sink, I discovered it was just a few inches beyond reach. I bent my left leg and pointed my right foot like an overweight ballerina but it was futile. It was impossible to stand at the sink and use the foot tap at the same time.

Frank entered the bar. 'Thought you might need this,' he said. He held out an old golf club, a nine-iron to be exact. 'It's one of Danny's. He'll never know, he's got loads.' I opened my mouth but words failed me. I stood back as Frank stood in front of the sink prodding at the foot pedal with the club. 'Hmm, you've still got to lean a bit. Might be better with a wood.'

'Frank, call me simple, but I kind of assumed you'd be able to use the foot pedal with your foot,' I said.

'You can,' he replied and stepped across to where the tap protruded from the wall. 'You just can't do it from the sink. Fucking stupid plumbing system you've got here. The water doesn't come in from under the sink, it comes in over here, so there's no way I could put the pedal there.'

'But that's no good. I can't be swinging a golf club in here every time I want some water,' I complained.

'Don't blame me. Blame the fucking idiot who did the plumbing in the first place. Should've been shot. Anyway, you'll get the hang of it. Here, stand there and give it a go.'

I shook my head in despair and jabbed the pedal with the nine-iron.

'There you go, water,' said Frank.

'Great,' I said with a sarcastic smile. 'Now, if I can just grow another hand, I can actually use the sink.'

The Czech girl had handed over 25,000 pesetas to Joy and asked if she could pay the other 25,000 in four days when she was paid by the hotel.

Joy had agreed, given her the keys and wrote a receipt, noting that the other half was due on the 1st of December. However, the 1st came and went without any sight of the girl. As did the 2nd and the 3rd. On the 4th, Joy received another call from the girl, apologising for not coming in to pay. She explained that she'd been working every night and had not had the chance. She promised to come in the following night and sort it all out.

Nobody had seen her since she moved in. She hadn't been back in the bar for a drink and hadn't been seen either entering or leaving her apartment. The girl now had only five nights left before Siobhan's friends arrived for a fortnight's stay and we were both beginning to wonder if she was intending to pay any more or was just going to do a runner on her last day, next Sunday. That night in the bar, we found out the situation was much worse than that.

It was busy, even for a Tuesday, one of the changeover days. With the nights starting to become colder, plummeting to a chilly 60 Fahrenheit, our customers were forsaking al fresco dining for the nine inside tables. Those in long sleeves and long trousers waited in the bar for their coach transfer to the airport and overnight flights home. The new arrivals, adamant that shorts and T-shirts would be worn no matter what the temperature dictated, studied their faces and exposed skin like it was a barometer for what they could expect.

There were also those foolish few who insisted on wearing beachwear all the way back to the arrivals gate at their UK airport. The wisdom of their choice would be seriously questioned when they stood, ruffled and shivering, shuffling from foot to foot at the luggage carousel as clouds of breath carried muttered obscenities across the empty luggage carousels.

The end of a holiday is like the day after Christmas. The thump of reality presents itself in many guises; the Hoover lying in wait when you return the suitcases to the cupboard under the stairs; the pile of florid laundry seemingly out of place in such familiar and faded surroundings; the thick waft of cold air as you put the cat out last thing at night. All serving to remind that the fortnight of fantasy is now just another memory, destined to fade as quickly as an Anglo-Saxon tan.

'Right, Joe, thanks for all your cooking. We're off now.' Another family had popped their heads into the kitchen to say goodbye. This always made me nervous as it was usually at this point that one of the hardier cockroaches that had somehow escaped the exterminator would be taking an evening stroll along the ceiling or one of the white-tiled walls.

'Take care. It was nice meeting you. See you next year.' I waved them off with a dripping spatula.

Most people only shouted a cursory farewell, aware that it required intense concentration to keep the orders flowing and not frazzle anything. Some however, took the opportunity to show off their 'special relationship' with the chef by spending as long as possible leaning on the serving shelf, forcing a conversation.

Despite the fact that David or I would be dashing around the kitchen in near panic, trying to concentrate on the matter in hand and only grunting when we guessed it was necessary to respond, they would still carry on with their chosen topic, getting in the way when Joy would try to take out the plates.

'Anyway, nice to talk to you. I can see you're busy,' they'd say eventually, unaware of just how close they were to being surgically fitted with a pair of catering tongs.

'Joe, look who's here!' Joy exclaimed, leading an old couple into the kitchen. She often did this. Not as any act of public relations, just because she liked to see me squirm. She may have had a photographic memory capable of remembering the names, preferred drinks, favourite food and collar size of every single customer that walked through our doors, but she knew damn well that I wouldn't have the slightest clue as to the identity of the people being paraded in front of me.

'Heeellooo,' I said with feigned sincerity. 'Nice to see you again. Long time no see.' Thankfully this was always enough to fool them into thinking that I really did remember. Behind them, Joy was knowingly shaking her head, dismayed at my lack of recognition.

'Yes, it's exactly a year,' said the man. He was dressed in a blue blazer, one of the old school of airline passengers.

'Well it's good to have you back,' I said with all the sincerity I could muster. 'I'll come out for a drink in a minute.' Joy would wheel them out making dumb gestures at me for my memory deficiency.

Not only was the night busy for orders, it was also busy with people bidding farewell and Joy trying to catch me out with new arrivals. However, I did recognise the next person she brought in and this time Joy wasn't smiling.

'Tell him what you've just told me.' Joy had her arms folded and was standing behind the Czech girl, blocking the doorway.

'I have problem. I no place to go Friday,' said the girl quietly.

'Well, I'm sorry but you have to leave. The owner's friends have booked the apartment from Friday. Sorry,' I said sympathetically.

'My boyfriend he know law. You not make me sleep on beach. He talk with lawyer. I not leave Friday. I use money I owe you for lawyer.'

'Whoa, hold on,' I said, waving a meat cleaver. The girl recoiled. 'You *are* leaving on Friday and you *are* going to pay the rest of the money.' I was leaning over the serving shelf, inches from the girl. She was nervous and understandably uncomfortable with the cleaver waving but still adamant that she wasn't moving out.

'I want speak with owner,' said the girl.

Siobhan still didn't know that there was someone renting her apartment. Joy was worried that she might think she was letting it out behind her back in order to keep the money, a common ploy in resort areas. She dialled Siobhan's number and told her what had happened, apologising at the end of every sentence.

'Put her on,' demanded Siobhan. She was not a woman to be messed with. We had seen her turn on Mike on several occasions, almost reducing the ex-soldier to tears. Joy handed the phone to the girl. The colour drained from her face as soon as Siobhan started.

'Right, you bitch. You get out of my apartment, do you hear? I have friends coming on Friday and I want you out. And if you don't pay the rest of that money, you're in deep shit, lady. Do you hear me? DEEP SHIT!' I could hear Siobhan's sharp, Northern Irish accent from across the kitchen.

'It's not me. It's boyfriend. He know law.' The girl was almost apologetic but Siobhan was having none of it.

'I don't care if it's you *or* your boyfriend. Get the fuck out of my apartment. Now put Joy back on.' She passed it back to Joy.

'Joy, get that fucking bitch out of my apartment.' The line went dead. Siobhan had slammed the phone down. The girl started to walk out.

'Hey, you're getting out on Friday,' said Joy, grabbing her arm.

'No,' said the girl, shaking her head. I rushed round the serving shelf still brandishing the cleaver.

'Yes-you-are,' I said, emphasising each word with a jab of the knife. I was furious at the girl's obstinacy. The girl quietly walked out with her head down.

'What are we going to do?' said Joy, panic in her eyes.

'She'll go,' I said. 'She'll *have* to.'

CHAPTER 18

The following day we visited the community president. Roger was a retired headmaster who spent every other month in Tenerife with his wife, Brenda.

'Ahh, our very own smugglers,' said Roger, looking down his nose. 'Do come in.'

Since taking over the bar and renting Roger's apartment for the first few weeks, we had tried to stay on the right side of the community committee, and Roger in particular. Residential committees can make life difficult for an on-site business owner, regarding commercial enterprises as a necessary evil.

We had only fallen foul of the community rules and regulations twice. The first occasion was when Gary and Michelle had forgotten to turn the outside speakers off as required at midnight. 'Good vibrations' were certainly not forthcoming the following day from residents and committee members after the Beach Boys had warbled well into the witching hour.

Fortunately the police weren't called. Any bar that gets stung three times by their decibel meter is immediately shut down and wrapped in pretty red and white crime scene-style tape for a period of time ranging from one week to three months – a pretty serious punishment for an overdose of the Beach Boys.

The second time was after our clothes maiden buckled under the combined weight of two dozen wet bar towels and Buster's acrobatics as he hunted for a soft surface to sunbathe on. Sheer apathy in the midsummer sun had prevented us from making a trip to the nearest hardware shop to replace it. Instead, we hung all our clean washing on the backs of the terrace chairs. It was not a pretty sight, I have to admit, especially as some of the bar towels were charred and fraying.

'Move those towels,' the president had bellowed, following murmurs of community discontent. The timeshare reps were also none too happy. Trying to persuade stubborn holidaymakers to invest in 'a piece of paradise' wasn't made easier when paradise looked like a Chinese laundry.

Being community president is a thankless task. It's a post that requires a thick skin, an authoritative tone and the ability to keep warring nations apart during disputes over what television channels should be made available to the community.

Who in their right mind would want to stir up the dust as chief castigator and troubleshooter in such a paradisiacal environment, and all for no reward, neither verbal nor financial?

Well, those who feel at a loss once retirement strips them of any authority. A retired headmaster for one. Roger certainly revelled in the role. Rarely would he be seen without a clipboard on his daily tours of inspection, jotting down notes and taking offenders' names should the opportunity to formally chastise arise.

Just as when members of the local police force would drop in for a drink, Roger's beer was always on the house. An obvious ploy but one that was seemingly appreciated, as it made his role seem even more authoritative. Joy of course, also managed to work her charm on the president, flirting like they were secret lovers.

It was because of this attention that Roger would overlook some of our less serious crimes, like not flattening our boxes in the rubbish container or keeping a pet on the premises. It was also why he was always willing to help if we had a problem that related to the community.

Inside Roger's apartment, Brenda sat on a large, pale orange sofa, reading a book. Her feet didn't quite reach the floor and the scale of the oversized furniture made her seem like a child. She looked up and smiled a shy smile.

Roger led us past and out onto the patio where two white, plastic sunloungers faced the sea. He insisted we sit down while he stood, arms folded, nodding sympathetically as we told him about the Czech girl and her threats of not moving. Having a squatter on the complex would certainly not look good for him as president and his cheeks grew red with rage as he listened intently.

'Right, well, we'll throw her out. Simple as that. I'm not having some hippy think she can take over my complex.

We made a plan to enter Siobhan's apartment when we knew the Czech girl was out, pack her things and change the locks.

The following day Wayne was set on detective duties and told to inform us the moment the girl left for work. Then we called for Roger who in turn commandeered Miguel, the *technico*, to follow with a new lock.

The four of us climbed the stairs quietly whilst Wayne maintained his vigil on Cardiac Hill.

'Have you got the keys?' he whispered to Joy.

'Yes, they're here,' she replied, handing him the bunch.

Roger took the key and put it in the lock.

'It won't turn,' he hissed.

'Here, let me try,' said Joy.

'They've changed the locks,' said Roger solemnly. The stakes had been raised.

David had become increasingly withdrawn over the past few weeks as his attempted reconciliation conversations with Faith were ending in a race to see who could slam the phone down first. He decided that, as it was quiet, he would go back to the UK for ten days in a last ditch effort to persuade Faith to return to Tenerife. If it proved that this was not going to happen, he could begin the process to sort out the sale of his house in Salford. This meant that Joy and I would be running the bar alone for the next ten nights. The extra worry of the squatters couldn't have come at a worse time.

Joy and I were unloading our car with what I hoped was enough stock to last us for a few days to spare the daily shopping routine but there was a limit to how much you could fit in a hatchback.

'*Pod mos hab ar?*' From over an armful of kitchen rolls, I could see no more than the receding hairline of a man standing in front of me.

'Sorry?'

'He said, can we talk?'

I recognised the voice of the Czech girl. I dumped the kitchen rolls back into the boot of the car and turned to face them. The girl was standing behind a wiry Spaniard in a blue checked shirt that was several sizes too big for him. A thin moustache partly obscured a wry smile. He stared, unblinking, waiting for my response, eyebrows raised, challenging me.

'Can you speak Spanish?' asked the girl. She kept her gaze on the floor. Her long brown hair was scraped back and up, fastened messily on top of her head making her look altogether more severe.

'No,' I replied curtly.

'Then we need a translator.'

'You translate,' I said.

'He doesn't want it.'

I led them to the Altamira where Marie, one of the receptionists, was picking her nose. I explained the situation and Marie agreed to help.

The man opened the conversation, claiming that because there was no contract, he wasn't moving out.

'Hang on a minute,' I said. 'You're not even in. How can you move out? Our agreement was with the girl, not you. As far as we're concerned, you're not even there.' I waited for Marie to translate. The man listened impassively. When she had finished, he told her that he was called Pedro and was the girl's boyfriend and he was living with her. He said it didn't matter who the initial agreement was with.

'This is the first we've heard about this scumbag,' said Joy to Marie but she just shrugged her shoulders and raised her hands defensively.

'Hey, I'm just translating, remember?'

Pedro turned round and mumbled to the girl quietly.

'Listen,' whispered Marie. 'Be careful. This man is dangerous. Just watch what you say.'

He continued to explain his side of the story to Marie.

'He says that he's lodged the money he owes you at the court in Granadilla until you settle the dispute. After that the owner of the apartment can go up there with a receipt and collect it.'

We repeated that the owner's friends were due out the day after tomorrow and asked if he expected us to make them sleep on the beach but as Marie translated, the man just shrugged.

'He says it's not his problem,' said Marie. She sighed. 'He says if you want him to leave your apartment you'll have to find him somewhere else to stay.'

Like us, Marie was realising that this was no ordinary chancer trying to get a few weeks' free rental. My stomach began to knot at the realisation that this wasn't going to be resolved easily.

'How long are you planning on staying there?' I asked.

Marie relayed that he was due to move into another apartment soon but it was being renovated. Maybe it would be ready in two weeks. I offered to pay for a room at a hostel in Los Cristianos for two weeks if he'd move out right now. He smiled. 'It's not that simple,' he told Marie. 'He'd have to speak to his lawyers and would meet us again tomorrow.'

Marie apologised and said she had to get back to work.

'I'd get a lawyer if I were you,' she whispered. 'This man is no good.' She walked back behind the reception, leaving Joy and me to face Pedro and the Czech girl alone. Pedro was staring at me, a smug smile on his face. The girl was pretending to study a rack of postcards on the reception desk.

Joy and I brushed past him, maintaining eye contact.

'*Mañana*,' he shouted after us as we crossed the car park on our way to get the bar ready.

'Have him done over,' said Frank, matter-of-factly. 'It's the only way you'll get him out.' The night had started slowly, allowing us time to tell him what had happened.

With two days to go before Siobhan's friends arrived, it was a serious consideration. The more people we told, the more we heard the same advice. Later that night, Wayne accompanied a familiar figure into the kitchen.

'Joe, this is Adam. He's offering his services.'

'Hi, we've met,' I said, shaking his hand. The blank look suggested it wasn't a mutual recollection.

'He's here to help you with your problem,' said Wayne.

This was all happening too quickly. I hadn't come to Tenerife to start employing hit men. I was a bar owner, a taxpayer, a nice guy. I also didn't want to seem ungrateful to a burly hit man who was standing in my kitchen expecting employment.

'I thought you worked for Micky?' I asked.

'I do,' he answered, 'but I do a bit of moonlighting. I've got a family to support.' He suddenly looked alarmed. 'Don't tell Micky though.'

'Err... course not. How much is it, out of curiosity?' I asked, not wanting to dismiss him without so much as a whiff of curiosity about his line of work.

'Depends what you want,' he barked. 'Here, take this. Give me a call.' He handed me a piece of paper.

In my hand was a typewritten list of services ranging from 'ruffed up a bit' to 'lost at sea'. The prices ran alongside. He must have been running a special on two broken legs, as the cost seemed much more economical than just having the one broken.

'Seems very reasonable,' I commented, failing to think of any other response that might be appropriate. 'I'll give you a shout.'

Adam left. What was I getting into? In just one short phone call I could change somebody's life forever – end it even. It would also change mine. I would have crossed the line, opened the door to gangland. The thought made me go cold, but it was also strangely empowering, like holding a loaded gun. I glanced again at the list. There was no listing for 'scare him a little but without hurting him'. I screwed the piece of paper up and threw it in the bin. Then I thought of the smug smile on his face and picked it out again, smoothing out the creases on the worktop. I filed it under the microwave with our health and hygiene certificate. Just as a last resort, I told myself.

Although deep down I had no intention of employing Dial-a-Hitman, the revelation that this kind of service was so readily available gave me an idea for our next meeting with the squatters.

They were already at the reception desk when Joy and I arrived. Pedro was attempting to make conversation with Marie but she had her head down and was busying herself shuffling papers.

'*Buenos días*,' he said to us with a smile.

'You don't mind me taking your photo do you?' I asked, revealing a camera that I was holding behind my back. Before he could answer I pressed the shutter. Pedro was startled but made no attempt to conceal his face.

'I have nothing to hide,' he said through Marie. With one arm resting on the reception desk and a hand placed cockily on his hip, he posed again.

The flash popped for the second time.

The Czech girl was standing behind him and looked away.

'Why do you want my picture?' he asked, as I pressed the shutter for a third time.

'I have a friend who wants to see it.' I emphasised the word 'friend'. His cheesy grin faltered and his bushy eyebrows that were raised in cocksure manner collapsed downwards.

He put out a hand to stop me taking any more and turned to Marie.

'He says he didn't manage to meet his lawyer and has arranged another appointment at 10.30 on Monday morning,' translated Marie. Pedro's speech was gaining momentum, his arms gesticulating wildly. Marie put her hands up in defence and turned to talk to me. 'I told you to be careful what you said,' she sighed. 'He's saying you called him a *bandid* and if you're not prepared to come to some agreement, he's taking you to court. He also wants me to give a witness statement but I told him I'm not getting involved. I don't mind translating as a favour for you and Joy, but I'm not being drawn into any legal battles.'

I apologised to Marie for involving her so far and asked her to arrange one more meeting for the following Monday. It was evident that the squatters had no intention of leaving soon. Tomorrow, Siobhan's friends arrived and we had little time to find them alternative accommodation.

I waved the Polaroids in Pedro's face and gave him what I hoped was a threatening a stare.

It worked. So much so that he had shared his anxiety with the *Guardia*

Civil, a high-booted member of which was now standing in the doorway of my apartment, waving a *d nuncia* at me for 'insulting and threatening behaviour'.

The *d nuncia*, or complaint, had been formally made by Pedro and required me to attend a court hearing to determine if the charge was to be upheld. Any thoughts of employing a leg-breaker were out of the window. If any harm came to Pedro now, having already informed the police that he had been threatened, a leather-gloved finger would be pointing my way quicker than I could say, 'One-way ticket to Manchester, please.'

Joy was in tears. Her emotions were divided between frustration, fear, hate and exhaustion. With David away, we had little time to be dealing with this added pressure, especially after a succession of sleepless nights.

There was also an overriding anger at the audacity of Pedro and his Czech girlfriend. He knew exactly what he was doing; he'd obviously pulled this stunt before. It was a thought that did little to raise any hope that we might beat him. We were up against a professional conman who knew the law and was smart enough to pre-empt a defence against one of our very few options.

The time had come to seek legal advice. We made an appointment with one of the top lawyers based in Las Americas.

The interior was a far cry from the clutter and mess of Julie's workplace. Joy and I sank deep into a brown leather sofa, soft music playing in the background. Our feet rested on a dark red carpet, the first carpet I'd seen in Tenerife. Gilt-edged certificates decorated the rich gold and claret flock wallpaper like record company awards and also, unlike at Julie's place, we were offered coffee that was served in china rather than re-used plastic cups.

The passing of time was marked by the clicking of a computer keyboard and a muffled conversation taking place behind one of three closed doors. Periodically we exchanged smiles with the receptionist, who was playing a frantic rhythm on the keys with long and glossy manicured nails.

Before we could finish our coffees, the receptionist opened the door that was concealing the conversation and gestured for us to go in.

The office was even more impressive than the waiting area. The view through smoked glass windows looked across a cluster of palms to the glittering ocean. Directly below, rental cars and taxis played dodgems, muted by the thick panes.

Across a broad glass table-top, Señor Santana, the lawyer, motioned for us to sit. At his side was a slender lady in her early twenties. The severe cut of her pencil skirt contrasted wildly with the curvature peeping between the buttons of a white cotton blouse.

'Good morning,' said the girl. 'I believe you don't speak Spanish, no?'

Joy and I shook our heads ashamedly. She tutted, half-joking.

'I am Josephine Perez, Señor Santana's assistant. I will translate for you.'

I explained all about the Czech girl, her boyfriend and the *d nuncia* that had been served on me. Josephine scrawled notes on a yellow-leaf A4 pad, nodding to add weight to Pedro's argument and shaking her head sympathetically as and when the story required.

She translated the tale to the lawyer, who rocked to and fro in a square-backed leather chair. When Josephine finished, he uttered a few words and motioned for her to speak on his behalf.

'This man, Pedro, he does know the law. I daresay he has done this many times before. As for the court case, do not worry, I will represent you. I doubt that Pedro will even show up, in which case the charge will be thrown out. But your immediate problem is how to get your friend's apartment back, yes?'

We nodded.

'The problem is this. Because there is no end date stated on the contract, he is legally allowed to stay there until he finds somewhere else. By Spanish law, you can't evict someone if it means they'll be homeless. I'm assuming he says he has nowhere else to go, yes?'

We confirmed the fact.

'Because this is the owner's second home, she can't claim that she is being made homeless by his living there. In the eyes of the law, he has more right to have that roof over his head than the owner.'

'So what can we do? There must be a way that we can get rid of him,' said Joy, exasperated.

'Oh, there is. We can file a *d nuncia*, take him to court and have him re-housed. We can start proceedings now, if you like.'

'Okay, let's do that,' I said, pleased that is seemed like a step forwards.

'But there's one catch,' said Josephine. 'It will take anywhere from two to five years.'

'We can't wait that long.' Joy had stood up, the anger rising again. 'I have to get him out. It's not my apartment. Siobhan will kill me.'

'Unfortunately the law always favours the tenant in these circumstances,' explained Josephine. 'I'm sorry.' She raised her palms in defeat.

We rose to leave.

'Let me talk to Señor Santana,' she whispered, holding the door open. 'Wait outside for a minute.'

We sank back into the sofa, dejected, despondent and defeated. My mind flicked to the shopping list under the microwave. *Denuncia* or no *d nuncia*, it was fast becoming the only option.

Joy had her head in her hands. 'I can't believe this is happening. I feel like asking Micky to sort him out.' I hadn't told Joy about the list. She was more likely to utilise the services than me, happy to ignore the future consequences. However, my logic told me that once we crossed that line we would be different people. We also didn't know if Pedro had connections. Having him beaten up may well have sparked gangland retribution. At this moment of last resorts, I was just pondering whether to tell her anyway when Josephine came out of the office and sat in an armchair next to us.

'There is another way,' she started, 'but you didn't hear it from me, OK?'

We both nodded, intrigued as she told us about the unofficial plan B.

Siobhan was in tears when Joy phoned to say that we'd failed to get the squatters to move out. Fortunately we had managed to find alternative accommodation for her friends in an apartment in the Altamira. A mutual friend had heard of our plight and offered to lend us her apartment for a nominal fee. Naturally this fee was to be paid by us, in addition to the lawyer's fee and any fines we may incur over the *d nuncia*.

Siobhan's mood did lighten however when we told her about the plan, and even though it meant that she would have to get on a plane to Tenerife herself, she was somewhat heartened that action was now being taken. In the meantime, we had appointed a 'team of detectives' to find out more about the couple of squatters.

Barry was put on static surveillance duty, keeping track of the movements in and out of Siobhan's apartment. He stationed himself at a bay window seat in Mrs Tanner's apartment, diagonally opposite Siobhan's. Not only did he have a clear view of the steps leading up to the one and only entrance to the apartment but he also had an unlimited supply of tea and home-made scones that Mrs Tanner forced on him with remarkable regularity.

Wayne was assigned to tail Pedro in the Smugglersmobile (when we weren't loading it with beans and tuna). We were curious to find out what the Spaniard did during the day and whether he worked or not. Wayne, not one of the world's most patient characters, said he would have preferred to just beat him up and torture the knowledge out of him. I explained that this would invariably lead to me being arrested and thus he would more than likely be out of a job with us.

Frank took on the last of our tasks, accompanied by his detective side-kick and Spanish translator, Danny. They were to take the Polaroids to the Hotel Conquistador and make enquiries as to whether the Czech girl was actually working there.

For our part, in between running the bar and making sure that Siobhan's friends were alright, we had to buy a list of items that were necessary for the implementation of plan B.

The first to report back with a breakthrough was Wayne. He'd followed Pedro to an apartment in Las Americas. After abandoning the car for a closer look, he'd seen Pedro opening the apartment with a key and leaving several hours later in different clothes.

'It seems like the slimy fucker has another home,' he beamed. This was a big breakthrough and was the first bullet we needed in the gun that was going to get rid of the two unwanted guests.

I flipped the lid off a bottle of Newcastle Brown for a job well done. As Wayne glugged down the contents, Frank trudged in with Danny in tow. He tossed the Polaroid on the bar.

'Nobody's ever seen her at the Conquistador. She doesn't work there now, never has.' It was bullet number two.

At the courts in Granadilla, a small army of wrong-doers and wrong-done-tos lined the curving staircase leading up to the two courtrooms. Both sides exchanged furtive, and some not-so-furtive, glances. Josephine joined Joy and me at the top of the stairs.

'Any sign of Pedro?' asked Joy.

'No, I'll be very surprised if he shows up,' she replied. 'Give me the photo you took of him, I'll ask some of my colleagues if they know him.'

A quarter of an hour later she was back.

'Just as we thought. Our friend Pedro is well known up here. He's a professional.'

Just then a clerk called our names and we entered the courtroom. The wooden floors creaked as we edged into a church-like pew facing a large arched window. In front of the window sat a man in his senior years. I thought he was sleeping, until he lifted his head to peer at us for a moment before continuing to study a ream of papers I could now see were resting on his lap.

'That's the judge,' said Josephine.

Unlike the theatre of British courtrooms, curly grey wigs and school-teacher cloaks were conspicuous by their absence. Instead, the man wore an open-necked, pale blue shirt under a slate grey jacket. A trio of ancillary workers busied themselves with their own paperwork, glancing at the judge occasionally to check if he was ready to proceed. He finally gave one the slightest of nods. An attendant cleared his throat and gave what I presumed was a summary of the case. The judge peered up again without lifting his head and mumbled something in Spanish. Josephine replied, indicating our presence with her hand. He then read out Pedro's name and waited for a response. Josephine said something back, to which the judge let out a long sigh and with his eyes still studying the paperwork, shooed us from the court with the back of his hand.

'That's it. It's over,' said Josephine as we closed the courtroom door behind us.

'That's it?' I repeated.

'Pedro didn't show up so the case was thrown out. I spoke with the judge before we went in. He's dealt with Pedro's games before. He knew he wouldn't show up again.'

Relief swept through me as we ran down the handful of steps outside the court. Pedro had gained nothing but he had cost us half a day of our time, several sleepless nights and the equivalent of two hundred pounds for Josephine's representation.

We had less than an hour to get back to the bar in time for opening. Our resolve to defeat him was strengthened as we sped back to El Beril. We passed through a succession of tiny white hamlets, thoughts of our own justice masking the beauty of Tenerife's pretty interior.

Black-frocked widows standing in low doorways paused their chatting to watch a car of foreigners speeding through their village. A huddle of old men, sitting on a bench beneath the shade of a sprawling laurel tree, eyed our hasty progress, shaking their heads disdainfully at this intrusion of fast forward in their world of slow motion.

We were not only in a rush to open the bar in time for the first wave of hungry holidaymakers but also we wanted to find out if Barry had gathered enough information to enable us to put the plan into action tomorrow.

First through the doors, as expected, was Siobhan. Pedro's abhorrent smugness had petrified our own anxiety into solid anger. Siobhan was without this advantage and was still clearly shaken at the events.

She was trembling, her face pale and drawn. From the puffiness round her eyes, it was obvious she had been crying on the plane. Although she preferred to portray a hard edge, it was merely protection, sheltering fraught nerves and an edgy temperament.

Living in Northern Ireland during the Troubles, especially when married to a British soldier, had wreaked havoc on her emotions and like many in the same situation, she had withdrawn deeper into her own personal bomb shelter.

None of the rage she had spat down the phone was evident now that the reality of confrontation was close. Instead of anger as a companion, she had brought her son-in-law and introduced us to him.

We had met Terry once before when he had stayed in Siobhan's apartment with his then fiancée, her daughter, for a week earlier in the season. They shared a common shyness as well as love and we hadn't seen much of them. But this time, the timidity was gone. He had shaved his head and the roundness of his body had been squared off, taut in every way, including his manner.

'How y'doing?' he said, accepting a handshake and without a smile.

'Terry insisted on coming,' explained Siobhan. 'I said there was no need, we were getting it sorted, but he wouldn't have it.'

'I'm going to teach that fucking slimeball a lesson,' said Terry. The muscles on his jawbone throbbed as he clenched his teeth. He looked like he was going to explode.

'Hold on, Terry,' said Joy. 'We've just come back from court today. We can't just wade in. This guy knows what he's doing. If we lay one finger on him Joe and I will be back in front of the judge again and this time we might not be so lucky. Let's just stick to the plan and then, down the line, when the dust has settled, you can do whatever you like.'

'Alright, but if I see him I can't promise he won't get a smack,' said Terry. 'Just keep him away from me.'

Joy gave Siobhan a key to our apartment. They were staying with us, hopefully only for a night if things went according to plan tomorrow.

'Tuesday 8.13 a.m., white Caucasian male leaves apartment.'

Barry was reading from a small, black notebook he had bought for 'the operation'. 'Tuesday 9.15 a.m., white Caucasian female leaves apartment.'

'Tuesday 5.10 p.m., white Caucasian female…'

'Barry?' Joy interrupted.

'Yes?'

'Call them Pedro and the Czech girl, will you?'

'Okay. Right, where was I? Ah, yes. Tuesday 5.10 p.m., white Cau… sorry… Czech girl and Pedro arrive back at the apartment together. Wednesday 8.10 a.m., Pedro leaves. At 9.22 a.m. the Czech girl leaves. Thursday is the same, give or take five minutes.'

'Thanks, Barry. That's great. We now know when the apartment's unoccupied,' said Joy.

'Unless they break the routine tomorrow,' I added. We exchanged glances.

'We'll just have to hope they don't, then,' said Joy.

CHAPTER 19

At 9.30 the following morning, Joy, Siobhan, Terry, Wayne, Frank and I were sitting in Roger's apartment, waiting for Barry to inform us that the squatters had left. An hour later, there was still no word.

I sneaked out of the apartment, careful not to be seen from Siobhan's balcony, which looked down on Roger's front door. Having taken a wide detour around the swimming pool to avoid any danger of being spotted, I knocked quietly at Barry's lookout post. After a few seconds, Mrs Tanner opened the door. She tilted her head and beamed radiantly.

'Tea?' she enquired, holding aloft a small brown teapot.

'Ah, no, no thanks. Is Barry here?'

'Yes, come in, he's just finishing his breakfast.' I followed Mrs Tanner inside. Barry was sitting at a table in the bay window finishing off the last remnants of a full fry-up. Three grey-haired ladies were sitting with him, watching his every mouthful. On seeing me, he started to choke on a piece of bacon rind. Mrs Tanner strode over and gave him a hearty whack between the shoulder blades.

'I… err… I was just coming to tell you,' he spluttered. 'They've left.'

'When?'

'About half an hour ago. Elsie here, was kind enough to make me breakfast while I was on stakeout. It would have been rude to refuse.' He looked at me apologetically. I rolled my eyes. Mrs Tanner gazed at Barry lovingly, then turned back to me.

'It's very exciting, isn't it? Would you like some breakfast before you… how did you put it, Barry… storm the apartment?' I politely declined. It was no surprise that Barry was happy to spend so much time watching Siobhan's with Mrs Tanner fussing over him. He'd obviously dramatised the situation, as Mrs Tanner had invited round several friends to watch the action.

'When are you smashing down the door?' asked one of them, excitedly.

'Err... as soon as Barry's finished his toast,' I replied.

'Good. I'll get my Kodak ready,' she replied.

Barry followed me back to Roger's apartment, where the rest of the group were growing anxious, particularly Siobhan.

'If we don't do something soon,' she whispered, 'Terry's going to start without us.' I looked over at Terry who was outside, pacing up and down the small patio at the back of the apartment.

'Right, Barry says they've gone, so if everybody's ready, let's go.'

Terry shot in from the patio and was already opening the front door to leave the apartment. I grabbed his arm.

'Remember, Terry, you can have him after we've sorted this out.'

Terry just grunted, picking up the holdall he had left at the entrance.

We marched in unison up two short steps of stairs and around the block to Siobhan's apartment. I motioned to the others to stay at the bottom while I quietly climbed the stairs leading up to Siobhan's door. After checking that there were no signs of life within, I called the others up.

Terry was first. He scaled the 20 or so stairs in just four bounds. In one swift motion, he pulled a portable drill out of the holdall and dropped the bag on the floor. Barry and Wayne were keeping watch either way at the bottom of the stairs.

'All clear?' I hissed.

Just as they both gave the thumbs up, my mobile rang. It was Joy. She'd gone to the top of Cardiac Hill to keep watch on the road. I put my hand on Terry's arm to halt him.

'He's coming back,' she hissed, 'Pedro's on his way back.'

'Quick,' I shouted to the others. 'He's coming back. Everybody back to Roger's.'

Wayne, Barry, Frank, Siobhan and Roger scattered like sprayed cockroaches but Terry was taking his time putting the drill back in the bag.

'You'll get your chance later, Terry. You agreed to do it my way first.' I grabbed the bag and pushed him towards the stairs. After just five minutes poised behind the front door of Roger's apartment, Joy phoned again to say Pedro had left.

We all filed out and assumed our previous positions. Terry carefully positioned the drill bit over the lock and pulled the trigger. Nothing happened. He shook the drill and slapped it a few times but still it refused to work.

'Fucking thing. Battery's dead.'

I was just about to ask, rather belatedly, whether he had charged it when my phone rang again.

'I have king prawn this week. You want?' It was Captain Birdseye, our fish deliveryman.

'Err... no thanks.'

'It's very fresh.'

'No, that's OK.'

'How about swordfish?'

'No thanks.'

'Nice swordfish steaks. You try?'

'No, listen, I'll call you back, OK?' I snapped shut the case and pondered the new dilemma. 'We need an extension lead,' I shouted to the five at the bottom of the stairs.

'I've got one!' shouted Siobhan.

'Great. Can you get it quickly?' I replied.

'Yes, I'll... oh... it's in my apartment.' Everybody turned to look at her.

'Well, go and get it then,' said Barry. He fluttered his hands at Siobhan, urging her on.

'My apartment. The one we're *trying* to get into,' explained Siobhan.

'Ah,' said Barry after a moment of pondering.

'I'll get mine,' said Roger. He bounded back around to his apartment.

'Barry, will you see if we can plug it in at Mrs Tanner's, then run the cable through the window? I pointed up at the bay window where four ladies were waving cheerily. We all waved back, dutifully.

With power restored, Terry began drilling the lock, ending what little discretion we had so far managed with a banshee squeal of twisting metal. After three choruses of high-pitched whining he managed to dismantle the lock and pushed the door open.

'We're in!' I waved the others up. My own preconception of what a squat would look like was immediately extinguished. Gone were Siobhan's family portraits and screen stars pictures. But instead of geometrical dust lines signalling their departure, new pictures and wall hangings had been hung in their place. The living room furniture had been rearranged around a new sunset-coloured rug and beanbags were scattered throughout the room. It was quite an improvement on Siobhan's design but I thought better than to mention it.

'The cheeky bastards,' said Siobhan, surveying 'the carnage'. 'They've changed everything around.'

'I think it looks better,' said Barry. His abysmal bar skills were only matched by his abhorrent lack of diplomacy.

Wayne shouted from the bedroom. 'Look in here!'

Siobhan recoiled and put her hand to her mouth. 'Oh sweet lord, the dirty bitch.'

The bed was decked in black silk. A pair of handcuffs rested on one of the pillows, still fastened to the headboard. On a chair in the far corner lay a short, leather whip and next to it, a video camera was mounted on a tripod.

Wayne broke the stunned silence. 'I hate to say it Siobhan but I think your place is now a brothel.'

'Just what this shithole needs,' said Frank, rubbing his hands together.

The suspicion was confirmed as we packed everything into bin liners. Next to the television was a stack of videos, the titles of which left no doubt as to their genre. Barry noticed there was one, unlabelled, half way out of the video recorder. He pushed it back in and turned on the TV.

We all turned to stare at the groans and heavy breathing emanating from a black-haired woman straddling a man. Her back was to the camera but the room furnishings were alarmingly familiar.

'That's my bedroom!' shrieked Siobhan.

We peered a little closer. Silent nods confirmed her suspicion. The girl flicked her hair, turning her face to the camera for a split second. There was no doubt that it was the Czech girl. Although the man was half concealed, it was evident that it wasn't Pedro. The legs were too flabby and even though we weren't exactly friends, I'd gauged enough of an opinion to surmise that he wasn't the sort to wear black socks whilst he had sex.

'Turn it off!' screamed Siobhan, crossing herself.

Barry and Frank were glued to the screen, arms folded.

'Barry! Frank! Turn that godforsaken filth off!' shouted Siobhan.

'Oh… sorry,' said Barry, as he fumbled with the remote control.

It took another half hour for the six of us to stuff everything into the bin liners. When we had finished, we taped a note on each. Josephine had warned Joy and me not to be around when the couple returned to Siobhan's apartment due to potential legal repercussions. While Siobhan and Terry remained behind to clear up and wait for their return, Joy, Barry, Frank, Wayne and I sat in the bay window of Mrs Tanner's apartment to await the showdown. Roger had made himself scarce. He deemed it unfit for the community president to become embroiled in possible physical altercations.

We nervously watched Mrs Tanner's carriage clock. The brass timepiece stood proudly between a pair of ceramic Siamese cats. It was a token of appreciation from British Aerospace to the late Mr Tanner for 45 years' loyal service tightening the nuts of Britain's airborne fighting fleet.

The dozens of photographs that were slipped in front of us as we waited showed a happy couple in various decades of courtship, each era proving that Mrs Tanner was a great believer in the old adage that suggested the way to a man's heart was indeed through his stomach. Her aim had been direct. A compulsion to force-feed him home-baked confectionery may well have been a contributing factor to her husband's expanding girth, and consequently, his fatal heart attack the day before his 64th birthday.

The hands ticked quietly towards 5.10 p.m. and the chat fell silent. Even Mrs Tanner's three excited friends ceased their merriment and gazed down across the narrow passageway to Siobhan's apartment.

By 5.30 p.m. Joy and I were starting to grow anxious. We had to open the bar in half an hour but we were determined to watch the climax. The couple had put us through so much worry over the past few weeks that we were desperate to witness the closure.

As the clock showed 5.45 p.m. we were beginning to think that Pedro and the Czech girl weren't going to come back that evening.

'Have you seen the time?' I asked Joy quietly. 'We're going to have to go and open.'

'Shh,' said Barry suddenly. 'They're here.'

Pedro was walking ahead of the Czech girl. Both had their heads down, looking glum. We all inched away from the window in order not to be seen. We watched them both trudge up the steps, still staring at their feet. It was only when Pedro was three steps from the top that he noticed the pile of black bags outside the apartment door. He stopped for a moment and gazed round, wondering if he'd come to the right apartment. The Czech girl had caught him up and began to look nervous again. She started to go back down the steps but Pedro grabbed hold of her elbow to halt her retreat. Stepping round the bin liners, he tried the key, then knocked loudly on the door. We quietly opened Mrs Tanner's window to hear the confrontation. Terry answered, his eyes ablaze with anger.

'Yes?' he barked.

'Who are you?' asked Pedro confidently, and in English.

'Who the fuck are you?' answered Terry, taking one step closer to the Spaniard.

Pedro didn't move. 'This is my apartment. What are you doing here?'

'This is my mother-in-law's apartment and I'm staying here with her,' said Terry.

'You... you can't be. We live here. We rented this apartment from Joy at the Smugglers Tavern.' Although Pedro had revealed his mastery of English, Terry's threatening demeanour was causing him to falter.

'Never heard of her,' snapped Terry. 'Do you have a contract?'

'Err... no.'

'Well I suggest you just fuck right off and stop wasting my time,' said Terry. He was clearly enjoying himself.

'You can't do this,' argued Pedro, raising his puny frame as much as he could. 'These are all my things,' he continued, pointing at the bin liners.

'Well move them off my doorstep before I tell the police you've been dumping rubbish outside my mother-in-law's apartment.'

At the mention of 'police' the girl turned and made her escape. She called to Pedro from the bottom of the steps, beckoning for him to follow but he wasn't giving in just yet.

'You can't throw me out,' he continued. His voice was getting louder now. 'Where am I going to go?'

Terry suddenly leaned closer, making him step back suddenly. He was reading the label on one of the bin liners.

'Why don't you go back to apartment 224, Playa Sol, Las Americas? That's where you live, isn't it?'

Pedro was speechless.

'I'm... I'm... I'm calling the police,' he spluttered.

'Go ahead,' said Terry, smiling, and closed the door.

'He won't do it,' whispered Wayne. 'He's bluffing.'

'He'll do it,' said Joy. 'He's got that much front.'

Instead of feeling relief that the confrontation had seemingly gone our way, and equally importantly that Terry had managed to resist assaulting Pedro, we now sat with knotted stomachs, awaiting the arrival of the police.

The two homeless squatters loitered at the bottom of the steps. The girl was trying to persuade Pedro to leave but he was resolute. After several failed attempts, they both sat down in silence.

It was now ten minutes past six but Joy and I had decided we had to stay around for the finale. We'd pay the consequences of an angry patronage later.

After half an hour, two uniformed policemen sauntered up to the couple, guns swinging on their hips. They listened to Pedro as he pointed up at the apartment and showed them the handwritten receipt that Joy had given to the girl. The volume and tone of his voice started to rise as he tried to evoke a sense of injustice. One of the officers held his hands up to halt the onslaught.

The two policemen led the way back up the stairs and knocked at Siobhan's door. This time Siobhan answered. In broken English, one of the policemen asked who she was. Siobhan told him her name, adding that she was the owner of the apartment.

'You have papers, say you owner?' asked the officer. Siobhan went back inside. Pedro tried to follow but the other policeman pulled him back. The two officers looked through the title deeds, bank statements, utility receipts, community payments and all the other reams of paperwork that Josephine had advised us to tell Siobhan to bring.

'This man say he live here,' said the officer glancing up.

'I've never seen him before in my life,' answered Siobhan, her eyes fixed on Pedro's. 'I don't know what he's talking about. I live here. I arrived last night and found all this stuff outside my house. I was about to throw it away. I assumed it was rubbish.'

The policeman handed the stack of papers back to Siobhan, turned to Pedro and shrugged his shoulders. He said something in Spanish and then nodded at his partner before descending the stairs and walking off. Pedro was left at the top of the stairs with his hands on his hips, staring at the closed door. He began to knock but gave up after realising that Siobhan was not going to open it. He snapped something at the girl, who was waiting at the bottom of the steps. She ran up and they grabbed two bin liners each before trudging back down the stairs and walking off dejectedly.

In Mrs Tanner's apartment, a cheer went out, perhaps a little too prematurely. Pedro looked up over his shoulder to see Wayne pressing his nose against the window giving a one-fingered farewell. It was over. I felt four stone lighter, and that was even after a fistful of homemade scones and choc-olate biscuits.

In the bar that night, Joy was in party mood. The bad-tempered rants of some of our more routine-bound customers couldn't shake her, nor could the protestations of Friedhelm, who stabbed at his watch with a finger and wobbled his jowls disapprovingly. 'Big problem,' he croaked, but for us the big problem had finally gone and we could get back to our intended mission of trying to run a successful Tenerife bar.

CHAPTER 20

Having a job that doesn't differentiate between weekdays and weekends means it's difficult to mark the passing of time. It was only when we noticed that our local cash and carry seemed to be stacking an inordinate amount of sweets and nuts that we realised Father Christmas had booked his flight and was halfway through packing. Panic set in as it dawned on us that we had made no preparations whatsoever, with only three weeks to go.

Although in Tenerife, British supermarkets are only second in supply to British bars, the ones we ransacked in order to buy traditional festive paraphernalia had either grossly underestimated the demand for tinsel et al or were having as much difficulty as us in importing it.

The only Christmas crackers we could find were small, pink and embossed with the somewhat discomforting smirks of Barbie and her plastic sidekicks. We bought them anyway in the over-ambitious hope that we may be able to use Blue Peter skills to turn them into more adult-orientated decorations.

Party poppers, tree baubles, sage and onion stuffing, chipolatas, cranberry sauce, parsnips, Christmas puddings and chocolate logs were also proving to be elusive, which meant our hastily put together Christmas menu had to be hastily disassembled again. A sprig of holly on chicken and wine was looking a distinct possibility until David remembered that our cousin Les was coming to spend Christmas with us and could perhaps bring over one or two items.

So it was that a fortnight before Christmas, Joy, David and I were helping to bundle Les's six cases onto two airport trolleys.

'A hundred and forty-five pounds excess,' Les chunnered as a red bauble fell out of one of the holdalls and shattered on the hard floor.

There appeared to be a lot more than we had asked him to bring and that was taking into the account the two cartons of party poppers and four boxes of crackers that had been confiscated before they left British soil.

'They're explosives,' the bag checker at Gatwick airport had countered, as baby-faced Les pleaded for their liberty.

Although he was 12 years our junior, our cousin's interests crossed over into both our spheres. He too was looking for an alternative to the 9-5 and had had limited success as a thespian, his peak of stardom portraying a sublimely camp Judas in a university production of *Jesus Christ Superstar* before pursuing more of a strict musical angle as an aspiring orchestra conductor.

Spending Christmas with us in Tenerife was just a way of avoiding the commercial expectations of UK festivities and also provided a way of 'going against the grain'. But it was with some disdain that he found himself humping half of Christmas over to Tenerife with him in return for three weeks of winter sunshine.

Although the offer was actually to spend a little time with his cousins helping out here and there, it wasn't long before he was drafted into full-time employment, such was our panic.

With the bar lacking even a trace of festive cheer, our first mission was to find some decorations. The four of us packed into the Renault 5 and headed up to the mountains to find the perfect tree.

The mercury was still loitering around the 75 degree mark when we left El Beril but our geographical naivety bit us like a rabid Jack Frost as soon as we reached the fringe of greenery marking the start of Teide National Park.

'Whoa, that's cold,' said Les, winding the window up as an icy, pine-scented gust breezed through the car.

The view until now had been one of stark ruggedness. The road had climbed through fields of sharp, black rock, a legacy of the frequent occasions when Mother Nature had decided to redecorate the island in hues of ash black and fiery red. Petrified rivers of grey tumbled over terraced ledges like molten lead poured down a staircase. Here and there, green cacti and mountain broom punctuated the apocalyptic vision, bursting resolute from the tiniest of fissures.

Eventually the road began to level off and lone stragglers were replaced by clumps, then a whole forest, of Canary Pine. Small patches of snow began to appear under rocky overhangs.

Travelling along a rare straight stretch of tarmac, the freshly painted centre lines rushed ahead like bursts of tracer fire. Then suddenly they disappeared, as a swirling wall of cloud rolled slowly across the mountain road. We slowed down, visibility reduced to little beyond the rusty red bonnet of our car. Then, as quickly as the scenery had vanished, it burst forth again as we drove out of the other side and back into brilliant, sharp sunshine.

Ahead of us, the towering pinnacle of Mount Teide, the highest peak in Spain, soared into the sky. To its right, the jagged rim of *Pico Viejo* serrated the bright blue. Side by side, the pair stood ominous, threatening future cataclysms. In front of them, lesser volcanic cones seemed to cower in their presence, minions of destruction softened with smooth slopes of loose ash and basalt.

We pulled to the side of the road and parked on a carpet of fallen pine needles. None of us had had the foresight to bring warm clothes. Joy was the least appropriately dressed, in shorts and T-shirt, but was the first to venture out. She hugged herself and blew into her hands. Whilst she gathered pine cones from the side of the road, Les, David and I ventured deeper into the forest in search of a suitable tree. We all took turns at sawing and dragged it back to the car, removing a handful of branches so it would fit in the back.

We knew it was an offence to cut down trees in the national park and raced back down the mountain, hoping we wouldn't be seen. Les and Joy, the smallest of the group, lay in the back, arms draped over the kidnapped pine in a token effort to hide its presence. Fortunately we fled unhindered by the strong arm of the park rangers and the Smugglers Christmas tree was planted in its new home, a sturdy potato pan festooned in bright foil wrapping paper.

The bookings for Christmas dinner were going well. Our biggest dilemma was the seating arrangements. A number of unexpected single reservations had thrown a spanner into the logistics. We had come to realize that the tens of thousands of British tourists who chose to escape the slush and sleet of Britain for sunnier climes over the festive period were not all happy holidaymakers. A number of individuals were also trying to escape from the cruel reality that Christmas was a time for family get-togethers and communal merriment.

For those unfortunate few who had lost their family and were drifting towards the end of their days in joyless isolation, the last thing they needed was to be surrounded by exaggerated mirth and the painful reminders that this particular time of year can inflict. Thus, a dash to a foreign land where at least the commercial pressure and the foreboding weather are far from the mind was the preferred choice for those less jubilant.

Plus there was Friedhelm. His closest relations were the scantily clad staff of Cleopatra's whorehouse, and it was highly unlikely that they would be joining him for a turkey dinner. Seating Friedhelm was the biggest problem. His English language skills were limited to, 'big problem', 'big beer' and 'fucky-fucky' – hardly the vocabulary necessary to kindle riveting conversation with fellow festive diners.

To sit him entirely on his own would be too cruel, cracker pulling is a two-man sport after all. To sit him at another party's table would conversely be too unfair on them. It was therefore, after a lot of name-tag swapping, that we arranged to squeeze all three of our lone diners on barrel tables just close enough to each other so that introductions could be made, yet just far enough away to make room for the cold shoulder approach, should it be preferred.

Despite the anxiety that cooking a five-course meal for 62 people for the very first time can bring, I awoke on the 25th feeling strangely content, mainly because it was another break in the routine.

Also, there was an element of personal pride in the fact that all of these people had decided that they wanted to spend Christmas Day with us, and were willing to pay a small fortune for the privilege.

Six months previously, such demanding situations would have caused a barrelful of consternation and acute hair loss. Now, having realised that the worst that could happen is that people get hungry, poisoned or pissed off – and occasionally all three – for once, apprehension was not one of the overriding emotions.

David, Les and I had spent the previous evening preparing the festive fare while Joy took care of the front of house business. Because of this advance preparation, the four of us took the liberty of opening some sparkling wine at ten in the morning. In hindsight this was not such a wise idea. Instead of double-checking that everything was on track, alcoholic complacency beset us all and we all managed to overlook one important element of Christmas dinner.

Joy and David were leisurely laying out the tables with green and red serviettes, Christmas crackers and scrawled name cards. Les and I were in the kitchen arranging where to place all the items that were to be plated up, shoved in the oven and heated to scalding point.

'Put the chipolatas, bacon and pastry cases for the cranberry sauce on the chest freezer,' said Les, clearing away two empty bottles of sparkling wine from the surface. Because every single work space was occupied with pre-prepared accompaniments, we had to implement a two-tier system on the freezer so that we could fit everything on. Tupperwares were precariously stacked two-high, overlapping the containers below. The plates were stacked three deep on the square table in the centre of the kitchen, waiting to be filled for the first orders. The wipe board on the fridge doors had been sectioned so we could tick off which course each table had been served. And the homemade French onion soup had started to gurgle atop one of the rings, waiting for a dash of champagne before being ladled into bowls and topped with slices of fresh crusty bread.

'I think we're ready,' I said, as Joy and David came to join us for one last drink before the rush.

'Cheers,' said David, raising a glass. 'Happy Christmas.'

'Happy Christmas,' we all replied, and took a slurp. The kitchen looked highly organised and we still had half an hour to spare before the diners arrived. We were feeling rather pleased with ourselves.

'Doddle,' said Les.

'We could have catered for a hundred,' added David.

'It's all gone too smoothly,' I said.

'Err… just one thing,' said Joy. Her eyes were scanning the worktops. 'Where's the turkey?'

Les and I looked at each other.

'SHIT!'

I began to frantically dismantle our Tupperware terrace on the freezer. We had forgotten to take it out last night. It was still frozen.

David looked at his watch and gulped down another glass of wine. As I held the lid open, Les reached into the chest freezer, leaning across the plastic containers of Brussel sprouts, mashed and roasted potatoes, sliced carrots and other foodstuffs that were now spilling onto the tiled floor.

Thankfully we had cooked and sliced the humongous bird three days earlier but the frozen breezeblock of white poultry that Les pulled out was like a block of super-glued Lego.

'We'll never defrost it in time,' I said, as I chiselled at it with a meat cleaver and rolling pin.

'Stick it in the microwave,' suggested David.

'It won't fit in,' said Les, who had taken to beating the disassembled bird with a meat tenderiser.

Finally, after the four of us had taken turns at assaulting it with various culinary implements, the block fell apart, but only in half.

'Stick one half in this microwave and take the other to our apartment,' said Joy. 'We'll have to defrost them separately.'

I threw the turkey into a smaller Tupperware, concealing it with a festive tea towel, one of a set bought by David for the occasion, and raced out of the doors. As I did, the first of our lone diners was making his way down the steps towards the bar.

'You shouldn't have,' said the man indicating the 'present' in my hands. I laughed and ran past him.

'We'll be with you in a minute!' I shouted over my shoulder.

By the time I returned, half of the tables were occupied. As I rushed through the doors a hand grabbed my arm and the Tupperware of turkey almost fell to the floor. It was Friedhelm.

'Joe,' he started. 'J-o-e…' His eyes were closed, his mind searching for the words in English. He shook his head, annoyed with himself but before he could fully release his grip in defeat he clenched my forearm tightly again. 'Joe…' he repeated again, even more slowly. His heavy eyelids lifted wearily like ageing window blinds. 'Happ-y Chrim-stas.'

'Yes, happy Christmas, Friedhelm,' I repeated, trying to release his grip.

In the kitchen, Les had also had similar success with the microwave and apart from one or two extraneous pieces that the radiation had morphed into shoe leather, the turkey was ready to serve.

Save for a spell of post-mince pie blubbering from Friedhelm, which we regarded as traditional for Smugglers' events, the paying guests were pleasantly surprised, stuffed and pie-eyed, though not necessarily in that order. We had also surprised ourselves. A little over six months ago I would have considered boiling an egg a fait accompli. Now I was standing in front of the washing-up for 62 people. These 62 had entrusted three people, who half a year ago couldn't tell a spatula from a cocktail twirler, to conjure up five courses of festive fare and lay on a congenial party for fifteen tables of relative strangers.

It felt like we had passed an exam, proof to ourselves that we could now finally call ourselves caterers and business people. It felt like the climax to what had seemed to be an endless period of meddling in the dark, learning by our mistakes and bluffing when all else failed. We had passed the crucial six-month honeymoon without falling prey to the lure of our own beer pumps.

None of us had been tempted into forbidden territory, despite our visitors' regular state of undress. We'd narrowly avoided a potentially fatal gas explosion and learned how dangerous boredom can be. We'd beaten all attempts by the electricity company to finish us before we had started, and refused to give in faced with the island's second biggest threat after the volcano – blindingly inefficient bureaucracy. We'd won over many of Mario's old customers and made the bar our own, then proceeded to poison the majority of the most faithful – but got away with it.

Neither small time gangsters nor squatting prostitutes, giggling health inspectors or jobsworth paper shufflers, thieving staff or lusty customers, ludicrously poor entertainers or demented locals had succeeded in thwarting our efforts to make the Smugglers Tavern a success. The six-month itch had left a few scabs but it hadn't proved fatal. I felt we were in the clear, we'd done it all. I mean, what else could running a bar abroad possibly throw at us?

END

And then what?

Read the next instalment right now. Just type the following into your browser for *Even More Ketchup than Salsa: The Final Dollop…*

http://getbook.at/EvenMoreK

Join me…

If you want to be one of the first to know when I publish another book, *and* you'd like me to send you the occasional photo from our Smugglers days, simply type the following into your browser…

http://eepurl.com/biSIL9

Pretty please…

If you enjoyed *More Ketchup than Salsa*, it would also be mighty useful if you could (pretty) please leave a review on Amazon.

More books by this author

Even More Ketchup than Salsa: The Final Dollop

If the first six months of running the Smugglers Tavern had been a baptism of fire, the subsequent years were about as much fun as bobbing for apples in a vat of acid.

Having swapped the tin roof of a cold British fish market for the sunny skies of a Spanish holiday island, Joe and Joy succeeded in thwarting the first wave of attacks from bungling bureaucrats, bewildered holidaymakers and their own spectacular ineptitude.

What they didn't realise was that their enemies were regrouping. Not only that, but those enemies had made camp a lot closer to home, enemies that would make their encounters with the exploding gas bottles, East European squatters and big-time Charlies featured in *More Ketchup than Salsa* seem like chapters from Enid Blyton.

The trials and tribulations of attempting to make a better life abroad continue... with disastrous consequences.

Buy *Even More Ketchup than Salsa: The Final Dollop* on Amazon

More books by this author

Moving to Tenerife: All You Need to Know…

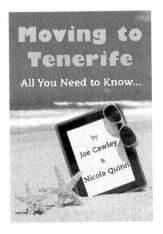

Hands up if you've ever been to Tenerife on holiday and toyed with the idea of making your stay a more permanent one.

No surprise, really – grey skies versus blue, roads clogged with stressed commuters versus a walk to work in the sunshine, wet weekends indoors versus days on the beach or round the pool.

In fact it's quite a wonder why more people don't bite the bullet and head for sunnier climes.

However, relocating can seem daunting – especially if you don't know much about the place. Hopefully with the help of this book, deciding if a move to Tenerife is right for you, actually taking the plunge, and doing all the stuff that follows a move, should become a lot clearer.

Moving to Tenerife is a useful guide that will show you the easiest path so you can begin enjoying your brand new life in the sun as soon as possible.

Buy *Moving o Tenerife* on Amazon

If you enjoyed *More Ketchup than Salsa*, you might also enjoy these other funny travel tales from fellow authors:

Free Country

The plan is simple. George and Ben have three weeks to cycle 1000 miles from the bottom of England to the top of Scotland. There is just one small problem... they have no bikes, no clothes, no food and no money. Setting off in just a pair of Union Jack boxer shorts, they attempt to rely on the generosity of the British public for everything from food to accommodation, clothes to shoes, and bikes to beer.

During the most hilarious adventure, George and Ben encounter some of Great Britain's most eccentric and extraordinary characters and find themselves in the most ridiculous situations. *Free Country* is guaranteed to make you laugh (you may even shed a tear). It will restore your faith in humanity, and leave you with a big smile on your face and a warm feeling inside.

Download *Free Country* on Amazon

If you enjoyed *More Ketchup than Salsa*, you might also enjoy these other funny travel tales from fellow authors:

That Bear Ate My Pants!

There comes a time in every man's life when he says to himself, "Holy Sh*t! I'm about to be eaten by a bear!"

Tony James Slater went to Ecuador, determined to become a man. It never occurred to him that 'or die trying' might be an option... The trouble with volunteering in a South American animal refuge is that everything wants a piece of you. And the trouble with being Tony is that most of them got one.

Just how do you 'look after' something that's trying its damnedest to kill you and eat you? And how do you find love when you a) don't speak the language, and b) are constantly covered in excrement and entrails? If only he'd had some relevant experience – other than owning a pet rabbit when he was nine. And if only he'd bought some travel insurance...

Check out *That Bear Ate My Pants!* On Amazon

Joe Cawley

Find out more about Joe and his upcoming books at **www.joecawley.co.uk** and follow Joe on Twitter **@theWorldofJoe**

If you'd like to be informed of when Joe's next book is available, please send a message to **writer@joecawley.co.uk** with any comments, opinions, requests or general waffle. Writing can be a lonely chore and any contact with the real world is gratefully appreciated.

Made in the USA
San Bernardino, CA
30 April 2017